THE INVESTIGATOR'S LITTLE BLACK BOOK 2

By
Robert Scott

Over 2,500 Sources of Information for Professional Investigators

Crime Time Publishing Co.
Beverly Hills, California

The Investigator's Little Black Book 2
(c) 1998 by Robert Scott

Published by:
Crime Time Publishing Co.
289 S. Robertson Blvd., Suite 224
Beverly Hills, CA 90211

 Printed on Recycled Paper

Printed in the United States of America
10 9 8 7 6 5 4 3 2
First edition.

Scott, Robert
The Investigator's Little Black Book 2
Over 2,500 Sources of Information for
Professional Investigators/by Robert
Scott — 1st ed.
p. cm.
Preassigned LCCN: 97-077171
ISBN: 0-9652369-2-7

1. Public records - Telephone directories.
2. Records — Telephone directories
3. Private investigators — Handbooks, manuals, etc.
I. Title

JK2445.P82S36 1998   352.3'87
                            QBI98-846

DISCLAIMER

This book is for informational purposes only and any reliance upon the information contained herein is at the sole risk of its user.

Inclusion in this book of any individual, company, service, product, or governmental agency does not constitute endorsement of the individual, company, service, product or governmental agency by the author or publisher.

Although every reasonable effort has been made to present accurate and complete information in this book, errors may be contained in the information presented. No warranties, either expressed or implied, are made by the author, publisher, or distributors of this book.

Acknowledgments

In June of 1996, no one had heard of *The Investigator's Little Black Book*, which was just being published. Through word of mouth, a little luck, and some good old fashioned American *hustle*, the book caught on and ended up in the briefcases and on the desks of thousands of investigators.

May I publicly offer a sincere thank you to a few from our community to whom I'm gratefully indebted?

Many thanks to Ralph Thomas, of Thomas Investigative Publications and NAIS, who saw the original *Black Book* before almost anyone else and declared that it would be a winner — and then put his support behind it. This was a welcome shot in the arm at a time when I was exhausted from just completing the book and uncertain if anyone would even care that it existed.

Thanks also to Bob Mackowiak, Editor and Publisher of *PI Magazine*, who reviewed the book very early on. Bob didn't wait to see which way the tide of public opinion would break on the book. He liked it and said so — in print.

Further gratitude goes to Richard Harer, a true investigator, for frequent sound advice, and to John Grogan, *PI Magazine* columnist, for being an all around nice guy.

Finally, I would like to thank the many investigators, law enforcement agencies and other "sources" who took time from their busy schedules to provide much of the information contained in this book.

Robert Scott
Los Angeles, CA

THE INVESTIGATOR'S LITTLE BLACK BOOK 2

ACADEMY OF MOTION PICTURE ARTS & SCIENCES

The *AMPAS* library contains a wealth of information on movie industry credits. 310/247-3020

>ACCIDENT RECONSTRUCTION

NHTSA, Auto Safety Hotline	800/424-9393
NHTSA, Office of Defects Investigation	202/366-2850
NHTSA, Crash Worthiness Research	202/366-4862
NHTSA, Office of Vehicle Safety Compliance	202/366-2832
Accident Investigation Quarterly & Accident Reconstruction Journal	301/843-1371
Vehicle Information Profiles, Inc.	800/772-6032

For classes and other information on the science of car crashes, contact the *Northwestern University Traffic Institute.* 800/323-4011

If you have access to the Internet, there's a searchable database of accident reconstructionists located at *www.tarsearch.com*

If you don't, here's some accident reconstruction experts:

Advanced Engineering Resources (North Carolina)	919/387-8811
Baxter Engineering (Phoenix)	602/832-7744
CLI International (Texas)	713/444-2282
Collision Investigation Associates (New Hampshire)	888/870-0900
Consolidated Consulting Services (California)	800/683-9847
Clark Accident Reconstruction (Florida)	941-455-2780
Crash Scene Dynamics (Virginia)	804/739-1754
CTL Engineering, Inc. (Ohio)	614/276-8123
Failure Analysis Associates (California)	415/326-9400
Kansas Accident Reconstruction Consulting (Kansas)	913/536-4333
Macinnis Engineering Associates, Ltd. (British Columbia)	604/277-3040
CD Pembleton Associates (Maryland)	301/843-0048
Rennenberg-Walker Engineering Associates (Alberta, Canada)	403/466-7709
Southeastern Safety Consultants	904/474-9607
Summit Engineering (South Carolina)	803/732-7979
Syder Research Labs, Inc. (California)	714/375-2166

Vidal Engineering (Missouri)	314/205-0088
VTS Investigations (Illinois)	847-888-4464
Willis, Kaplan & Associates (Illinois)	847/215-7757

AERIAL & SATELLITE PHOTO-GRAPHS

Earth Science Information Center, a project of the U.S. Geological Survey, has a massive collection of aerial photographs of the entire United States. Both recent and vintage shots are available. Cost ranges between $7.50 and $50 per shot.   800/USA-MAPS

When the United States Air Force evaluated satellite photographs taken during Operation Desert Storm by *Spot Image Corp.*, they declared the photographs "invaluable to mission success". Since then, this private company's satellites have been relied upon by the Department of Defense for operations in Somalia, Bosnia and elsewhere. *Spot Image Corp.'s* satellites are also available to the private sector for a variety of uses. Custom photographs can be taken from the satellites of any spot on Earth. Resolution is 10 meters -- meaning you'll see buildings, not people. Custom shots cost approximately $1845 each. Also available is an extensive library of pre-existing shots taken over the last few years. These go for $845 each.   703/715-3100

>*Geographic Earth Mapping Information* (GEMI) acts as a broker for various sources of archived aerial and satellite photographs.   888/333-GEMI

The *Research Source* offers a pre-existing data bank of satellite photos of industrial plants.   302/738-7335

API offers aerial photographs from a unique, low flying tethered blimp.   714/744-2729

>AGENCY RECORDS

Agency Records is a service offering driver's license information from all 50 states. Information is available online, by fax, or by phone. You'll need to establish an account to use their service. Cheap prices.   860/667-1617

Also see...*DRIVER'S LICENSE INFORMATION*.

AIRCRAFT THEFT INVESTIGATIONS
The Aviation Crime Prevention Institute aids in the detection and prevention of aircraft theft. A monthly bulletin of stolen aircraft and aircraft parts is published. Also available is a database of stolen aircraft dating back to 1974.

800/969-5473
301/791-9792

AIRCRAFT TITLE INFORMATION
Insured Aircraft Title Service, Inc. offers aircraft ownership searches.

800/654-4882
405/681-6663

AIR FORCE PERSONNEL LOCATOR
To locate a current active member of the *Air Force*.

210/652-5774
210/652-6377

ARISTOTLE PUBLISHING
See...VOTER REGISTRATION RECORDS

>ALPHA DOT
Alpha Dot is a new and unique high tech tool for use in theft detection and counterfeiting investigations. *Alpha Dots* are very small silicon dots. To the naked eye they appear to be a speck of dirt, if they're noticed at all. Under microscopic examination, however, they're encoded with a unique, registered serial number that make the dots unique, identifiable, and traceable. The dots can be placed on paper currency, or on goods or products for future identification. The complete kit, including everything you'll need plus an instructional video sells for around $265. Because the *Alpha Dots* are encoded with the serial number of your choice (mine contain my phone number), there's a two week turnaround time to receive your kit.

509/533-6956

>ALTERNATIVE PRESS INDEX
The Alternative Press Index, published quarterly, offers a subject index to articles appearing in approximately 250 alternative, radical, and otherwise left wing publications.
Alternative Press Center

410/243-2471

Also see...*NAMEBASE.*

Also see...*CENTER FOR INVESTI-GATIVE REPORTING.*

AMERICAN BAR ASSOCIA-TION (ABA)

The *ABA* offers a Discipline Database which tracks reported disciplines, nationwide, against attorneys. They will also indicate if an attorney's law school is accredited312/988-5000

AMERICAN CIVIL LIBERTIES UNION

*Information*212/549-2500

AMERICAN CORRECTIONAL ASSOCIATION

*Information*800/222-5646

>AMERICAN INSURANCE SER-VICES GROUP, INC.

What happens when 1,700 insurance companies send information on persons making insurance claims to a single source? You end up with a set of powerful databases useful in identifying bogus or questionable insurance claims. Access to the databases is restricted to member insurance companies, self-insureds and third-party administrators. The primary databases are T*he Index System* (for bodily injury claims history) and *PILR* (Property Insurance Loss Registry for property losses).

AISG Marketing Department	212/669-0406
The Index System, Customer Support	732/388-0332
PILR, Customer Support	732/388-0157

>AMERICAN RACING MANUAL

Conducting a financial investigation of a subject who owns race horses? Did you know that winnings from an owner's horses are public record? *American Racing Manual* (put out by the same people behind the Daily Racing Form) is a CD ROM which shows amounts paid to owners of winning horses. Published annually, sells for $20.800/306-3676

>AMERICAN WAR LIBRARY

American War Library is a very in-

teresting database that is seeks to
identify every service person who has
ever served in the U.S. armed forces
during both peace and war from the
Revolutionary War through to the
present day. Currently, there are over
16,000,000 names in the database.
The information comes from several
different sources. One potential use
of the information is to verify a person's
claim of past military service. The
database is available by computer
only. Using common communication
software, like HyperTerminal, dial
into *310/715-2912*. Subscriptions
are necessary to access the main database. Cost is $15 for 30 days of
access; $39 for a full year.   310/530-0177

>AMERICANS WITH DISABILITIES ACT
The United States Department of
Justice has oversight over compliance
with the Americans with Disability
Act. Violations of this law can lead
to what's referred to as an "ADA lawsuit". Call the *ADA Information Line*
for technical questions and general
ADA information.   800/514-0301

ANIMAL MUTILATIONS
Located in Paris, TX, Tom Adams'
Project Stigma investigates the my-
sterious mutilation of animals. Mostly
livestock. Often found with surgically
removed organs and a near total loss
of blood.   903/784-5922

ARMY - PERSONNEL LOCA-TOR SERVICE
To locate active members of the
Army.   703/325-3732

ARSON INVESTIGATION
Pragmatics, Inc. manufactures fire investigation equipment, including ac-
celerant detectors.   314/225-6786

Applied Technical Services is a private forensics lab that offers fire caus-
ation analysis.   800/544-5117

Analytical Forensic Associates, Inc.
uses chemical analysis of fire debris
to identify accelerants.   770/246-1711

Fire Science Technologies, Inc. are fire and explosion investigators with offices in Massachusetts, New Jersey and Seattle.

800/852-5073
413/283-7003

The Insurance Committee for Arson Control sponsors an annual arson investigation seminar.

212/669-9245

International Association of Arson Investigators

502/239-7228

National Fire Protection Association

800/344-3555

The *Bureau of Fire and Aviation Management* tracks forest fires currently burning in the United States.

202/205-1500

The *U.S. Fire Administration* maintains a nationwide database of fire incidents, as submitted by participating local fire agencies. It's known as the Fire Incident Reporting System.

301/447-1024

ART - STOLEN
>*International Foundation for Art Research* offers an authentication service to make sure your Picasso *really* is a Picasso. They also publish *IFAReports* with a focus on stolen art.

212/391-6234

Art Loss Register has offices in London and New York City. Their database includes 70,000 stolen works of art and art objects and is relied upon by both insurance companies and law enforcement.

212/391-8791

Trace Publications, Ltd. circulates a monthly publication of stolen art to collectors, dealers, and museums. Company owner Phillip Saunders is an internationally known art theft consultant. Their website is at *http://www.trace.co.uk*

011-44-01983 826000

Robert E. Spiel Associates, Inc. is a Chicago based international art theft consultant.

312/258-0646

Trans-Art Professionals is staffed by attorneys who provide legal services to collectors to protect their

rights under U.S. law. Company
principal Dr. Willie Korte is widely
known as an expert in World War II
era art .hefts.   202/737-4913

ASSASSINATIONS
See...*Coalition on Political Assassinations.*

**>ASSET FORFEITURE FINANCIAL
RECOVERY**
Need a collection agency to pursue recovery of a debt on behalf of your
agency or a client? *Asset Forfeiture*,
a Glendale, California based collection
company has a set fee of 25% of moneys
recovered, with no minimum placement.   888/4ASSET4

AT&T DIRECTORY ASSISTANCE
AT&T offers its own nationwide directory assistance. For 95 cents (as of
publication date) they will look up
any name, nationwide. They find the
area code, and search local directory
assistance. If a non-published number
is found, they search old directories.
If the number was previously published, they will provide it. They allow
two look ups per call.   900/555-1212

**AT&T EMPLOYEE VERIFICA-
TION**
Provide the SSN of an AT&T employ-
ee to verify employment.   800/266-4014

AT&T LANGUAGE LINE
AT&T offers interpreters by phone in
140 languages. No appointment is
necessary. You call them, they connect you to an interpreter, then to the
subject of your interview. Payment
accepted by credit card. Cost ranges
from $4.15 per minute (Spanish) to
$7.25 per minute (Swahili). A great
resource!   800/843-8420

AT&T TELE-CONFERENCING
Need to have a phone call with up to
fourteen other parties at once? *AT&T
Tele-Conferencing* will connect all of
you. Charge based on the number of
lines and length of call.   800/232-1234
                                                 700/456-1000

>AT&T TRUE MESSAGES
You might think of this as a "Reverse
Answering Machine". Have a witness

or other party that you need to contact, but their telephone is never answered? It just rings and rings and rings? Then consider *AT&T True Messages*. You record a message for the person you're trying to contact. AT&T will then attempt to send the message to the number once every half hour for the next ten hours. If they're successful, there's a $1.75 charge. If they're not successful, there's no charge.   800/562-6275

After you've recorded your message, you can learn the delivery status of it, and whether on not it has been delivered, by calling this number: 800/TRUE123

ATTORNEYS
To determine if an attorney's law school is one of the 176 law schools accredited by the *American Bar Association*.   312/988-5000

The *ABA* also offers a Discipline Database which tracks reported disciplines, nationwide, against any given attorney.   312/988-5000

Also see STATE BAR ASSOCIATIONS for additional biographical, licensing, and discipline information.

>AUDIO ENHANCEMENT
Have an audio tape that needs to be enhanced or authenticated?

National Audio Video Forensic Laboratory   818/989-0990

Secure Audio Services   602/812-9420

AUTOPSIES
See....*DEATH INVESTIGATIONS*.

>AUTOMATIC NUMBER IDENTIFICATION (ANI)
What is an ANI number? When you don't know the number of a telephone line, you call an ANI number from that telephone line and a computer tells you what the number is. Many local phone companies have their own local ANI's (For example, 211-2345). Nationwide, however, you can call this AT&T number, while you're on hold, their com-

puter will tell you what phone you're
calling from. If you call and an operator
answers, hang up and call back until
you get put on hold. | 800/222-0300

Need to know who the long distance
carrier is for any given phone line?
From that line, call this number and
a computer will tell you. | 700/555-4141

>AUTO REPOSSESSION
Here's some professional groups for
auto repossessors:

Time Finance Adjusters | 800/874-0510
| 904/274-4210

National Finance Adjusters | 410/728-2800

American Recovery Association | 504/366-7377

*California Association of Licensed
Repossessors* | 916/781-6633

Professional Repossessor magazine is
a nicely done magazine that includes
how-to-tips, products reviews, and
war stories. | 888/REPONEWS

AUTO SAFETY HOTLINE
*Auto Safety Hotline, Dept. of Trans-
portation*, maintains information on
auto safety related information, in-
cluding auto recalls. | 800/424-9393

AVERT, INC.
Avert, Inc. offers nationwide pre-employment investigations of job applicants, covering such areas as criminal
histories, educational verification, and
driving records. | 800/367-5933
| 303/221-1526

AVIATION
*>The International Society of Air
Safety Investigators* is an organization
of air accident investigators with members in 35 countries. The Society maintains a technical library with copies of
600 plus air accident reports and information on over 9,000 accidents in its
computerized databases. | 703/430-9668

>NASA Headquarters Library is a
good starting point for space and
flight related inquiries. | 202/358-0168

>*Aircraft Owners & Pilots Association*
is the world's largest aviation association with over 340,000 pilots and
aircraft owners as members.   301/695-2000

>Databases of FAA registered pilots
and airplanes are available for free on
the Internet, and at a low cost through
many online database providers. *Aviation
Research Group* has produced a CD
ROM containing this information as well.
Sells for around $113.   609/737-9288

>*Jane's World Airlines* is available in
book form, diskette, or CD ROM
(Price range $890 - $1,500). Inside
you'll find detailed data on the world's
major airlines, including financial
associations, fleet sizes, aircraft type
and names of key decision makers.
Jane's Information Group   703/683-3700

*Insured Aircraft Title Service,
Inc.* has information on aircraft
owners, pilots, mechanics,
and manufacturers.   800/654-4882
                                               405/681-6663

Also see....*FEDERAL AVIATION
ADMINISTRATION.*

BANKRUPTCY COURTS
Bankruptcy filings can open the door
to the financial affairs of a given person or business.

Some courts have a 24 hour touch
tone automated information system
called Voice Case Information System (VCIS). Punch in the name or
Social Security Number of a person
and the computer will tell if there has
been a bankruptcy filing. Courts without VCIS must be contacted by phone
during normal business hours:

Also see....*PACER.*

Alabama, Northern District:
Decatur Division   205/353-2817
Birmingham Division   205/731-1614
Anniston Division   205/237-5631
Tuscaloosa Divison   205/752-0426
Alabama, Middle District   334/206-6300
Alabama, Southern District   vcis   334/441-5637
Alaska   vcis   907/271-2658

Arizona:		
Phoenix Division	vcis	602/640-5820
Tucson Division	vcis	520/620-7475
Yuma Division		602/783-2288
Arkansas, Eastern District	vcis	501/324-5770
	vcis	800/891-6741
Arkansas, Western District	vcis	501/324-5770
	vcis	800/891-6741
California, Northern District:		
San Jose Division	vcis	800/457-0604
San Francisco Div.	vcis	800/570-9819
	vcis	415/705-3160
Oakland Division		510/273-7212
Santa Rosa Division		707/525-8539
California, Eastern	vcis	800/736-0158
	vcis	916/551-2989
California, Central District:		
Los Angeles Division	vcis	213/894-4111
San Fernando Division	vcis	818/587-2936
Santa Ana Division	vcis	714/836-2278
Santa Barbara Division	vcis	805/899-7755
Riverside Division	vcis	909/383-5552
California, Southern District		
San Diego Division	vcis	619/557-6521
Colorado	vcis	303/844-0267
Connecticut	vcis	203/240-3345
	vcis	800/800-5113
Delaware	vcis	888/667-5530
	vcis	302/573-6233
District of Columbia	vcis	202/273-0048
Florida, Northern District:		
Pensacola Division		904/435-8475
Tallahassee Division		904/942-8933
Florida, Middle District:		
Jacksonville Division	vcis	904/232-1313
Orlando Division	vcis	407/648-6800
Tampa Division	vcis	813/243-5210
Florida, Southern District	vcis	800/473-0226
	vcis	305/536-5979
Georgia, Northern District	vcis	404/730-2866
	vcis	404/730-2867
Georgia, Middle District	vcis	912/752-8183
Georgia, Southern District:		
Augusta Division		706/724-2421
Savannah Division		912/652-4100
Hawaii		808/541-1791
Idaho	vcis	208/334-9386
Illinois, Northern District:		
Chicago Division	vcis	312/408-5089
Rockford Division	vcis	815/987-4487
Illinois, Central District	vcis	217/492-4550
	vcis	800/827-9005
Illinois, Southern District	vcis	618/482-9365
	vcis	800/726-5622
Indiana, Northern District	vcis	800/726-5622
	vcis	219/236-8814

Indiana, Southern District	vcis	800/335-8003
Iowa, Northern District	vcis	800/249-9859
	vcis	319/362-9906
Iowa, Southern District	vcis	800/597-5917
	vcis	515/284-6230
Kansas	vcis	800/827-9028
	vcis	316/269-6668
Kentucky, Eastern	vcis	800/998-2650
	vcis	606/233-2657
Kentucky, Western	vcis	800/263-9385
	vcis	502/625-7391
Louisiana, Eastern	vcis	504/589-7879
Louisiana, Middle	vcis	504/382-2175
Louisiana, Western	vcis	800/326-4026
	vcis	318/676-4234
Maine	vcis	888/201-3572
	vcis	207/780-3755
Maryland	vcis	410/962-0733
Massachusetts	vcis	617/565-6025
Michigan, Eastern District		
(Includes Detroit)	vcis	313/961-4940
Michigan, Western District	vcis	616/456-2075
Minnesota	vcis	800/959-9002
	vcis	612/290-4070
Mississippi, Northern District	vcis	601/369-8147
Mississippi, Southern District:		
Biloxi Division	vcis	800/293-2723
	vcis	601/435-2905
Jackson Division	vcis	800/601-8859
	vcis	601/965-6106
Missouri, Eastern District		
(includes St. Louis)	vcis	314/425-4054
Missouri, Western District	vcis	816/842-7985
Montana	vcis	406/782-1060
Nebraska	vcis	800/829-0112
	vcis	402/221-3757
Nevada:		
Las Vegas Division	vcis	800/314-3436
	vcis	702/388-6708
Reno Division		702/784-5515
New Hampshire	vcis	800/851-8954
	vcis	603/666-7424
New Jersey	vcis	201/645-6044
New Mexico	vcis	888/435-7822
	vcis	505/248-6536
New York, Northern District	vcis	800/206-1952
New York, Southern District:		
New York City Division	vcis	212/668-2772
White Plains Division		917/682-6117
New York, Eastern District	vcis	800/252-2537
	vcis	718/852-5726
New York, Western District	vcis	800/776-9578
	vcis	716/551-5311
North Carolina, Eastern District	vcis	919/234-7655
North Carolina, Middle District	vcis	910/333-5532
North Carolina, Western District	vcis	704/344-6311

North Dakota	vcis	701/239-5641
Ohio, Northern District	vcis	800/898-6899
	vcis	330/489-4731
	vcis	216/489-4771
Ohio, Southern District:		
Columbus Division	vcis	800/726-1006
	vcis	513/225-2562
Dayton Division	vcis	513/225-2544
Oklahoma, Northern District		918/581-7181
Oklahoma, Eastern District	vcis	918/756-8617
Oklahoma, Western District	vcis	800/872-1348
	vcis	405/231-4768
Oregon	vcis	800/726-2227
	vcis	503/326-2249
Pennsylvania, Eastern District	ycis	215/597-2244
Pennsylvania, Middle District:		
Harrisburg Division		717/782-2260
Wilkes-Barre Division		717/826-6450
Pennsylvania, Western District	vcis	412/355-3210
Rhode Island	vcis	401/528-4476
South Carolina	vcis	800/669-8767
	vcis	803/765-5211
South Dakota	vcis	800/768-6218
	vcis	605/330-4559
Tennessee, Eastern District	vcis	800/767-1512
	vcis	423/752-5272
Tennessee, Middle District		615/736-5584
Tennessee, Western District	vcis	888/381-4961
	vcis	901/544-4325
Texas, Northern District:		
Amarillo Division		806/376-2302
Dallas Division	vcis	214/767-8092
Fort Worth Division		817/334-3802
Lubbock Division		214/767-8092
Texas, Southern District	vcis	800/745-4459
	vcis	713/250-5049
Texas, Eastern District	vcis	903/592-6119
Texas, Western District (includes San Antonio and El Paso)	vcis	210/229-4023
Utah	vcis	800/733-6740
	vcis	801/524-3107
Vermont	vcis	800/260-9956
	vcis	802/747-7627
Virginia, Eastern District	vcis	800/326-5879
Virginia, Western District:		
Harrisonburg Division		540/434-8327
Lynchburg Division		804/845-0317
Roanoke Division		540/857-2873
Washington, Eastern District (includes Spokane)		509/353-2404
Washington, Western District (includes Seattle)	vcis	888/436-7477
	vcis	206/553-8543
	vcis	206/442-6504
West Virginia, Northern District	vcis	304/233-7318

West Virginia, Southern District	vcis	304/347-5337
Wisconsin, Eastern District	vcis	414/297-3582
Wisconsin, Western District	vcis	800/743-8247
Wyoming		307/772-2037

BANKS & BANKING
>*Office of Thrift Supervision*   202/906-6000
> *Office of Thrift Supervisor, National Complaint Hotline*   202/906-6237

>The *FDIC's Division of Compliance and Consumer Affairs* offers financial reports on FDIC insured institutions, information on failed and problem banks and more.   800/934-3342
    202/942-3100

>*Board of Governors of the Federal Reserve*   202/452-3000

BICYCLE THEFT
The *National Bike Registry* seeks to deter bicycle theft through registration.   800/848-BIKE

BLOODHOUNDS
The *National Police Bloodhound Association* promotes the usage of purebred bloodhounds in law enforcement and search and rescue operations.   717/547-1543
    717/547-7155

BOATING ACCIDENT DATABASE
Statistician, U.S. Coast Guard, maintains a database of boating accidents.   202/267-0955

Also see...*MARITIME INFORMATION SYSTEM.*

BODILY INJURY CLAIMS
See...*THE INDEX SYSTEM.*

Also see...*MARINE INDEX BUREAU.*

For statistical information on injuries, including such information as costs, frequency and demographics, consider obtaining an annual publication from the *National Safety Council* called *Accident Facts.* The current book is 160 pages and sells for $29.95.   800/621-7619

>BOOKS IN PRINT
Books in Print is *the* database of books

currently in print. Most major bookstores have it on their computers, as do virtually all libraries. It's the quickest, fastest way to either find a book, or locate books by a given author or publisher. Books in Print is run by R.R. Bowker – but don't call them for a look up, call your local bookstore or library.

R.R. Bowker Data Collection Center   813/855-4635

If you're on the Internet, *Barnes & Noble's* website has an extensive database of books that can be searched by title, author or subject. Go to *www.barnesandnoble.com*

BRB PUBLICATIONS
BRB publishes several directories on where and how to obtain public records, including from local, state, and federal courthouses.   800/929-3764

>BROADCAST INTERVIEW SOURCE
Ever wonder how TV news shows and other media outlets come up with experts to provide sound bites on short notice? One way is through usage of *Broadcast Interview Source*. It's a directory of experts and spokespersons on subjects ranging from UFO's to tax reform. Although *Broadcast Interview Source* wouldn't be a core source for investigators, its an interesting resource to know about.   202/333-4904

BROADCAST TRANSCRIPTS
Datatimes offers transcripts of many CNN, PBS, and NPR programs.   800/642-2525

Or, call this number for CNN transcripts.   800/CNN-NEWS

Or, call this number for ABC News transcripts.   800/CALL ABC

Or, call this number for NPR (National Public Radio) transcripts.   888/NPR-NEWS

For CBS News programming transcripts, call: 800/777-TEXT

BUREAU OF ALCOHOL, TOBACCO & FIREARMS
Headquarters   202/927-7777

15

>Direct Freedom of Information Act Requests to *Bureau of Alcohol, Tobacco, and Firearms, Freedom of Information Request, 650 Massachusetts Ave. N.W., Washington, DC 20226*

>HOTLINES:

Arson Hotline	888/ATF-FIRE
Bomb Hotline	888/ATF-BOMB
Illegal Firearm Activity	800/ATF-GUNS
Firearms Theft Hotline	800/800-3855

To determine if an individual or business maintains a Federal Firearms License for gun sales, importation, or manufacture, call the *ATF Licensing Center*. 404/679-5040

ATF Academy 912/267-2251

National Laboratory Center	301/413-5227
Atlanta Forensic Science Laboratory	404/679-5100
San Francisco Laboratory Center	510/486-3170

National Tracing Center aids law enforcement agencies by tracing the history of firearms from manufacture through current ownership. 800/788-7133
304/274-4100

Explosive Enforcement Branch 202/927-7920

ATF FIELD OFFICES:
Atlanta Field Division:

Atlanta, GA	404-331-6526
Macon, GA	912-474-0477
Savannah, GA	912-652-4251

Baltimore Field Division:

Baltimore, MD	410-962-0897
Hyattsville, MD	301-436-8313
Wilmington, DE	302-573-6102

Birmingham Field Division

Birmingham, AL	205-731-1205
Gulfport, MS	601-863-4871
Huntsville, AL	205-539-0623
Jackson, MS	601-965-4205
Mobile, AL	334-441-5338
Montgomery, AL	333-223-7507
Oxford, MS	601-234-3751

Boston Field Division:

Boston, MA	617-565-7042
Burlington, VT	802-463-3238

Hartford, CT	203-240-3185
New Haven, CT	203-773-2060
Portland, ME	207-780-3324
Concord, NH	603-225-1547
Providence, RI	401-528-4366
Springfield, MA	413-785-0007
Worchester, MA	508-793-0240

Charlotte Field Division:
Charlotte, NC	704-344-6125
Charleston, SC	803-727-4275
Columbia, SC	803-765-5723
Fayetteville, NC	910-483-3030
Greenville, SC	864-232-3221
Greensboro, NC	910-547-4224
Raleigh, NC	919-856-4366
Wilmington, NC	910-343-4936

Cleveland Field Division:
Cleveland, OH	216-522-7210
Cincinnati, OH	513-684-3354
Columbus, OH	614-469-6717
Toledo, OH	419-259-7520
Youngstown, OH	216-747-8285

Chicago Field Division:
Chicago, IL	312-353-6935
Oakbrook, IL	708-268-0986
Springfield, IL	217-492-4273
Merrillville, IN	219-791-0702

Dallas Field Division:
Dallas, TX	214-767-2250
Fort Worth, TX	817-334-2771
Lubbock, TX	806-798-1030
Oklahoma, TX	405-297-5060
Tyler, TX	903-592-3927
Tulsa, OK	918-581-7731

Detroit Field Division:
Detroit	313-393-6019
Flint, MI	810-766-5010
Grand Rapids, MI	616-456-2566

Houston Field Division:
Houston, TX	713-449-2073
Austin, TX	512-349-4545
Beaumont, TX	409-835-0062
Corpus Christi, TX	512-888-3392
El Paso, TX	915-534-6449
McAllen, TX	210-687-5207
San Antonio, TX	210-805-2727
Waco, TX	817-741-9900

Kansas City Field Division:
Kansas City, MO	816-421-3440

Colorado Springs, CO	719-473-0166
Des Moines, IA	515-284-4372
Denver, CO	303-866-1173
Omaha, NE	402-221-3651
Springfield, MO	417-864-4707
Wichita, KS	316-269-6229

Los Angeles Field Division:
Los Angeles, CA	213-894-4812
Long Beach, CA	310-980-3434
Riverside, CA	909-276-6031
San Diego, CA	619-557-6663
Van Nuys, CA	818-756-4350

Louisville Field Division:
Louisville, KY	502-582-5211
Ashland, KY	606-329-8092
Bowling Green, KY	502-781-7090
Ft. Wayne, IN	219-424-4440
Indianapolis, IN	317-226-7464
Lexington, KY	606-233-2771

Miami Field Division:
Miami, FL	305-597-4800
Jacksonville, FL	904-232-2228
Ft. Lauderdale, FL	954-356-7369
Ft. Myers, FL	813-334-8086
Hato Rey San Juan, PR	809-766-5084
Orlando, FL	407-648-6136
Pensacola, FL	904-435-8485
St. Croix, VI	809-692-9435
St. Thomas, VI	809-774-5757
Tallahassee, FL	904-942-9660
Tampa, FL	813-228-2184
West Palm Beach, FL	407-835-8878

Nashville Field Division:
Nashville, TN	615-781-5364
Chattanooga, TN	423-855-6422
Knoxville, TN	423-545-4505
Memphis, TN	901-766-2904

New Orleans Field Division:
New Orleans, LA	504-589-2350
Baton Rouge, LA	504-389-0485
Little Rock, AR	501-324-6181
Shreveport, LA	318-676-3301

New York Field Division:
New York, NY	212-264-4658
Albany, NY	518-431-4182
Buffalo, NY	716-551-4041
Melville, NY	516-694-8372
Newark, NJ	201-357-4070
Rochester, NY	716-262-2110
Syracuse, NY	315-448-0889

Philadelphia Field Division:
Philadelphia, PA	215-597-7266
Atlantic City, NJ	609-625-2228
Camden, NJ	609-968-4884
Harrisburg, PA	717-782-3884
Pittsburgh, PA	412-644-2911
Reading, PA	610-320-5222
Trenton, NJ	609-989-2155
Wheeling, WV	304-232-4170

Phoenix Field Division:
Phoenix, AZ	602-640-2840
Albuquerque, NM	505-766-2271
Tucson, AZ	520-670-4725

San Francisco Field Division:
San Francisco, CA	415-744-7001
Bakersfield, CA	805-861-4420
Fresno, CA	209-487-5393
Las Vegas, NV	702-388-6584
Reno, NV	702-784-5251
Oakland, CA	510-637-3431
Sacramento, CA	916-498-5100
Salt Lake City, UT	801-524-5853

Seattle Field Division:
Seattle, WA	206-220-6440
Agana, GUAM	671-472-7129
Anchorage, AK	907-271-5701
Billings, MT	406-657-6886
Boise, ID	208-334-1983
Cheyenne, WY	307-772-2346
Helena, MT	406-441-1101
Honolulu, HI	808-541-2670
Portland, OR	503-326-2171
Spokane, WA	509-353-2862
Yakima, WA	509-454-4403

St.Paul Field Division:
St.Paul, MN	612-290-3092
Fargo, ND	701-239-5176
Milwaukee, WI	414-297-3937
Sioux Falls, SD	605-330-4368

Washington Field Division:
Washington, DC	202-219-7751
Bristol, VA	540-466-2727
Falls Church, VA	703-285-2551
Norfolk, VA	804-441-3190
Richmond, VA	804-560-0005
Roanoke, VA	540-857-2300

>ATF Regulatory Enforcement Districts:
SOUTHEAST (Atlanta)	404-679-5001
MIDWEST (Chicago)	312-353-1967

SOUTHWEST (Dallas)	214-767-2280
NORTH ATLANTIC (New York)	212-264-2328
WESTERN (San Francisco)	415-744-7013

BUREAU OF PRISONS (FEDERAL)
Available to anyone is the *Federal Prison Locator* which tells if a person has been incarcerated in a federal prison, since 1981.   202/307-3126

Also available to anyone is the *Federal Prison Archives* which has pre-1981 information.   202/307-2934

Bureau of Prisons, Library   202/307-3029

Also see...*STATE PRISONS.*

BUSINESS BACKGROUND IN-VESTIGATIONS
EyeQ from *Datatimes* is an online business news service. The monthly cost is $39. In return, you'll have access to a large data bank of business media, with small additional charges for stock and company profiles.   405/751-6400

A simple and often effective way to locate any business is to call *800 Directory Assistance*. If the company has a toll free 800 number, the operator should be able to provide the location.   800/555-1212

The *U.S. Dept. of Commerce Library* reference desk will check standard business reference publications for basic background information on businesses.   202/482-5511

This company sells CD ROM databases including Companies International, which profiles a quarter million companies worldwide.   800/877-GALE

CT Corporation is a private company with offices nationwide that serve as the registered agents for service of process for many large corporations.   212/246-5070

Also see...*CORPORATIONS* section for state departments of corporations which can identify the officers of corporations within their jurisdictions.

Also see...*DOW JONES NEWS RE-*

TRIEVAL.

Dun & Bradstreet is the leading business credit reporting company. Their business information reports typically contain a corporate history, profiles of current officers, information on the company's activities, and pertinent derogatory data such as lawsuits, tax liens and UCC filings.

Customer Service	800/362-3425
International	800/932-0025

Standard & Poor's Online Registry provides information on public and private companies, their owners and key executives. Also available through *Dialog* online service.   800/237-8552

For $100, this *U.S. Dept. of Commerce* unit will provide a credit report & background info on foreign companies. Ask for *World Trade Data Reports.*   202/482-4204

Graydon America offers business credit reports on overseas companies.   800/466-3163

For just $6.95 per month (as of publication date) *Infoaccess* offers up to 100 reverse directory look ups, company "profiles" (which tell the most basic facts about a business), and/or "Business Directory Assistance" inquiries (the equivalent of a national yellow pages).   800/808-INFO

Also see...*ECONOMIC NEWS.*

BUSINESS ESPIONAGE
The *Business Espionage Controls & Countermeasures Association* is a professional organization of investigator's specializing in the detection of the secret destruction or theft of business information or assets. This includes the detection of "bugs" and other illegal electronic interceptions, as well as more conventional methods, such as the use of undercover agents or informants.   301/292-6430

Also see...*DEBUGGING.*

CABLE TV - THEFT OF SERVICE
"Black Boxes" and other forms of

signal theft are to cable TV companies what fast fingered shoplifters are to five and dimes. *Signal Audit Services, LLC* specializes in busting cable crooks through a variety of interesting investigative secrets. Hint: "Black Boxes" leak frequency that can be detected through a variety of measures. The company also uses other techniques that we can't put into print. Although *Signal Audit Services'* primary clients are cable TV companies, they also offer consulting services to PI's and others.

Los Angeles (Headquarters)   818/376-0291
Englewood, CO   303/290-9500

Also see....NATIONAL ANTI-PIRACY ASSOCIATION.

>CALIBRE PRESS

Although its target is law enforcement, *CALIBRE PRESS* puts out a unique and interesting book and video catalog that many PI's will find worthwhile. Titles available include *Inside the Criminal Mind*, *Going Undercover* and *Death Scenes*, possibly the single most shocking book *ever* published. (It features photos from the 1920's through '40's "scrapbook" of an L.A.P.D. homicide detective.)   800/323-0037

CAMBRIDGE STATISTICAL RESEARCH ASSOCIATES

CSRA made its name by providing easy access to the Social Security Administration's Master Death Index. They still offer that, but have also broadened their scope to include some other interesting databases. One searches for active military personnel. Further details and online searching can be done at their website, *www.csra.com*   800/327-2772
    714/653-2101

CANADIAN CORPORATIONS

>Infomart Online is an online information service focusing on Canadian business. Includes newspapers, newswires, corporate profiles, more.   800/668-9215

Control Data Systems Canada Ltd offers access to Canadian corporation records.   613/723-1174

>CANADIAN GOVERNMENT

Reference Canada	800/667-3355
Revenue Canada	416/954-3500
Ministry of Corporate and Consumer Relations	416/326-8555
Ministry of Justice and Attorney General	613/992-4621
American Consulate, Toronto	416/595-1700

For information on Canadian Motor Vehicle Licensing, see *DRIVER'S LI-CENSE INFORMATION.*

CANADIAN INVESTIGATIONS

>*Canadian Investigation Network* is an Ontario based private investigation agency available to assist in north of the border investigations. 888/CIN-8590
416/241-0009

Tracer's Worldwide Service offers locates of persons in Canada. 800/233-9766

CASINO FRAUD

International Casino Monitoring provides intelligence on casino cheats 011-44-1322-554124

The *Nevada State Gaming* Control Board publishes its "Black Book" of cheats barred from the state's casinos. 702/687-6500

New Jersey Division of Gaming Enforcement 609/441-7464

>*New Jersey Casino Control Commission* 609/441-3200

Also see...*THE EXCLUDED PARTY INDEX*....which includes the names and other information on persons banned from casinos in Nevada and New Jersey for cheating and other abuses.

CDB INFOTEK

CDB Infotek offers the most extensive selection of public and private databases available. Their reliability is excellent, too. See...*DATABASE PROVIDERS* for more details. Information is available online, or by fax, or call in service:

California	800/427-3747
Outside California	800/992-7889

CELEBRITY ADDRESSES

Axiom Information Resources publishes contact addresses for celebrities, politicians, and athletes. Most of the addresses are to mail services or publicists employed by the celebrities.　　　　313/761-4842

>Locating a celebrity for the purpose of legal service of process can present unique challenges. *Gold Star Investigations* is a Los Angeles based firm with a track record of serving the rich and famous.　　　　818/883-6969

CENTER FOR ANTISOCIAL & VIOLENT BEHAVIOR

Research group studies violence, crime, police issues　　　301/443-3728

CENTERS FOR DISEASE CONTROLL

Main #　　　　404/639-3311

Centers for Disease Control, Traveler's Advisory Hotline　　404/332-4559

Press Office, CDC　　404/639-3286

CENTER FOR INVESTIGATIVE REPORTING

The *Center for Investigative Reporting* is a non-profit group that, among other things, funds the investigation of hard to tackle stories and issues that the mainstream media tends to shy away from.　　415/543-1200

Also see...*ALTERNATIVE PRESS INDEX.*

Also see...*NAMEBASE.*

CENTRAL INTELLIGENCE AGENCY

Headquarters　　　703/482-1100
Job Opportunities　　800/562-7242

CHARITABLE ORGANIZATIONS

Most states and many municipalities register charitable organizations. Contact one of these numbers to receive background on charitable organizations:

Arizona　　　　800/458-5842

California	916/445-2021
Florida	800/435-7352
Maryland	401/974-5534
New Jersey	201/504-6262
>New York	518/486-9797
	212/416-8430
North Carolina	919/733-4510
Pennsylvania	800/732-0999
Virginia	804/786-1343

The *Internal Revenue Service's* SOI
(Statistics of Income) database includes data extracted from IRS form
990 — which tax exempt/charitable
organizations are required to file. The
information includes asset and income
data and employer identification numbers, among other things. Sorry, this
information is not available by phone.   202/874-0410

This information can be found on a
BBS by computer, using communication software, such as HyperTerminal.
The number to dial into is 202/874-9574.
However, you won't find a searchable
database online. You'll have to down-
load their data into your own database.

>The *IRS* also maintains a master list
of all tax exempt organizations that contains basically the same information. It's
available for free, on the Internet, at
*www.irs.ustreas.gov/plain/tax_stats/
soi/ex_imf.html*

You can also request a hardcopy of a
non-profit organization's tax return by
filing *Form 4506A* with the Internal
Revenue Service. It's public record.   800/829-1040

Form 4506A can also be downloaded
directly off the Internet from the IRS
website. Go to *www.irs.ustreas.gov/
forms_pubs/forms.html* and scroll
down the list of forms to 4506A.

>**CHECK FRAUD**
One highly knowledgeable source of
how counterfeit and other bad check
schemes are run is *Frank Abagnale* —
who himself is a former convicted
check forger. Today, he's relied upon
by the FBI, major banks, and corporations to stem losses from check
schemes. Believing that punishment
for fraud and restitution is rare,

Abagnale now focuses primarily on prevention. He's designed numerous checks and cashier's checks with fraud proof features.   800/237-7443

These companies maintain databases of persons who have written checks with insufficient funds, or on closed accounts. These aren't databases set up for investigators, though. Rather, they're geared toward merchants who must typically open an account and pay a monthly minimum charge:

TeleCheck	713/599-7600
ETC	206/483-2500
Equifax	404/885-8000

CHEMICAL SPILLS - EMERGENCY HOTLINE
Chemtrec is the chemical industry's emergency hotline for chemical and hazardous substance spills   800/424-9300

Also see...*TOXIC CHEMICALS.*

CHICAGO CRIME COMMISSION
The Chicago Crime Commission is a not for profit organization that has been gathering information on mobsters since 1919. Once the scourge of Al Capone, the group has broadened its focus to include modern day street gangs. *CCC* maintains an extensive library of local news clippings on mobsters, going back decades.   312/372-0101

CHILD ABUSE
There are many organizations set up to aid in the search for missing children. Only one has quasi-governmental status which includes partial access to NCIC and other usually law enforcement only resources. *The National Center for Missing and Exploited Children* is active in not only the recovery of abducted children, but also in the prevention of various types of sexual exploitation. Assistance offered to law enforcement includes photograph and poster preparation, technical case assistance and forensic services. *NCMEC* collaborates with the U.S. Secret Service's Forensic Division to provide handwriting, poly-

graph, fingerprint and other technical
forensic assistance.   800/THE-LOST
                                                  703/235-3900

Child Help U.S.A.   800/422-4453

Child Maltreatment is a two volume
clinical guide/reference book on child
abuse. Contact *GW Medical Publish-
ers, Inc.*   800/600-0330

*California's Child Molester Indenti-
fier* is a state run hotline that maintains
a database of registered child molesters. When the pay per call line is
called, the operator will determine if
a proposed baby-sitter, teacher, or
???? is a registered sex offender.
Cost is $10 per call. Two names can
be checked per call: 900/463-0400

>CHILD SUPPORT ENFORCEMENT
Here's a list of telephone numbers for
state agencies who enforce child support
orders:

Alabama	334/242-0606
Alaska	907/269-6801
Arizona	602/274-7646
Arkansas	501/682-6047
California	916/654-1556
Colorado	303/866-2214
Connecticut	203/424-5251
Delaware	302/577-4807
District of Columbia	202/724-5154
Florida	904/922-9590
Georgia	404/657-3851
Hawaii	808/587-3698
Idaho	208/334-0666
Illinois	217/524-4604
Indiana	317/232-4894
Iowa	515/281-4597
Kansas	913/296-3237
Kentucky	502/564-5988
Louisiana	504/342-7397
Maine	207/287-2886
Maryland	410/767-7674
Massachusetts	617/621-4990
Michigan	517/373-7570
Minnesota	612/297-4450
Mississippi	601/359-4863
Missouri	314/751-4301
Montana	406/444-3338
Nebraska	402/471-9390
Nevada	702/687-4744
New Hampshire	603/271-4578

New Jersey	609/588-2401
New Mexico	505/827-7200
New York	518/474-9081
North Carolina	919/571-4120
North Dakota	701/328-3582
Ohio	614/752-6561
Oklahoma	405/522-5871
Oregon	503/986-6083
Pennsylvania	717/787-3672
Rhode Island	401/277-2847
South Carolina	803/737-5870
South Dakota	605/773-3651
Tennessee	615/313-4880
Texas	512/463-9888
Utah	801/536-8911
Vermont	802/241-2319
Virginia	804/692-1501
Washington	360/586-3162
West Virginia	304/558-3780
Wisconsin	608/267-0926
Wyoming	307/777-7193

Also see...FEDERAL PARENT LOCATOR SERVICE.

>CLAIMS INTELLIGENCE REPORT

Claims Intelligence Report is a notable monthly newsletter produced by Hawaii PI John Wood. The newsletter focuses on legal and other developments relevant to insurance claim handling and investigation. Regular subscription cost is $144 per year. Mention *The Investigator's Little Black Book* for a special rate of $75. Want to review a free sample copy before subscribing? E-mail a request to *pi@ilhawaii.net* or fax the request to 808/885-5622.   808/885-5090

>COALITION ON POLITICAL ASSASSINATIONS

Comprised of medical and forensic experts, academics, authors and investigators, *COPA* has led the charge into reopening the investigations of the murders of the Kennedys, Martin Luther King, Jr. and others. Their primary focus is on unlocking secret government files through legal action. When you see something in the news about new information being released on one of these high profile assassinations, chances are *COPA* has had a hand in it.   202/785-5299

COAST GUARD - U.S.
Information   202/267-2229

Boat Ownership Records is a Coast
Guard database of every hull number
on every recreational boat in the
U.S., from which the vessel's manufacturer can be identified   202/267-0780

Contact the *Coast Guard, Personnel
Locator Service,* to locate an active
member   202/267-1340

Law Enforcement at Sea and *Defense
Operations*   202/267-0977

The *U.S. Coast Guard* maintains a
database of past search and rescue
operations   202/267-1948

Statistician, U.S. Coast Guard, maintains a database of boating accidents   202/267-0955

>COMBINED DNA INDEX SYSTEM (CODIS)

The future of law enforcement is here
and its name is *CODIS*. Short for the
Combined DNA Index System, this
FBI run program is a little known but
rapidly growing database of DNA
samples taken from hundreds of thousands of convicted violent offenders.
The system is most valuable in the
investigation of crimes where there
are no suspects. When trace evidence
is left behind at a crime scene – such
as hair, saliva, blood or semen – a
DNA profile is made and a computerized search is begun of the *CODIS*
database. Although still in its early
stages, with roughly half of the states
participating, *CODIS* has already
produced several dozen "cold hits".   202/324-3000

COMMERCIAL PROPERTY – CALIFORNIA

*Experian's Commercial & Industrial
Database* contains information on
commercial properties that have been
sold in California in the last ten years.
The information often includes a
photograph of the site.   800/345-7334

COMMODITY FUTURES TRADING

To report fraud and/or make com-

29

plaints, contact the *Commodity Futures Trading Commission.* 202/418-5000

The *National Futures Association* is the commodity futures industry's self-regulatory organization. Disciplinary and background information are kept on file on persons and firms involved in commodity futures trading. 800/621-3570
312/781-1410

COMPUTER DATA EXTRACTION
The Chelsea Group, Inc. specializes in retrieving information from computers when the access code is not available. 208/765-9181

Access Data Recovery Service also recovers data from computers where the password is missing or not available. 801/377-5410

Drivesavers specializes in rescuing data from fire, water, and trauma damaged computers. 415/883-4232

Computer Forensics specializes in computer evidence/information recovery, including E-mail as physical evidence. Are you sure that was deleted? 206/324-6232

As does *Electronic Evidence Discovery.* 206/343-0131

COMPUTER SECURITY
The *FBI's National Computer Crime Squad* investigates intrusion into governmental, financial, and medical computers. It also has jurisdiction over intrusion into the phone systems, privacy violations, and pirated software. 202/324-9164

>*The National Computer Security Center* is a section of the National Security Agency that sets security standards for government computer systems. 301/859-4371

>*Computer Crimes Unit, General Litigation Section, Department of Justice.* 202/514-1026

>As of our publishing deadline, there was a very interesting report on the Internet from a federal interagency group called the *Computer Search and*

Seizure Working Group. The site gives detailed guidelines for how and when federal agents should seize computers as evidence. Members of the interagency group include the FBI, IRS, DEA, ATF and others. The site is located at *http://www.io.com/~asrcs/fedguide.html*

U.S. Secret Service, Electronic Crimes Branch — 202/435-5850

>*National Computer Security Association* is a technically oriented group focusing on the establishment of standards and certification. — 800/488-4595

>Have a computer security problem along the lines of hacking, counterfeit e-mail, or other security breaches? Consider seeking assistance from computer expert David Tubbs of Talon Technology International. (Website: *http://www.talontech.com*) — 714/434-7476

>*Information Systems Security Association* has a membership of persons who protect computerized information. — 847/657-6746

>*Janus Associates* provides information security, computer forensics, and business recovery consulting services. They audit computer systems for vulnerability to intrusion and fraud. They also offer data recovery services for legal purposes in situations where the data has been "deleted". (When a file is deleted on a computer, it isn't destroyed. Rather, the information is simply parked on the hard drive, waiting to be overwritten. Until the data is overwritten, it is recoverable.) This Stamford, CT based firm is woman owned and claims numerous major corporations and governmental agencies among its clients. — 203/964-1150

Internet Security Systems is a security consulting company. — 770/441-2531

Computer Security Institute — 415/905-2310

The *National Institute of Standards and Technology Computer Security Lab* offers publications and a BBS on computer security — 301/975-2000

>If you have a security concern or discover a leak in any *Microsoft* product, send e-mail to *secure@microsoft*

>To report suspected counterfeit Microsoft products, call the *Microsoft Anti-Piracy Hotline:* — 800/RU-LEGIT

>If you want to know what's on the collective mind of the hacker community, check out *2600: The Hacker Quarterly*. It's also referred to as "The Hacker's Bible" by some. Can be gotten through subscription and also at many bookstores. — 516/751-2600

>CONFI-CHEK INVESTIGATIONS
There are giant vendors of on-line data and there are smaller ones who offer a more limited menu of information, but with more personal service. One of these is *Confi-Chek Investigations*, who offer database searches over the internet, *www.confi-chek.com* — 800/821-7404 / 916/443-4822

CONGRESSIONAL INFO
Pending legislation in the U.S. House of Representatives and Senate can be identified through the *Bill Status Office*. Computerized searching can be done by topic or keyword. — 202/225-1772

For hourly recorded updates of activity on the House or Senate floor, use these numbers:
House Cloakroom (Republicans) — 202/225-7430
House Cloakroom (Democrats) — 202/225-7400
Senate Cloakroom (Republicans) — 202/224-8601
Senate Cloakroom (Democrats) — 202/224-8541

COPYRIGHT INFORMATION
U.S. Copyright Office, Library of Congress — 202/707-3000

Dialog online service includes a database of copyright registrations. — 800/334-2564

To investigate who owns the copyright on a given work, call the *Copyright Office Hotline* and request a copy of Circular 22. — 202/707-9100

CORONERS
Coroners, also known a *Medical Examiners*, are an early source of information in any death investigation:

National Association of Medical Examiners	314/577-8298
Anchorage	907/264-0690
Atlanta	404/730-4400
Baltimore	410/333-3250
Boston	617/267-6767
Charlotte	704/336-2005
Chicago	312/666-0500
Cincinnati	513/221-4524
Cleveland	216/721-5610
Columbus	614/462-5290
Dallas	214/920-5900
Denver	303/436-7711
Detroit	313/224-5640
Honolulu	808/527-6777
Houston	713/796-9292
Kansas City	816/283-3553
Las Vegas	702/455-3210
Los Angeles	213/343-0512
Miami	305/545-2400
Milwaukee	414/223-1200
Minneapolis	612/347-2125
New Orleans	504/524-6763
New York	212/447-2030
Oakland	510/268-7300
Philadelphia	215/823-7457
Phoenix	602/506-3322
Pittsburgh	412/355-0990
Portland	503/248-3746
St. Louis	314/622-4971
Salt Lake City	801/584-8410
San Antonio	210/615-2100
San Diego	619/694-2895
San Francisco	415/553-1694
San Jose	408/299-5137
Seattle	206/223-3232
Washington, D.C.	202/724-4330

CORPORATION RECORDS

CT Corporation offers online access to corporation records nationwide. In addition, they have offices in fifty states that are the registered agents for service of process for numerous corporations   212/246-5070

Also check our *DATABASES PROVIDERS* section. Most of these companies offer access to corporate filing records.

CORPORATIONS - REGISTER-ED AGENTS

CT Corporation functions as the registered agent for service of process for hundreds of major corporations. Ask for "Service of Process" to determine if they represent any given corporation.

212/246-5070

Also see *CORPORATIONS - STATE DEPARTMENTS OF.*

CORPORATIONS - STATE DE-PARTMENTS OF

Each state has a department of corporations that registers corporations doing business in that state. Many will provide information by phone. All will by mail. Information typically includes corporate officers, registered agents, location, and history:

Alabama	334/242-5324
Alaska	907/465-2530
Arizona	602/542-3026
Arkansas	501/682-3409
California	916/657-5448
Colorado	303/894-2251
Connecticut	860/566-8570
Delaware	302/739-3073
D.C.	202/727-7278
Florida	904/487-6053
Georgia	404/656-2817
Hawaii	808/586-2727
Idaho	208/334-2300
Illinois	217/782-7880
Indiana	317/232-6576
Iowa	515/281-5204
Kansas	913/296-4564
Kentucky	502/564-7330
Louisiana	504/925-4792
Maine	207/287-4190
Maryland	410/225-1330
Massachusetts	617/727-2850
Michigan	900/555-0031
Minnesota	612/297-1455
Mississippi	601/359-1633
Missouri	573/751-4153
Montana	406/444-3665
Nebraska	402/471-4079
Nevada	702/687-5203
Nevada Corporate Status Line	900/535-3355
New Hampshire	603/271-3246
New Jersey	609/530-6400
New Mexico	505/827-4504
New York	518/473-2492

(Pay-Per-Call line, faster service)	900/835-2677
North Carolina	910/733-4201
North Dakota	701/224-4284
Ohio	614/466-3910
Oklahoma	900/820-2424
Oregon	503/378-4166
Pennsylvania	717/787-1057
Rhode Island	401/277-2357
South Carolina	803/734-2158
South Dakota	605/773-4845
Tennessee	615/741-2816
Texas	512/463-5555
Utah	801/530-4849
Vermont	802/828-2386
Virginia	804/371-9733
Washington	360/753-7115
West Virginia	304/558-8000
Wisconsin	608/266-3590
Wyoming	307/777-7311

COUNTERFEIT CURRENCY

The *U.S. Secret Service, Counterfeit Division*   202/435-5756

>*Office of the Comptroller of the Currency, Enforcement and Compliance Division*   202/874-5301

Data Impressions offers magic markers that are claimed to identify counterfeit currency.   800/677-3031
310/630-8788

>**COUNTERFEIT PRODUCTS**
In March of 1997, 26,000 counterfeit copies of Windows 95 were seized in downtown Los Angeles. Pound for pound, the software had a greater street value than more traditional forms of contraband. To report suspected counterfeit Microsoft products, call the *Microsoft Anit-Piracy Hotline*.   800/RU-LEGIT

To report counterfeit music tapes and CD's, contact the *Recording Indusrty of America Piracy Hotline*.   800/BAD-BEAT

International Counterfeiting Coalition   202/223-5728

Also see...*NATIONAL ANTI-PIRACY ASSOCIATION.*

Also see...*VIDEOTAPE PIRACY.*

Also see...*CABLE TV - THEFT OF SERVICE.*

Also see...*ALPHA DOT.*

COURTROOM EXHIBITS
LSI Graphic Evidence specializes in
graphics for courtroom evidence:

Chicago	312/482-8395
Houston	713/655-0503
Los Angeles	310/568-1831

CREDIT BUREAUS
Three "Super Bureaus" collect and
disseminate personal financial information on millions of Americans. Release of the information is regulated
by the Fair Credit Reporting Act and
various State statutes:

Equifax	800/685-5000
	800/685-1111
Trans Union	800/858-8336
	800/851-2674
Experian (Formerly TRW)	800/422-4879
	800/682-7654

**CREDIT CARD & FINANCE
COMPANIES**
American Express:

Fraud & Security	*(NYC)*	212/640-3415
Fraud & Security	*(LA)*	213/688-0825
Purchase Protection Plan		800/322-1277
AMEX/Centurion		305/472-3787
AMEX/Optima		954/503-3787
American Express Card		954/503-3787
AT&T Universal Bank		904/954-7500
Bank of America		800/423-3811
		800/247-3409
		800/582-4332
Bank of Hoven		605/948-2278
Bank of New York (DE)		800/777-9379
Bay Bank (MA)		617/329-3700
BMW Financial Services		800/398-3939
BP Oil		216/586-6373
Broadway		602/929-3187
Capital Bank of Miami		305/279-7900

Chase Bank	602/731-3009
Chemical Bank	516/934-3639
Chevron	510/602-7020
Chevy Chase	800/685-0800
Chrysler Credit	714/251-2300
	619/497-3300
Citibank	800/843-0777
Skip Trace	972/664-4113
Student Loans	800/967-2400
Colonial National Bank	215/956-0482
Diner's Card	
(Merchant Verification)	800/525-9040
Discover Card	800/DISCOVER
	800/347-2683
Education Loan Service	617/849-1140
First Card	847/888-6000
	800/862-9356
First National Bank of Chicago	708/888-6000
Ford Consumer Finance	714/855-7114
Ford Motor Consumer Loan	800/753-3673
Ford Motor Credit	800/727-7000
	916/920-3600
	810/244-5924
GE Capital Mortgage Services	800/222-0238
	800/544-3466
GE Credit Auto lease, Inc.	800/488-5208
GMAC	800/200-4622
Home Savings of America	800/874-9718
Household Bank	800/477-6000
	800/685-1000
ITT Financial Services	503/779-9994
JC Penny	503/652-4700
	800/542-0800
Lord & Taylor	800/654-0520
Marine Midland Bank	800/874-2100

MBNA America	302/456-8926
Mercedes Benz Credit	800/654-6222
	503/293-6100
Mellon Bank	800/753-7011
Montgomery Wards	800/950-0345
National Bank of Detroit	616/771-7000
	813/484-0461
Nationsbank	800/274-5060
Neiman Marcus	800/753-0407
Nordstrom	206/233-5904
Sanwa Bank	818/312-5560
Sears	800/877-8691
Standard Oil (CA)	510/602-7020
Student Loan Marketing Association	800/233-1193
Visa :	
Customer Service	800/847-2911
Law Enforcement Assistance	800/367-8472
Wells Fargo Bank	800/642-4720
Zales Jewelers	602/829-5800

CREDIT CARD FRAUD

International Association of Credit Card Investigators	415/897-8800
Mastercard - Law Enforcement Assistance	800/231-1750
American Express:	
Fraud & Security *(NYC)*	212/640-3415
Fraud & Security *(LA)*	213/688-0825
Visa Law Enforcement Assistance	800/367-8472
>Discover Card Law Enforcement Assistance	800/347-3102

CREDIT CARD IDENTIFIER

Have a credit card number, but don't know the bank of issuance? By calling *Chase Merchant Service's* toll free number, authorized users can identi-

fy the bank of issuance. Authorized
users should choose option 5, then enter
the first six digits of the credit card number, then hit the * key. The phone number
of the bank which issued the credit card
will be read by an automatic attendant.   800/326-7991

>FYI: Credit card numbers that start with
a "5" are Mastercards; with a "4" are Visa
cards.

>CRIME LABS - PRIVATE
Private crime or "forensic" labs can
be used for everything from establishing
paternity to trace evidence and ballistic
analysis. There is no nationwide association of private crime labs.

The Society of Forensic Toxicologists
is limited to the study and identification
of various types of poisons, including
drugs. For a referral to a forensic toxi-
cologist in your area, call: 602/839-9106

PoisonLab is a lab specializing in forensic toxicology. They'll identify
drugs, poison, and other toxins from
biological specimens.   619/279-2600

ChemaTox Laboratory, Inc. is a Colorado based lab that offers a number of services, including drug identification, soil
pollutants, and arson (accelerant) testing. 800/334-1685

Forensic Science Consulting Group
is a private crime/forensics lab whose
specialties include crime scene analysis, ballistics, fingerprints, and trace
evidence.   760/436-7714

National Medical Services is a Pennsylvania based crime lab offering a
range of services, including examina-
tion of trace evidence.   800/NMS-LAB1
                                            215/657-4900

Chemical Toxicology Institute is
located in Northern California and
focuses on drug and other laboratory
tests.   650/573-6222

Also see...*DNA LABS.*

Also see...*DRUG DETECTION.*

CRIME LABS - GOVERNMENT

American Society of Crime Lab Directors has a membership limited to governmental crime lab directors. — 813/341-4409

Clandestine Laboratory Investigating Chemists Association can be contacted through Ken Fujii, membership secretary. — 510/646-2455

The *U.S. Department of Fish & Game's National Fish & Wildlife Forensic Lab* has been called the first full service wildlife crime lab in the world. — 541/482-4191

CRIME STATISTICS

FBI, Uniform Crime Reporting Section — 202/324-5038

Juvenile Justice Clearinghouse maintains statistics and data on juvenile justice. — 800/638-8736

U.S. Department of Justice, Bureau of Justice Statistics — 800/732-3277

CRIMINAL JUSTICE ORGANIZATIONS

American Criminal Justice Association — 916/484-6553

American Society of Criminology — 614/292-9207

Corrections Information Center disseminates information on prison issues — 303/444-1101

Justice Research & Statistics Association — 202/624-8560

The Center for Antisocial and Violent Behavior studies violence, crime, and police issues — 301/443-3728

National Crime Prevention Institute   502/852-6987

National Criminal Justice Reference Service is the National Institute of Justice's massive repository of over 130,00 documents, publication and books. Information Specialists are available to consult by phone on crime and justice related research matters. This is a department of the U.S. Department of Justice.   800/851-3420

CRIMINAL RECORDS
The National Crime Information Center (NCIC) is law enforcement's massive nationwide criminal history program. Run by the FBI, *NCIC* has over 33 million records and is available, nationwide, to over 76,000 federal, state and local authorized users. Access to *NCIC* is through a tightly monitored computer system over dedicated telephone lines maintained by the FBI. Access by unauthorized users is a federal crime.

NCIC currently consists of seventeen separate databases or "files". Soon there will be a eighteenth, a nationwide Sex Offender Registry.

>The most recently added files include *The Violent Gang/Terrorist File, The Protective Order File*, and *The Deported Felon File*.

By far the largest file is the *Interstate Identification Index* (also commonly known as the "Triple I") which has over 25 million criminal records from all 50 states. Most of these are felonies, but some serious misdemeanors are also included. The *"Triple I"* is only as complete as the records which are supplied to the FBI by the states. Felony arrests could have been occured which would not be reflected in a person's *Interstate Identification Index* record due to shortcomings in the reporting process.

Other *NCIC* files include the *ATF Violent Felon File* which shows felons with convictions where a firearm was used, or where a subject was killed; the *Foreign Fugitive File* which tracks wanted persons from abroad; the *Wanted*

Person File which catalogs persons with outstanding federal, felony or serious misdemeanor warrants; the *Missing Person File* which is a database of the lost, missing, and mysteriously disappeared; the *Unidentified Person File* which tracks John and Jane Doe corpse information, unidentified catastrophe victims, living persons who are uncertain of their own identity, and miscellaneous recovered body parts; the *Vehicle File* which lists stolen cars; the *Gun File* which lists stolen and abandoned firearms; the *License Plate File* which lists stolen license plates; the *Boat File* which lists stolen watercraft; the *Securities File* which lists serial numbers of stolen securities including currency; the *Articles File* which lists the serial numbers of stolen items valued in excess of $500; the *Originating Agency Identifier* which keeps track of the criminal justice agencies authorized to access NCIC; and finally, the *U.S. Secret Service Protective File* which keeps track of individuals who pose a threat to the President.

304/625-6200

For where NCIC is headed in the future, see...*NCIC 2000*.

Anyone can request a copy of their own criminal record. Contact this *FBI* number for more information. However, be forewarned that the process is cumbersome.

202/324-5454

Available to anyone is the *Federal Prison Locator* which tells if a person has been incarcerated in a Federal prison, since 1981.

202/307-3126

Also available to anyone is the *Federal Prison Archives* which has pre-1981 information.

202/307-2934

Several states provide access to statewide criminal records where no release from the subject is required:

>*Alabama* allegedly offers a statewide criminal check without the consent of the subject. However, when we contacted the *Alabama Bureau of Investigation* for details, we couldn't find anyone there who knew what to do. Practically speaking, this is a waste of time.

800/216-8860

> In *California*, statewide criminal checks are limited to law enforcement only. However, there is a legal, backdoor way to access much of the same information. By calling the *California Department of Corrections* with a subject's name and DOB, you can learn if the subject has a history of incarceration in the state's prison system since 1977. Only felony convictions result in state prison incarceration in California. However, a felony conviction does not automatically mean that incarceration in state prison will result. The line is operated 24 hours a day, 7 days a week.　916/445-6713

>*Colorado* allows rap sheets (arrests and convictions) to be obtained. You'll need to pay a $7 fee per name checked and complete a form called *Public Request for Information*.　303/239-4680

>*Connecticut* offers a statewide criminal conviction history for $15 per name. You'll need to call and request their form, *Criminal History Conviction Information Request*. Requests are filled by mail only.　860/685-8480

>*District of Columbia* criminal checks can be done through the *DC Superior Court* by telephone. Includes felony convictions since 1978. Have the subject's name and DOB ready when you call.　202/879-1373

>*Florida* allows criminal history checks without the permission of the subject. The cost is $15 per name checked. Requests should be made on the State's *Criminal History Information Request* form. The form can be found on the Internet at *www.fdle.state.fl.us*. The form can also be requested by sending a SASE to *Florida Department of Law Enforcement, CJIS User Services, P.O. Box 1489, Tallahassee, FL 32302*　904/488-4931

>Although *Georgia* doesn't have a statewide criminal check available to non-law enforcement parties, the state will release information about a person who is under active parole supervision. Call the *Georgia Board of Pardons & Parole*.　404/656-5330

>*Hawaii* will release a subject's adult criminal history, including both felonies and mis-

demeanors. Send the subject's name, DOB and SSN plus a $10 fee. (They prefer payment by money order or cashier's check.) Send your request to *Department of Attorney General, Hawaii Criminal Justice Data Center, Room 101, 465 S. King Street, Honolulu, HI 96813.*

808/587-3106

>*Iowa* will release the adult criminal conviction history of a subject, including both felonies and serious misdemeanors. Arrest information without a disposition will also be included from the past 18 months. The fee is $13 per name checked, plus your request must be made on a special state provided form. If you want a person checked under two names (ie., a married name and maiden name), two fees and two request forms must be submitted. The forms and further instructions can be obtained by calling this number and asking for a *Non-Law Enforcement Record Check Request* form and a *Billing* form. They'll fax you what you need. The same form can also be obtained over the Internet at *www.state.ia.us/government/dps/dci.*

515/281-5138

>In *Kansas*, statewide criminal histories are available to non-law enforcement personnel. A user agreement, called the *Criminal History Record Request and Agreement*, must be requested from the Kansas Bureau of Investigation. After executing the agreement, names can be checked for $10 each. Turnaround time is 8 - 10 weeks.

913/296-8200

>*Kentucky* is one of the few states with the centralized collection of criminal court conviction records. The person whose record is being checked is notified, however. The name checks are done by mail only. Cost is $10 each and they take a week to fulfill. Call this number, ask for *Records*, and then request to be faxed a *Record Request Form.*

502/573-2350

>*Maine* offers adult criminal conviction histories to anyone requesting the information. The state's criminal records aren't computerized yet, so there's a slow turnaround time - possibly three months. Send $7.00, the subject's name and date of birth to *Maine State Police, Bureau of Identification, 3600 Hospital*

Street, Augusta, ME 04330.   207/624-7009

>A statewide felony check can be done in *Maryland* via the *JIS* system which should identify whether or not a subject has been arraigned on felony charges in the state's circuit courts. For a $15 fee, private company *Document Resources* will check the *JIS* system.   800/777-8467

>*Massachusetts* is another state that's on the books as offering a statewide criminal history. Look at the details, though, and you'll realize it's all but worthless. In short, the state will tell if a person's had a felony conviction - but only if they've completed their sentence or probation within the last two years. A convicted murderer, who has completed his sentence and parole more than two years ago would come up clean.   617/660-4600

>*Minnesota* will release felony and certain misdemeanor conviction information without a release. Record checks are not done by phone. Public record information released will be for the last 15 years only. Send the subject's full name and DOB with a SASE to *Bureau of Criminal Apprehension, 1246 University Ave, St. Paul, MN 55104.* Include a fee of $4 per name checked. Indicate that you are requesting a *Public Record Criminal History Check.* Payment accepted by money order or company check *only.*   612/642-0670

>*Missouri* statewide criminal record checks are available without the subject's consent. Send a check or money order for $5 per name checked to *Missouri State Highway Patrol, Attn: Criminal Records, P.O. Box 568, Jefferson City, MO 65102.* Include the subject's name, DOB and SSN. All convictions, pending charges, and a 30 day arrest history will be released.   573/526-6153

>*Montana* will provide criminal history information. Included are felony criminal convictions going back to the subject's 18th birthday, plus misdemeanor convictions for the past 5 years. Turnaround time is 7 to 10 days. Fee is $5 per name checked. Include the subject's name, any known aliases, DOB, SSN and SASE. Phone checks not done. Mail request to: *Identi-*

fication Bureau, 303 N. Roberts, #374, Helena, MT 59620. .... 406/444-3625

>*Nebraska* allows criminal history checks without the consent of the subject. Their records include all arrests and convictions when the arrestee's fingerprints have been taken. In practical terms, this means for felonies and serious misdemeanors. There's a 15 day turnaround time. Fee is $10 per name checked. Send the subject's name, DOB, SSN and any aliases to *Nebraska State Patrol, Attn: CID, PO Box 94907, Lincoln, NB 68509-4907.* 402/471-4545

The State of New York doesn't offer statewide criminal records without a signed authorization from the subject. To conduct searches at local criminal courts, including in *New York City,* you might want to contact *Fidelifacts.* Cost is around $31 per name checked. Turnaround time is roughly two days. 800/678-0007
212/425-1520

>*North Dakota* will release a person's statewide conviction history for felony and some misdemeanor convictions. Also included are certain events from the preceding 12 months, including arrests. Call this number and request a *Non-Criminal Justice Records Release Form.* After completing the form, return it with a $20 fee to the *North Dakota Bureau of Criminal Investigation.* (Note: The person whose name is checked is notified by the State that his or her criminal history has been re-quested. However, the identity of the requester is kept confidential.) 701/328-5500

Ohio Professional Electronic Net-work (AKA *OPEN*) offers a computer-ized database of county arrest records from 82 of Ohio's 88 counties. The information is available online, on a subscription basis. This is one of the very few databases of arrest records (as opposed to conviction records) publicly available anywhere. 800/366-0106
614/481-6980

>*Oklahoma* has an open criminal re-cord release policy. For a fee of $15 per name checked, the *Oklahoma State Bureau of Investigation* will conduct

46

a statewide criminal arrest and conviction history.   405/848-6724

>*The Oklahoma Department of Corrections* will tell if a subject has spent time in
a state prison.   405/425-2500

>*Oregon* criminal records are available
without the subject's consent - but there's
one catch: The subject of the inquiry is
sent a letter and told that you have requested his or her criminal history. Felony and misdemeanor conviction information going back to the subject's 18th
birthday is included. Limit requests to one
name per letter, include the subject's name,
DOB and last known address. Send payment in the amount of $15 per name
to *Oregon State Police, Attn: Open Records, PO Box 430034, Portland, OR
97208.*   503/378-3070

Also in Oregon, the state's civil and
criminal court records can be accessed
through *OJIN* — the *Oregon Judicial
Information Network*. Access is by computer, 24 hours a day. There's a set up
fee involved, too, of around $100.
Toll Free, from Oregon only: 800/922-7391
From out-of-state dial: 503/986-5582

If you're in need of a statewide criminal search in Oregon, but don't need
to sign up with OJIN, contact local investigators, *Agrue, Beers & DeLapp.*
They're all hooked up to OJIN and will
do a statewide criminal search for $35.   503/246-7561

>*Pennsylvania* offers felony conviction
data by mail only. Call this number
and request their form, *Request for
Criminal Record Check.* Complete
the form and mail back with a $10
fee per name checked. No release from
subject required.   717/783-5592

>*South Carolina* will release criminal
conviction and arrest
information that is less than one year
old. There's a 7 -10 day turnaround.
Send payment in the amount of $25
per name checked, payable by money
order or company check *only.* Include
the subject's name, DOB and SSN
(if available). Also include a SASE.
Mail request to: *South Carolina Law*

Enforcement Division, Attn: Records, PO Box 21398, Columbia, SC 29221.   803/737-9000

>*Texas* statewide criminal histories are now available thanks to a new public records act which took effect September 1, 1997. A subject's misdemeanor and felony conviction criminal history and/ or felony deferral record will be released without the subject's consent. Send a $10 fee, plus as many identifiers as possible on the subject, including name, DOB, SSN, race and sex. Requests are currently turned around in about 48 hours. Send your request to *Texas Department of Public Safety, Attn: Crime Records Service, PO Box 15999, Austin, TX 78761-5999.*   512/424-2474

Also in Texas, you'll want to know about a fine company called *Quick Search* which specializes in criminal court look ups in all Texas counties. For just $3 (as of publication date) they will perform a criminal court look up in Dallas County. For another $5 they'll check Harris County (Houston). Other Texas counties are $3 - $8 each.   214/358-2840

In *Utah*, probation and parole records are public information. Therefore, to learn if a person is on probation or parole, call the *Utah Department of Corrections:*   801/265-5500

>*Virginia* has broken new ground with a program that releases information on offenders who are currently under parole supervision. (It's known informally as the *Know thy NeighborLaw*, but in fact it isn't a law at all. A gubernatorial directive authorized the release of this information beginning in September of 1996.) For a fee of $5 any person can request a print out of all persons on parole within a given zip code. For $37.50, you can receive a similar list (on paper or computer disk) for the entire state. The lists are updated monthly. Currently, there are roughly 9,000 names on the list which is being read and used by employers, homeowner's associations, neighborhood watchgroups, and others. For 24 hour automated information, call this telephone number. To obtain the list, mail your

payment and request to: *Virginia Department of Corrections, Attn: Victim Services Unit, 6900 Atmore Dr, Richmond, VA 23225*.   804/674-3243

>In the *State of Washington*, statewide criminal conviction histories are public record. Request a *Background Check Form* from: *Washington State Patrol, P.O. Box 42633, Olympia, WA 98504-2633*. You'll need to complete the form and provide the name and DOB of the person to be checked, plus a $10 fee. You'll receive back a print out of his or her criminal convictions, and whether or not he or she is on the sex offender list. Eventually there will probably also be an Internet site with the information available online. In the meantime, further questions can be directed to the *Washington State Patrol's Identification and Criminal History Section*.   360/705-5100

>*Wisconsin* arrest and conviction information from 1971 through the present is available without the subject's consent. Include the subject's name, DOB, sex, race, a SASE, and payment in the amount of $13 per name checked. Mail your request to: *Crime Information Bureau, Attn: Record Check Unit, PO Box 2688, Madison, WI 53701-2688*   608/266-5764

The next best option is to research criminal court indexes in the counties and municipalities where the subject has been known to live. Contact *directory assistance* in the local area and ask for the local criminal court, then contact the court directly. Some courts will provide information over the phone. Most, however, require a written or in person inquiry.

>*Crime Search* is a public record retrieval company that offers nationwide criminal court record checks at bargain basement prices.   847/679-9595

Criminal court convictions are also available via computer in many areas. Work though one of the many public record providers in our *DATABASE PROVIDER* section.

The *U.S. Department of State* monitors the arrests/trials of U.S. citizens in foreign lands through its *Overseas Citizens Services* Unit   202/647-5226

Also see...*SEX OFFENDER REGISTRIES*.

Also see...*STATE PRISONS*....where in certain states a de facto criminal history can be obtained by requesting an individual's prison history.

CSRA
See...*Cambridge Statistical Research Associates*.

CURRENCY EXCHANGE RATES
To determine current exchange rates, call *Thomas Cook*   800/287-7362

CUSTOMS, U.S.
Main #   202/927-2109

>Direct Freedom of Information Act Requests to: *United States Customs Service, Freedom of Information Request, 1099 14th St NW, Washington, DC 20229.*

>To report customs violations, or fraud or corruption within the *U.S. Customs Service*   800/BE ALERT

DATABASE PROVIDERS
CDB Infotek offers the most extensive selection of public and private databases available. Their reliability is excellent. The company has *two* identical computer systems. If one goes down, they switch to the other. *CDB's* other big plus is customer service. When honest mistakes happen, they'll usually credit your account, if asked. This saves you from having to eat the cost of a search run in error. There are other database providers that are cheaper, but of the ones that I have personally used, *CDB* sets the standard. Databases offered are too numerous to list here, but include civil and criminal court records, DMV records, corporation records, real property ownership, birth/marriage/death records and much more. The information is available online, by fax, or by call in service:
California   800/427-3747
Outside California   800/992-7889

Merlin Information Services has carved out its own growing niche in data land through a library of public record CD ROMS. They take much of the same information that the online providers offer on a pay-by-search basis and package it into a CD ROM. You just pop the disc into your computer and do unlimited searching for just the initial cost of the disc. If your company does a sufficient volume of searches, you'll find *Merlin's* cost per search to be very attractive. (The CD ROMS range in cost from $69 to $699, with an average being around $299 .) Other advantages include being able to search a database by address, and a nifty "browse" feature. Many of *Merlin's* discs are available on a quarterly subscription basis to keep the information reasonably fresh. However, they've recently begun offering updated information over the Internet, too. If having the very latest information is mandatory, consider a "hybrid" search, using a CD ROM and also a low cost web based search to obtain the most recent filings. The *Merlin* website, *www. merlindata. com,* also offers a free search, called *The Ultimate Weapon.* Several databases, mostly of California public records, can be searched for free. If hits are made, you only pay for the "details" you choose to download. For more information, call and ask for *Merlin's* most recent newsletter.   800/367-6646

Database Technologies aka *DBT Online* aka *DBT Autotrak* is a database provider that's caught a small buzz in certain circles of investigators. The main reason is a database called *Faces of the Nation,* a skip-tracing tool made up of browsable credit bureau header files. Master *Faces of*

The Excluded Party Index™

the Nation (which isn't hard to do) and you'll have a very powerful locate tool to rely upon. The cost for most searches is $1.50 per minute, with a surcharge added for certain premium items. Once you learn to navigate the system, you'll be able to search more cheaply. There are no monthly fees. If you could have just one database provider, it wouldn't be *DBT*. However, it would make a very handy secret weapon to keep on the side.   800/279-7710

Integrated Database Software has been used by collection agencies, skip trace firms, and a select few PI's in the know for conducting dirt cheap locates. For more details, see...*INTEGRATED DATABASE SOFTWARE.*   630/530-9962

Many database providers offer essentially the same information, just wrapped in different colored paper. *DCS Information Services* out of Dallas first caught many investigator's attention by offering their DNIS database. It was the first non-MVR database made widely available to PI's that was driven by date of birth information, instead of social security numbers. If you were looking for a subject named John Smith and you had his birth date, the database wouldn't just spit out a list of John Smiths. It would give you a list of John Smiths whose birth date matched that of your subject. The results were remarkable. Since then, DCS has grown and added social security number searches, real estate ownership, driver's license, and other data. Their costs are very reasonable.   800/299-DNIS

Lexis-Nexis is a massive provider of computerized information, a favorite child of the legal profession. Few PI's use the service, because the core information PI's use most can be found more cheaply elsewhere. Nevertheless, *Lexis-Nexis* boasts 1,100 sources of information. Much of this, though, is geared toward the needs of lawyers, not PI's. Included is a vast archive of case law, constantly updated state and federal statutes, and state insurance regulations. Also available are numerous public record databases, plus some interesting specialty databases. *M-Find* is a locator database of US Military personnel. Another data-

base features FEIN (Federal Employer
Identification Numbers).   800/227-4908

Now, if you don't want to subscribe
to *Lexis-Nexis*, but would like to make
spot buys from their many databases,
consider *Lexis-Nexis Express*. Non-
subscribers can use the aid of staff
Lexis-Nexis researchers to buy information ala carte. Payment accepted by
credit card.   800/843-6476

Information America is another
well known database provider, offer-
ing numerous searches.   800/532-9876

Info Americall is the research on
demand service of InfoAmerica.
Their researcher will conduct the
searches on an hourly fee basis.   800/235-4008

Know X is a database provider, owned
by Information America, that offers
public record information for sale over
the Internet (*www.knowx.com*).Their
current menu of databases is quite limited and wouldn't be satisfactory to most
PI's. *Know X* doesn't advertise a phone
number. Here's their e-mail address: *support@knowx.com*

*Information Resource Service Com-
pany (IRSC)* is a major provider
of public and private records, similar
to CDB Infotek.
California   800/640-4772
                                            714/526-8485

If you don't have a computer, don't
worry — you can still obtain all of
this marvelous information by fax or
phone using these resellers. Be ready
to pay for the extra service, though.
Here's some companies that sell database information by fax and/or telephone:
Research Data Service   702/733-4990
Atlas Information Services   352/666-4371
Tracers Worldwide Services   800/233-9766
Super Bureau   800/541-6821

DATABASES - SPECIALTY
Aristotle offers a database of register-
ed voters.   800/296-2747
                                            202/543-8345

Art Loss Register has a database of
stolen works of art and art objects.   212/391-8791

CQ Washington Alert is an online
information service specializing in
congressional information.   800/432-2250

Dataquick offers real property
ownership records.   800/523-3765
                                              310/306-4295

DataStar is an online information service operated by the same folks behind
Dialog. Focus is from a European per-
spective and covers business, medical
and pharmaceutical sources. For a more
detailed description of the databases
available, check out Datastar's homepage
on the Net, *www.rs.ch/www/rs/datastar.
htm*   800/334-2564

Datatimes offers access to text previously appearing in over 5,000 publications and news sources, worldwide. Current fee is $39 per month for
unlimited searching of headlines, plus
a charge of $2.95 per article printed.   800/642-2525

Dialog is an online information service
for researchers, corporate librarians
and information professionals. Some
of the databases are familiar -- such
as news text retrievals, company profiles, and airline schedules. Others
are highly specialized on hard to find
subjects.   800/334-2564

EyeQ from *Datatimes* is an online business
news service. The monthly cost is $39.
In return, you'll have access to a large
data bank of business media, with small
additional charges for stock and company
profiles.   405/751-6400

The *Federal Railroad Administration*
maintains a database of railway acci-
dents.   202/366-4000

FAA Accident & Incident Histories
monitors aircraft accidents.   405/954-4173

The *Public Records Section, Federal
Election Commission*, maintains a
database of financial information dis-
closed by all federal candidates and
contributors since 1977.   800/424-9530

FamilySearch, a CD rom database, includes SSA death records and is available at most of the 2,000 *Church of the Latter Day Saints Family History Centers*, located throughout the fifty states. Free. Call this number to find your nearest *Family History Center:*   800/346-6044

The FDA maintains a database of known poisonous substances:
Poison Control Branch   301/827-3223

The *Governmentwide Information Systems Division* maintains a database of all federal procurements over ten thousand dollars since 1979.   202/401-1529

The Index System is the insurance industry's mega database of persons who have filed bodily injury claims.
AISG Marketing   212/669-0406
The Index System, Customer Support   732/388-0332

Jewelers Board of Trade is a jewelry trade organization that maintains a database of background information on persons in the jewelry business.   213/627-4238

Jury Verdict Research has profiled over 100,000 personal injury cases verdicts and settlements on CD ROM.   800/341-7874

Metronet offers access to nationwide surname scans, and reverse directory look ups through a 900 pay-per-call line.   900/288-3020

The Marine Index Bureau maintains a database of injury claims made by maritime personnel.   800/929-0654

The Maritime Information System offers databases culled from U.S. Coast Guard records, including *Boating Accidents, Merchant Vessel*, and *Manufacturer Identification Code*.   800/325-8061

>*Namebase* is a unique database of over 96,567 persons who have been named in at least one of hundreds of investigative journalism books.   210/509-3160

>*The National Driver Register* is a computerized database of information on the most dangerous drivers in America.   202/366-4800

The *National Reference Center* is a free
program of the Library of Congress
which maintans a huge database of
experts and organizations on virtually
any technical or scientific subject.   202/707-5522

NTIS maintains a computerized database of over one million reports on a
wide range of technical subjects.   800/553-NTIS
                                                        703/487-4650

OSHA's *Office of Management of
Data Systems* maintains a database
of all OSHA workplace inspections
made since 1972.   202/219-7788

>*Ohio Professional Electronic Net-
work* (OPEN) offers in depth online
access to public records in Ohio, in-
cluding criminal arrest data.   800/366-0106
                                                        614/481-6999

>*Producer Database* is the first national
database of licensing information on
insurance agents and brokers, including
disciplinary information from state li-
censing authorities.   913/599-8085

Property Insurance Loss Registry
is the insurance industry's mega
database of property claims.
AISG Marketing   212/669-0406
PILR Customer Support   732/388-0157

Questel-Orbit, Inc. is an online provider of patent and trademark filings
information.   800/456-7248

>*The Southern Poverty Law Center's*
website names names of militia members
and organizations in a growing, publicly
available database. (*www.splcenter.org/
klanwatch/kw-1.html*)   334/264-0286

Standard & Poor's Online Registry
is a database of information on publicly and privately owned companies,
their owners, and key executives.   800/237-8552

The Trademark Register offers online
access to the federal trademark registry
on a subscription basis. Reasonable
rates   202/662-1233

The United States Geological Survey
has a database called the *Geographic*

Names Data System (AKA National Geographic Names Database), which stores the names of over two million places in the United States.   703/648-4550

The *U.S. Fire Administration* maintains a nationwide database of fire incidents, as submitted by participating local fire agencies. It's known as the Fire Incident Reporting System   301/447-1349
301/447-1024

VISTA Environmental Information, Inc. offers databases compiled from state and federal environmental records   800/767-0403
619/450-6100

West Law offers an extensive database of legal information for attorneys   800/937-8529

Also see......*NATIONAL INSURANCE CRIME BUREAU ...NATIONAL PRACTITIONERS DATA BANK...THE EXCLUDED PARTY INDEX....CRIMINAL RECORDS ...SEX OFFENDER REGISTRIES...MEDICAL DOCTORS ...MILITARY PERSONNEL...NEWSPAPERS...NEWS SOURCES.*

>DEATH INVESTIGATIONS
A very good guide to conducting death investigations is *Death Investigator's Handbook* by Louis N. Eliopulos. The author is a Chief Forensic Investigator in Jacksonville, Florida. The book provides detailed guidelines on collecting evidence and investigative procedures for just about every conceivable cause of death. Available through these publishers, the book is nearly 900 pages long and sells for $40.00.
Paladin Press   800/392-2400
Thomas Investigative Publications   512/420-9292

Death Investigator's Handbook author Louis N. Eliopulos is also available as a consultant to law enforcement agencies and insurance companies.   904/630-0977

>Need to obtain a court admissible autopsy? Consider the services of *Autopsy/ Post Service, Inc.* This Los Angeles based company specializes in conducting autopsies for civil and criminal cases and includes Johnnie Cochrane as a regular customer. The firm is operated by former LA County Coroner's Investi-

gator *Vidal Herrera*. Also available is
expert medical review and testimony in
death cases. If you're outside of Los
Angeles, *Herrera* may still be able to
help – his company has a growing num-
ber of associates around the country.   800/AUTOPSY

Planning on taking a dirt nap soon your-
self? Looking to pinch pennies down to
the bitter end and beyond? Consider
Direct Casket for savings on your under-
ground condo. They sell direct, cutting
out the middleman.   800/77-CASKET

Also see…HOMICIDE INVESTIGATIONS.

Also see…HUMAN REMAINS.

Also see…CORONERS.

Also see...*FORENSIC ENTOMOLOGY*.

Also see...*NECROSEARCH*.

DEATH PENALTY
Death Penalty Information Center   202/293-6970

>Published annually, *Death Row* is
a large format, soft cover book ($20))
that includes the name of every prisoner
currently on death row in the United
States, plus other vital information.
Also includes articles, interesting facts
and other information related to the death
penalty.   310/553-2400

>*Capital Punishment Project, ACLU*   202/675-2319

>*Capital Punishment Research
Project*   205/693-5225

>See the appendix of this book for
a chart of which states implement
the death penalty, and by which mode
of execution.

DEATH RECORDS
The Social Security Administration
maintains a master file of all deaths
in the United States since 1962 in
which a Social Security death claim
has been made. Information includes
full name of decedent, social security
number, and zip code where the death
benefit was directed to.

Cambridge Statistical Research Associates offers inexpensive access to the Social Security Administrations death master file.

714/509-9900
614/432-5400

Most, if not all, of the companies in our *DATABASE PROVIDERS* section also offer access to this information.

FamilySearch, a CD rom database, includes SSA death records and is available at most of the 2,000 *Church of the Latter Day Saints Family History Centers*, located throughout the fifty states. Free. Call this number to find your nearest *Family History Center:*

800/346-6044

DEBUGGING
Comsec offers "electronic eavesdropping detection".

800/990-0911
818/502-0000

>*Microsearch* provides electronic surveillance detection and counter espionage services for business and government.

714/952-3812

>*IntelTech Data Systems, Inc.* offers advanced high tech sweeps to detect electronic eavesdropping.

708/460-7927

>*Micro Electronic*s is to bugging devices as Maytag is to washing machines. This is the internationally known manufacturer of electronic surveillance devices, including micro-transmitters shaped like a credit card, pen transmitters and more. Most of these items are ILLEGAL to possess or attempt to possess in the United States unless you are an authorized law enforcement agency. All inquiries to the company must be on departmental letterhead. Here's their telephone and fax numbers in Tokyo:

Tel. 011-81-3-5399-2315
Fax 011-81-3-5399-2317

Also see...*BUSINESS ESPIONAGE CONTROLS & COUNTER-MEASURES ASSOCIATION.*

DECEPTION DETECTION
See...*JOHN E. REID & ASSOCIATES.*

Robert Scott

DECODE TAPED NUMBERS
Telephone touchtones recorded onto standard audio tape can be decoded into the actual numbers dialed. Devices to decode these tones can be purchased relatively inexpensively. (See *Shomer-Tec* in our *Telephone Security* section for one company that might have them in stock.)

There are other ways to decode touchtones as well. Here's a free way:

>*2600*, the magazine for hackers, has a free "Phone services" option when you call their main switchboard. Enter the "phone services" section and once inside, you'll have the opportunity to play recorded touchtones, which will then be decoded.   516/473-2626

DEMOGRAPHICS
Slater Hall Information Products offers demographic information, nationwide   202/393-2666

Also see...*U.S. CENSUS BUREAU.*

DETECTION DOGS
Global Training Academy, Inc. trains canines for drug, explosives, and arson detection.   210/622-9460

>*Canine Academy* trains dogs to detect narcotics. DEA certified.   512/267-2275

Canine Training Center, U.S. Customs trains dogs to work for Uncle Sam   540/635-7104

Drug Detection Dogs is a Southern California based company specializing in drug sniffing canines   800/NARC DOG

United States Police K-9 Association   612/484-2537

The National Police Bloodhound Association   717/547-1543

DETECTIVE SCHOOLS
>*Henry Ford Community College* in Dearborn, Michigan offers a degree program in Private Investigation.   313/845-9856

>*Academy of Legal Investigators*   800/842-7421
                                          503/393-8488

>*National Investigation Academy* ad-
ministers the *CMI* (Certified Master
Investigator) certification. Available
through correspondence.   818/883-6969

Lion Investigation Academy offers a
home study course with degrees and/
or diplomas offered in Private Investigation and Security, Bloodstain Pattern Interpretation, Polygraph Examination, Questioned Document Examina-
tion and more.   610/868-2637

Nick Harris Detective Academy   818/343-6611

West Coast Detective Academy has
three California campuses. Check out
their website to learn more, *www.
wcdetective.com*
Headquarters, North Hollywood   800/752-5555
                                          818/752-8700
Oakland, CA   510/595-8391
Anaheim, CA   714/237-1540

William Dear School of Investigation   214/630-9834

DIALOG
Dialog is an online information service
for researchers, corporate librarians
and information professionals. Some
of the databases are familiar -- such
as news text retrievals, company profiles, and airline schedules. Others
are highly specialized on hard to find
subjects. Specialty databases include
foreign trademark registrations, called
Trademarkscan. Another, *Toxline*,
details the toxic effects of drugs, pesti-
cides, and other chemicals. *Public
Opinion Online* contains public opinon
surveys. Over 500 databases in all.
Sign up fee is $295. The average cost
of a search is $50.   800/334-2564

For those who would prefer to have
the research done by a *Dialog* researcher, contact *Dialog's DialSearch*
service. Average cost of a research
project is $300   800/634-2564

DIPLOMATIC IMMUNITY
There are over 118,000 representatives of foreign governments in the
United States who enjoy either partial
or total diplomatic immunity against

criminal prosecution.

The *Department of State* offers the following numbers to verify the validity of the status of diplomatic and consular personnel. (Limited access may be available to non-law enforcement personnel.)

For *Diplomatic Agents and their family members* and *Consular Personnel and their families*   202/647-2663

For *Administrative, technical, and service staff*   202/647-1405

For *International Organizations* other than the U.N.   202/647-1402

For current status of *diplomatic license plates and motor vehicle registration*   202/895-3532

For current status of *Department of State Driver's Licenses*, which are issued to diplomatic/consular personnel: 202/895-3512

For *Reporting Traffic Accidents and Citations* involving diplomatic personnel   202/895-3512

After normal business hours, call *(24 hours)*   202/647-7277

United Nations Personnel can be verified as follows:

U.N. License Plates and motor vehicle registration   212/826-4505

Personnel Verification   212/415-4131

After normal business hours verification   212/415-4444

DIPLOMATIC SECURITY
Department of State, Diplomatic Security   202/663-1814

DISASTER INFORMATION
American Association of Avalanche Professionals   916/587-3653

The National Geophysical Data Center tracks earthquakes and other earth

movements.	303/497-6477
The Natural Hazards Research and Applications Information Center studies natural disasters.	303/492-6819
Their *library* contains over 14,000 books and periodicals on all aspects of natural disasters.	303/492-5787
The Office of Hydrology is the federal agency that tracks flooding.	301/713-0006
Federal Emergency Management Agency	800/462-9029
>USGS National Earthquake Information Center	800/525-7848
The National Geophysical Data Center tracks earthquakes and other earth movements.	303/497-6477
The *Bureau of Fire and Aviation Management* tracks forest fires currently burning in the United States.	202/205-1500
The *Federal Railroad Administration* maintains a database of railway accidents.	202/366-4000
FAA Accident & Incident Histories monitors aircraft accidents.	405/954-4331

>DNA TESTING

These private laboratories offer DNA testing for forensic purposes. Some are limited to paternity testing only; others offer a full range of testing options for criminal or civil cases.

Genescreen	800/DNA-TEST
Genetic Design	800/247-9540
>Alpha Genetics	513/475-6667
>Cellmark Diagnostics (Used by the LA County District Attorney in the OJ case.)	301/428-4980
>DNA Paternity Services	800/DNA-1005
> Reliagene	800/256-4106
>DNA Diagnostics Center specializes in paternity testing.	800/DNA-CENTER

>*Identi-Gene* also specialized in pater-
nity testing . 800/DNA-TYPE

DOG BITES
Richard Polsky, Ph.D. is a dog behavior specialist available as a consultant
/expert witness in dog attack matters. 800/605-2227
310/474-3776

**>DOW JONES NEWS RETRIEV-
AL**
One worthwhile source fo business and
financial investigations is Dow Jones
News/Retrieval. After you pay a one time
start up charge of $29.95, you'll receive
software to install in your computer that
will give you access to a wide variety of
business information. Included are
searchable daily editions and archives
of The Wall Street Journal, The Los
Angeles Times, The New York Times
and Financial Times. Also available is
company and industry data, including
SEC filings, Insider Reports, and real
time quotes on stocks, commodities,
futures and indexes. Searching headlines
is free, you pay $2.95 per article down-
loaded. 800/369-7466
609/520-4088

>DRIVER'S LICENSE INFORMATION
There are several on-line information
providers (see *DATABASE PROVIDERS*)
from whom authorized users can obtain
driver's license information. The same
information is also often available directly
from many state motor vehicle agencies
by written request. Three states offer the
information in some form, by phone.
Dealing directly with the state agencies
can be a time consuming hassle. Not
recommended unless other options are
not available.

The best published information containing
details on accessing motor vehicle related
information is *THE GUIDE TO BACK-
GROUND INVESTIGATIONS.* (See...*THE
GUIDE TO BACKGROUND INVESTIGA-
TIONS.*)

Also see...*AGENCY RECORDS* which offers
driver's license and motor vehicle infor-
mtion from all states.

Also see...*INSURANCE INFORMATION EXCHANGE.*

Also see...*NATIONAL DRIVER REGISTRY.*

These are state agencies who maintain driver's license information. Michigan, Georgia, and Texas offer driver's license information by phone, although sometimes in limited form.

Alabama	334/242-4400
Alaska	907/465-4335
Arizona	602/255-8359
Arkansas	501/682-7207
California	916/657-6525
Colorado	303/205-5613
Connecticut	860/566-3720
Delaware	302/739-4343
District of Columbia	202/727-6761
Florida	904/488-9145
Georgia: Hit "3" for status, then follow the prompts. You'll have the option of entering a DL number to learn status.	404/657-9300
Hawaii	808/538-5530
Idaho	208/334-8736
Illinois	217/782-2720
Indiana	317/232-2894
Iowa	515/244-9124
Kansas	913/296-3671
Kentucky	502/564-6800
Louisiana	504/925-6009
Maine	207/287-2733
Maryland	410/787-7758
Massachusetts	617/351-7200
Michigan: This number includes an option to obtain DL information through an automated attendant, 24 hours per day. Cost is $6.55 each and is payable by credit card.	517/322-1624
Minnesota	612/296-6911
Mississippi	601/987-1200
Missouri	573/751-4300
Montana	406/444-3292
Nebraska	402/471-4343
Nevada	702/687-5505
New Hampshire	603/271-2251
New Jersey	609/292-6500
New Mexico	505/827-2234
New York	518/474-2381
North Carolina	919/715-7000
North Dakota	701/328-2603
Ohio	614/752-7500
Oklahoma	405/425-2226
Oregon	503/945-5000
Pennsylvania	717/787-3130
Rhode Island	401/277-2994

South Carolina	803/251-2940
South Dakota	605/773-6883
Tennessee	615/741-3954
Texas:	
To learn the status of a Texas	
DL, call:	512/424-2600
Utah	801/965-4430
Vermont	802/828-2050
Virginia	804/367-0538
Washington	206/902-3900
West Virginia	304/558-0238
Wisconsin	608/266-2353
Wyoming	307/777-4800

CANADIAN MOTOR VEHICLE LICENSING AUTHORITIES:

Alberta	403/427-5127
British Columbia	604/387-6824
Manitoba	204/945-7370
New Brunswick	506/453-2810
Nova Scotia	902/424-4597
Newfoundland	709/576-2519
Ontario	416/235-4686
Prince Edward Island	902/566-2474
Quebec	418/528-3184
Saskatchewan	306/787-4800
Yukon	403/667-5811
Northwest Territories	403/873-7402

DRUG DEALER EVICTIONS
The U.S. Department of Housing and Urban Development operates a program to evict drug dealers from public housing.   202/708-1422

>DRUG DETECTION
When any one of several different illegal drugs are used, trace amounts of the substance are left deposited in the cortex of the hair of the user. *Psychemedics*, a Los Angeles area firm, has developed a patented process to detect these trace amounts. The tests offer two advantages over standard urinalysis testing. One is that the test in non-evasive — and can even be conducted without the knowledge of the subject — as might be the case of a parent concerned about his or her teen's possible drug use. Another is that the trace amounts of drug will remain in the users hair for up to 90 days. (Some urinalysis tests only have a 2-3 day time window.) Drugs tested for in-

clude marijuana, cocaine, heroin, methamphetamine and PCP. *Psychemedics* includes Fortune 500 companies and the Federal Courts among its customers. The firm has now begun marketing its test on a retail level. The tests can be purchased at many pharmacies and can also be mail ordered directly from the company. Cost is approximately $75 per test. The company recommends approximately 60-80 strands of hair for the test. Hair from hairbrushes is not recommended as these are older and may not indicate recent drug use. Results will be available in around 5 days through a confidential and anonymous 800 number.

Psychemedics, Customer Service   800/800-5447
Psychemedics, Workplace Testing Program   800/628-8073

Identa-A-Drug is a handbook which uses a three step identification system to identify street drugs. Sells for around $30.
Gall's, Inc.   800/477-7766

Drug Detection Services, Inc. offers drugs of abuse screening. Mail in kits available.   800/748-2742
                                                     505/880-1432

3D Ltd. Drug Detection Devices offers drug screening services, too.   888/768-6786
                                                     770/886-6226

F. Morton Pitt Co. offers law enforcement products, including drug and alcohol test kits.   800/533-2838
                                                     805/658-5133

Alcohol Countermeasure Systems sells breath alcohol analyzers.   800/440-3784

Also see...MISTRAL SECURITY.

Also see...DETECTION DOGS.

Also see...CRIME LABS - PRIVATE.

DRUG ENFORCEMENT ADMINISTRATION (DEA)
National Headquarters   202/307-1000

>*DEA Special Agent Recruiting*   800/DEA-4288

>*DEA FOIA Office*   202/307-7709

>*National Controlled Substances
Registrations* is a little known database of the *DEA* which registers doctors,
dentists, veterinarians, pharmaceutical
manufacturers and others who are authorized to handle controlled substances.
(Take a look at the next prescription
you receive from your doctor. In small
print there should be a DEA number.)
Available through:
Database Technologies   800/279-7710

Report sale of illegal drugs to the *Enforcement Section*   202/633-1151

El Paso Intelligence Division   915/564-2000

Aviation Unit   214/767-4813

Laboratories:
Special Testing & Research Lab   703/285-2583
Mid-Atlantic Lab   202/275-6478
Northeast Lab   212/399-5137
Southeast Lab   305/591-4830
North Central Lab   312/353-3640
South Central Lab   214/767-7211
Southwest Lab   619/557-6490
Western Lab   415/995-5131

DEA Field Offices:

ATLANTA DIVISION:
Atlanta, GA   404/331-4401
Charleston, SC   803/724-4531
Charlotte, NC   704/371-6188
Columbia, SC   803/765-5251
Columbus, GA   404/649-7850
Greensboro, NC   919/333-5203
Knoxville, TN   615/549-9334
Chattanooga, TN   615/855-6600
Memphis, TN   901/521-3396
Nashville, TN   615/736-5271
Savannah, GA   912/944-4286
Wilmington, NC   919/343-4513

BOSTON DIVISION:
Boston, MA   617/557-2100
Bridgeport, CT   203/579-5591
Burlington, VT   802/658-4931
Concord, NH   603/225-1574
Hartford, CT   203/240-3238
Portland, ME   207/780-3331
Providence, RI   401/528-4130

Springfield, MA	413/785-0284
CARIBBEAN DIVISION:	
Santurce, PR	809/253-4200
CHICAGO DIVISION:	
Chicago, IL	312/353-7875
Fargo, ND	701/239-5771
Hammond, IN	219/937-5321
Indianapolis, IN	317/269-7977
Milwaukee, WI	414/297-3395
Minneapolis, MN	612/348-1700
Springfield, IL	217/492-4504
DALLAS DIVISION:	
Dallas, TX	214/640-0801
Ft. Worth, TX	817/334-3455
Oklahoma City, OK	405/231-4141
Tulsa, OK	918/581-6391
El Paso, TX	915/534-6400
Alpine, TX	915/837-3421
Lubbock, TX	806/798-7189
Midland, TX	915/686-0356
Tyler, TX	214/592-1160
Amarillo, TX	806/376-2339
DENVER DIVISION:	
Denver, CO	303/784-6300
Cheyenne, WY	307/772-2391
Salt Lake City, UT	801/524-4156
Albuquerque, NM	505/262-6283
Glenwood Springs, CO	303/945-0744
Colorado Springs, CO	719/471-1749
Las Cruces, NM	505/523-8337
DETROIT DIVISION:	
Detroit, MI	313/234-4000
Cincinnati, OH	513/684-3671
Cleveland, OH	216/522-3705
Columbus, OH	614/469-2595
Grand Rapids, MI	616/456-2541
Louisville, KY	502/582-5908
Lexington, KY	606/233-2479
Saginaw, MI	517/754-4541
HOUSTON DIVISION:	
Houston, TX	713/693-3000
Corpus Chrisi, TX	512/888-3236
Galveston, TX	713/766-3568
Beaumont, TX	409/839-2461
McAllen, TX	512/618-4800
Waco, TX	817/741-1920
Brownsville, TX	512/546-7575
Laredo, TX	512/722-5201
San Antonio, TX	512/824-9457
Austin, TX	512/482-5631

Eagle Pass, TX	512/773-5378

LOS ANGELES DIVISION:

Los Angeles, CA	213/894-2650
Agana, Guam	011-671/472-7384
Honolulu, HI	808/541-1930
Las Vegas, NV	702/388-6635
Reno, NV	702/784-5617
Riverside, CA	909/351-6642
Santa Ana, CA	714/836-2892
Santa Barbara, CA	805/964-6299

MIAMI DIVISION:

Miami, FL	305/590-4870
Ft. Lauderdale, FL	305/527-7220
Ft. Myers, FL	813/275-3662
Gainesville, FL	904/371-2077
Jacksonville, FL	904/791-3566
Key Largo, FL	305/852-7874
Altamonte Springs, FL	407/648-6155
Panama City, FL	904/769-3407
Tallahassee, FL	904/681-7412
Tampa, FL	813/228-2178
West Palm Beach, FL	407/659-3660
San Juan, PR	809/754-6450

NEWARK DIVISION:

Newark, NJ	201/645-6060
Atlantic City, NJ	609/625-1119
Camden, NJ	609/757-5407

NEW ORLEANS DIVISION:

New Orleans, LA	504/840-1010
Baton Rouge, LA	504/389-0254
Birmingham, AL	205/731-0621
Fayettville, AR	501/442-2612
Gulfport, MS	601/863-2992
Jackson, MS	601/965-4400
Oxford, MS	601/234-8542
Little Rock, AR	501/378-5981
Mobile, AL	205/223-7429
Shreveport, LA	318/226-5078

NEW YORK DIVISION:

New York, NY	212/337-3900
Albany, NY	518/472-3425
Buffalo, NY	716/551-4421
Rochester, NY	716/263-3180
Long Island, NY	516/420-4500
JFK Airport Station	718/917-1666

PHILADELPHIA DIVISION:

Philadelphia, PA	215/597-9530
Allentown, PA	215/770-0940
Harrisburg, PA	717/782-2270
Pittsburgh, PA	412/644-3390

Wilmington, DE	302/573-6184

PHOENIX DIVISION:
Phoenix, AZ	602/664-5600
Yuma, AZ	602/344-9550
Tucson, AZ	602/629-6845
Sierra Vista, AZ	602/459-2232
Nogales, AZ	602/281-1727

SAN DIEGO DIVISION:
San Diego, CA	619/616-4100
Calexico, CA	619/357-6831
Tecate, CA	619/293-7072
San Ysidro, CA	619/428-7115
Carlsbad, CA	619/557-6247

SAN FRANCISCO DIVISION:
San Francisco, CA	415/436-7900
Fresno, CA	209/487-5402
Sacramento, CA	916/978-4225
San Jose, CA	408/291-7235
Salinas, CA	408/755-3784

SEATTLE DIVISION:
Seattle, WA	206/553-5443
Anchorage, AK	907/271-5033
Blaine, WA	206/332-8692
Boise, ID	208/334-1620
Eugene, OR	503/687-6861
Medford, OR	503/776-4260
Great Falls, MT	406/771-0333
Portland, OR	503/326-3371
Spokane, WA	509/353-2964
Yakima, WA	509/575-5813

ST. LOUIS DIVISION:
St. Louis, MO	314/425-3241
Cape Girardeau, MO	314/425-4819
Carbondale, IL	618/457-3605
Des Moines, IA	515/284-4700
Cedar Rapids, IA	319/399-2259
Kansas City, KS	913/236-3176
Omaha, NE	402/221-4222
Sioux Falls, SD	605/334-7393
Springfield, MO	417/831-1040
Rapid City, SD	605/343-4947
Wichita, KS	316/838-2500

WASHINGTON, DC DIVISION:
Washington, DC	202/401-7834
Charleston, WV	304/347-5209
Clarksburg, WV	304/623-3700
Norfolk, VA	804/441-3152
Richmond, VA	804/771-2871
Baltimore, MD	301/962-4800

DEA FOREIGN OFFICES:

Ankara, Turkey	011-90-41-265-47
Istanbul	011-90-11-61-3602
Asuncion, Paraguay	011-505-21-201041
Athens, Greece	011-30-1-721-2951
Bangkok, Thailand	011-66-2-253-2917
Chiang Mai	011-66-53-221509
Songkhla	011-66-074-313-523
Bern, Switzerland	011-41-31-43-7367
Bogota, Colombia	011-571-285-1300
Barranquilla	011-57-845-9353
Bonn, Germany	011-49-228-339-2307
Frankfurt, Germany	011-49-69-56002-771
Brasilia, Brazil	011-55-61-321-7272
Sao Paulo, Brazil	011-55-11-881-6511
Bridgetown, Barbados	809/436-4950
Brussels, Belgium	011-32-2-513-3830
Buenos Aires, Argentina	011-541-774-7611
Canberra, Australia	011-6162-7333-470
Cairo, Egypt	011-20-2-355-7371
Caracas, Venezuela	011-58-2-285-3111
Copenhagen, Denmark	011-45-1-42-31-44
Curacao, Netherlands	011-599-9-613066
Guatemala City. Guatemala	011-502-231-8563
Hong Kong	011-852-5-239011
Islamabad, Pakistan	011-92-51-826161
Karachi	011-92-21-515081
Lahore	011-92-42-870-221
Peshawar	011-92-521-42424
Kingston, Jamaica	809/829-4850
Kuala Lumpur, Malaysia	011-60-3-248-9011
La Paz, Bolivia	011-591-2-322-925
Santa Cruz, Bolivia	011-591-333-485
Cochabamba, Bolivia	011-591-42-40476
Lagos, Nigeria	011-234-1-619837
Lima, Peru	011-51-14-24-4236
London, England	011-44-1-499-9000
Madrid, Spain	011-34-1-274-3400
Manila, Phillipines	011-632-521-7116
Mexico City, Mexico	011-525-211-00422
Guadalajara, Mexico	011-52-36-2530-84
Hermosillo, Mexico	011-52-621-7-4732
Mazatlan, Mexico	011-52-678-21760
Tegucigalpa	011-504-323121
Merida, Mexico	011-52-99-25-5742
Monterrey. Mexico	011-52-83-44-5261
Nassau, Bahamas	809/322-8179
New Delhi, India	011-91-11-600-651
Bombay, India	011-91-22-822-3611
Nicosia, Cyprus	011-357-2465-182
Ottawa, Canada	613/238-5633
Montreal, Canada	514/261-1461
Paris, France	011-33-14-296-1202
Marseilles, France	011-38-91-54-92-90
Port-Au-Prince, Haiti	011-509-120-868
Quito, Ecuador	011-593-2-230053

Guayaquil, Ecuador	011-593-4-323-715
Rome, Italy	011-39-6-4674-2225
Milan, Italy	011-39-2-652-841
San Jose, Costa Rica	011-506-20-3939
Santiago, Chile	011-562-71-0133
Santo Domingo, Dominican Republic	809/541-2171
Seoul, South Korea	011-82-2-732-2601
Singapore	011-65-338-0251
The Hague, Netherlands	011-31-70-62-4911
Tokyo, Japan	011-81-3-224-5000
Vienna, Austria	011-43-222-514-2251

DRUG INFORMATION
The Food & Drug Administration
maintains a database of pharmaceuti-
cals. Provides information on a cost
basis.   301/827-4420

DUN & BRADSTREET
Dun & Bradstreet is the leading business credit reporting company. Their
business information reports typically
contain a corporate history, profiles
of current corporate officers, information on the company's activities, and
pertinent derogatory data such as
pending lawsuits, tax liens and UCC
filings. >You'll get the best prices on
D&B products by subscribing to
their services. However, if you don't
want to subscribe, most products,
including Business Information Reports ($79.00), are available ala carte
from the *D&B Express Services* number below.

Customer Service	800/362-3425
International	800/932-0025
D&B Express Service	800/879-1362

>However, Business Information Re-
ports can also be obtained for a
limited time through a special
promotion. Call the *D&B Express
Service* number below and ask for
extension 3400. Tell the rep that you
want the Office Depot customer dis-
count and the Business Information
Report will be discounted from $79
to $55.   800/879-1362

EARTHQUAKE DATA BASE
>*USGS National Earthquake Information
Center*   800/525-7848

*The National Geophysical Data Cen-
ter* tracks earthquakes and other earth

movements.   303/497-6477

>ECONOMIC ESPIONAGE

Private Investigators in every state
need to familarize themselves with
the *Economic Espionage Act of
1996* (USC Title 18, sections 1831
- 1839).

Certain activities that might be conducted by private investigators -
including certain types of competitor
intelligence - could constitute a violation of the Act and carry a penalty of
up to a $500,000 fine and/or 15
years in federal prison. The law
makes it a federal crime to obtain by
unauthorized means any type of
trade secret where release of the
secret will cause economic harm to
its rightful owner. "Unauthorized
means" includes usage of pretexts,
undercover agents, and confidential
informants. For more information,
contact your nearest FBI office and
ask to speak with the ANSIR (Aware-
ness of Security Issues and Response)
coordinator.

>ECONOMIC NEWS

Need to know about fast breaking
economic news…like whether or
not the Fed is going to raise
interest rates, or what Treasury
cash balances are? *Dow Jones
Telerate* is a subscription service,
delivered electronically, that posts
government and market information
direct from the source. This is for
those who can't wait to read about
it in the next day's paper, but need
the information *now*.   800/472-3859
In Canada: 416/365-7171

Need current or historical cost of
living information, also known
as Consumer Price Information?
The Bureau of Labor Statistics
collects such data for much of
the federal government.   202/606-5886

800# DIRECTORY ASSISTANCE

A simple and often effective way to
locate any business is to call *800 Directory Assistance*. If the company
has a toll free 800 number, the opera-

tor should be able to provide their
location.   800/555-1212

ELECTION FRAUD
William C. Kimberling, Deputy
Director of the *Office of Election
Administration, Federal Election
Commission,* is a recognized expert in election fraud, voter registration and election procedures.
He advises state and local officials
on the development of anti-election
fraud safeguards. The two most
common forms of election fraud
(other than politicians who break
their promises)? Vote buying and
voter impersonation, according to
Kimberling.   202/219-3670

Craig C. Donsanto is Director
of the *Election Crimes Branch*
of the *United States Department
of Justice*. He both investigates
and prosecutes election fraud and
campaign finance law violations. He
isn't able to take complaint calls
personally from the general public.
(He advises that these should be
sent in writing to him at P.O. Box
27518, Central Station, Washing-
ton, D.C. 20038.)   202/514-1421

Robert Naegele was a principal
author of the Federal Election
Commission's Voting System
Standards, and is Chief Technical
Advisor to the National Association
of State Election Directors.   408/655-2648

**EL PASO INTELLIGENCE CEN-
TER (EPIC)**
U.S. Customs tracks and maintains
information on persons exiting and
entering the U.S. for law enforcement
purposes through the *El Paso Intelli-
gence Center*   800/USE-EPIC
                                                915/564-2000

EMBASSIES
Afghanistan   202/234-3770
Albania   202/223-4942
Algeria   202/265-2800
Angola   202/785-1156
Antigua and Barbuda   202/362-5211
Argentina   202/939-6400
Artienia   202/628-5766

Azerbaijan	202/842-0001
Bahamas	202/319-2660
Bahrain	202/342-0741
Bangladesh	202/342-8372
Barbados	202/939-9200
Belarus	202/986-1604
Belgium	202/333-6900
Belize	202/332-9636
Benin	202/232-6656
Bolivia	202/483-4410
Bosnia and Herzegovina	202/833-3612
Botswana	202/244-4990
Brazil	202/745-2700
Brunei	202/342-0159
Bulgaria	202/387-7969
Burkina Faso	202/332-5577
Burundi	202/342-2574
Cambodia	202/726-7742
Cameroon	202/265-8790
Canada	202/682-1740
Cape Verde	202/965-6820
Central African Republic	202/483-7800
Chad	202/462-4009
Chile	202/785-1746
China	202/328-2500
Colombia	202/387-8338
Congo, Republic of	202/726-0825
Costa Rica	202/234-2945
Cote D'Ivorie	202/797-0300
Croatia	202/588-5899
Cuba c/o Swiss Embassy	202/797-8518
Cyprus	202/462-5772
Czech Republic	202/363-6315
Denmark	202/234-4300
Djibouti	202/331-0270
Dominica	202/364-6781
Ecuador	202/234-7200
Egypt	202/895-5400
El Salvador	202/265-9671
Equatorial Guinea	914/738-9584
Eritrea	202/429-1991
Estonia	202/789-0320
Ethiopia	202/234-2281
Fiji	202/337-8320
Finland	202/298-5800
France	202/944-6000
Gabon	202/797-1000
Gambia	202/785-1399
Germany	202/298-4000
Ghana	202/686-452?
Greece	202/939-5800
Grenada	202/265-2561
Guatemala	202/745-4952
Guinea	202/483-9420
Guinea-Bissau	202/872-4222
Guyana	202/265-6900

Haiti	202/332-4090
Holy See	202/333-7121
Honduras	202/966-7702
Hungary	202/362-6730
Iceland	202/265-6653
India	202/939-7000
Indonesia	202/775-5200
Iraq c/o Algerian Embassy	202/483-7500
Ireland	202/462-3939
Israel	202/364-5500
Italy	202/328-5500
Jamaica	202/452-0660
Japan	202/939-6700
Japan Information Center	202/939-6900
Jordan	202/966-2664
Kazakhstan	202/333-4504
Kenya	202/387-6101
Korea	202/524-9273
Kuwait	202/966-0702
Kyrgyzstin	202/628-0433
Laos	202/332-6416
Latvia	202/726-8213
Lebanon	202/939-6300
Lesotito	202/797-5533
Liberia	202/723-0437
Lithuania	202/234-5860
Luxembourg	202/265-4171
Malawi	202/797-1007
Malaysia	202/328-2700
Mali	202/332-2249
Malta	202/462-3611
Marshall Islands	202/234-5414
Mauritania	202/232-5700
Mauritius	202/244-1491
Mexico	202/728-1600
Micronesia	202/223-4383
Mongolia	202/333-7117
Morocco	202/462-7979
Mozambique	202/293-7146
Myanmar	202/332-9044
Namibia	202/986-0540
Nepal	202/667-4550
Netherlands	202/244-5300
New Zealand	202/328-4800
Nicaragua	202/939-6570
Niger	202/483-4224
Nigeria	202/986-8400
Norway	202/333-6000
Oman	202/387-1980
Pakistan	202/939-6200
Panama	202/483-1407
Papua New Guinea	202/745-3680
Paraguay	202/483-6960
Peru	202/833-9860
Phillipines	202/467-9300
Poland	202/234-3800

Portugal	202/328-8610
Qatar	202/338-0111
Republic of Congo (formerly Zaire)	202/234-7690
Romania	202/332-4846
Russia	202/298-5700
Rwanda	202/232-2882
Saint Kitts and Nevis	202/686-2636
Saint Lucia	202/364-6792
Saint Vincent and the Grenadines	202/462-7806
Saudi Arabia	202/342-3800
Senegal	202/234-0540
Seychelles	212/687-9766
Sierra Leone	202/939-9261
Singapore	202/537-3100
Slovakia	202/965-5161
Slovenia	202/667-5363
South Africa	202/232-4400
Spain	202/452-0100
Sri Lanka	202/483-4025
Sudan	202/338-8565
Suriname	202/244-7488
Swaziland	202/362-6683
Sweden	202/467-2600
Switzerland	202/745-7900
Syria	202/232-6313
Tanzania	202/939-6125
Thailand	202/944-3600
Trinidad and Tobago	202/467-6490
Tunisia	202/862-1850
Turkmenistin	202/737-4800
Uganda	202/726-7100
United Arab Emirates	202/338-6500
United Kingdom	202/462-1340
Uruguay	202/331-1313
Uzbekistan	202/638-4266
Venezuela	202/342-2214
Vietnam	202/861-0737
Western Samoa	212/599-6196
Yemen	202/965-4760
Yugoslavia	202/462-6566
Zaire (See Republic of Congo)	
Zambia	202/265-9717
Zimbabwe	202/332-7100

EMPLOYMENT SCREENING
Avert, Inc. offers nationwide pre-employment investigations of job applicants, covering such areas as criminal histories, educational verification, and driving records.

800/367-5933
970/221-1526

ENGLAND - INVESTIGATORS
Association of British Investigators, Ltd

011-44-1815-463368

ENGLAND - MISSING PERSONS
British Tracing Service, Ltd locates
missing persons throughout England.   011-44-1923-859444

**ENGLAND - REAL PROPERTY
RECORDS**
Land Registry Information does real
property ownership searches throughout England.   011-44-1812-881418

ENVIRONMENTAL INVESTIGATIONS
>*Environmental Protection Agency,
Information Resource Center*   202/260-5922
Environmental Protection Agency   202/260-2090

>The Environmental Protection Agency's
Public Information Center publishes an
annual directory of agency personnel sit-
uated at its headquarters. Free.   202/260-5922

>*Environmental Protection Agency,
Safe Drinking Water Hotline*   800/426-4791

>*EPA Office of Investigations* keeps
watch over EPA administered programs
for fraud, bribery, and false claims.   617/565-3928
   703/308-8283
   404/321-6016

>*Society of Environmental Journalists*
(website: *www.sej.org*)   573/882-5431

>*Conservation Directory* is published by
the National Wildlife Federation and
contains a comprehensive listing of
environmental agencies and groups.   800/432-6564

*VISTA Environmental Information,
Inc.* offers databases compiled from
state and federal environmental records.   800/767-0403
   619/450-6100

>*National Radon Hotline* (Operated by
the National Safety Council.)   800/SOS-RADON

>*National Pesticides Telecommunications
Network* maintains information on pesti-
cides, including their effects on health
and what to do when a spill occurs.   800/858-PEST

*The U.S. Department of Fish &
Game's National Fish & Wildlife Forensic Lab* has been called the first full
service wildlife crime lab in the world.   541/482-4191

Also see...TOXIC CHEMICALS.

EQUIFAX
One of the big three credit bureaus.
Maintains detailed financial infor-
mation on millions of Americans.   800/456-6432

EVIDENCE PHOTOGRAPHERS
*Evidence Photographers Internation-
al Council* is a professional group of
crime scene and civil evidence photographers. Referral service available.   717/253-5450

>THE EXCLUDED PARTY INDEX
Exclusion lists are one of the best kept
secrets in the world of public records.
Very few PI's, even those with expert
credentials, know about the existence
of this information. So what exactly is
an exclusion list? It's a database of
persons and firms who have run afoul
of one governmental agency or another
for some type of misconduct. As a result,
they're placed on an exclusion list and
are excluded or banned from engaging in
certain types of activity. Example: A
medical clinic is busted for ripping off
Medicare through bogus billings. The
clinic and its principals are then excluded
from doing further business with the
federal government by being placed on
an exclusion list. *The Excluded Party
Index* is a compilation of exclusion lists
from over 60 state and federal agencies
including the United States Department
of Justice. Included are persons who have
defrauded the federal government, convicted drug dealers, casino cheats, California Vexatious Litigants and many
others. *EPI* now comes on a CD ROM
($99.00) which includes a unique
"Political Associations" database which
identifies political contributions made
to federal election campaigns.
Crime Time Publishing Co.   310/840-5317

EXPERIAN
One of the three mega credit bureaus,
formerly called TRW.   800/422-4879

EXPERT WITNESSES
Expert Resources, Inc. specializes in
providing expert witnesses for court
cases:

Atlanta   404/577-3592

Boston	617/451-5351
Chicago	312/327-2830
Cincinnati	513/241-8648
Dallas	214/698-1881
Detroit	313/964-0505
Honolulu	808/531-5464
Houston	713/223-2330
Los Angeles	213/669-1660
Miami	305/372-5259
Minneapolis	612/338-2788
New Orleans	504/525-8806
New York	212/288-1120
Peoria, IL	309/688-4857
Philadelphia	215/829-9570
San Diego	619/232-4618
San Francisco	415/398-8854
Seattle	206/587-0745
St. Louis	314/241-9669
Washington, DC	202/397-1177

Profnet is a network of university research professionals available as background sources, technical consultants, and expert witnesses.

800/PROFNET
516/941-3736

American Academy of Forensic Sciences is a professional organization that offers an expert referral service. Also maintains a reference library.

719/636-1100

National Consultant Referrals, Inc. is another company that specializes in providing expert witnesses.

800/221-3104

National Forensic Center provides expert witnesses and litigation consultants. They also train consultants to serve as expert witnesses.

609/883-0550

The National Reference Center is a free program of the Library of Congress which maintains a huge database of experts and organizations on virtually any technical or scientific subject.

202/707-5522

FATAL ACCIDENTS
The *U.S. Department of Transportation* maintains a computerized database of fatal motor vehicle accidents from all 50 states, called the *Fatal Accident Reporting System*. The information is chiefly statistical and does not provide identifying information on persons involved in the accidents.

202/366-4820

FEDERAL AVIATION ADMINISTRATION (FAA)

Hotline Information Center	800/322-7873
Accident & Incident Histories	405/954-4173
Airmen Registry	405/954-3205

Requests for information can also be
faxed to the *Information Management Section* — 405/954-4655

>*Investigations Division* — 202/267-3378

Kolbenschlag Aviation Services
is an aviation information service
that offers customized searching
of the FAA's databases. Their
agents have both piloting and aircraft maintenance experience.
Normal turnaround time is 24 hours,
but in a pinch they promise to do
it in one. — 503/787-8700

Also see...*AVIATION.*

FEDERAL BUREAU OF INVESTIGATION (FBI)

National Headquarters — 202/324-3000

The *National Crime Information Center (NCIC)* is law enforcement's massive
nationwide criminal history system, run
by the FBI. Access by unauthorized users
is a federal crime. For more on NCIC,
see *Criminal Records.* — 304/625-6200

>The world's largest repository of
fingerprints is maintained at the FBI's
new *Criminal Justice Information
Services Division* complex in Clarksburg,
West Virginia. Roughly 50,000 fingerprint
checks a day are requested through this
$200 million facility. More than 220
million fingerprint cards are archived here.
NCIC (National Crime Information Center),
law enforcement's national crime database,
is now located here, too. — 304/625-6200

>The FBI's *Fugitive Publicity Office*
leads the PR charge on high profile
Most Wanted cases. It's also the
agency's contact point for book
authors needing information. — 202/324-5348

>Non-book media should direct inquiries
to the FBI *Press Office.* — 202/324-3691

>Freedom of Information Act requests

to the FBI are seriously backlogged, with fulfillment taking years. However, hundreds of pre-processed files (on well known persons) are available for viewing without a wait. To view one of these files, call the *FBI FOIA Reading Room* at least 48 hours in advance.

202/324-5520

>The *FBI* has started to post some of its most requested FOIA files on the Internet. FBI files on Amelia Earhart, Elvis Presley, Jackie Robinson and others can now be viewed at *www.fbi.gov/foipa/document.htm*

>FOIA requests to the FBI should be directed to: *FBI FOIA Unit, Records Resources Division, Federal Bureau of Investigation, 9th & Pennsylvania Avenue N.W., Washington, DC 20535.*

>*The Society of Former Special Agents of the FBI* provides networking and other support for Special Agents in their post-bureau life. The organization also assists in job placement of former agents in the private sector.

703/640-6469

>*Violent Criminal Apprehension Program(VICAP)* is a little known FBI data collection center that catalogs information relating to serial murder

The FBI's new Criminal Justice Information Services Division in Clarksburg, West Virginia.

(Photo courtesy Federal Bureau of Investigation.)

and other crimes of violence. Information collected focuses on unsolved , apparently random killings. The purpose is to cross index the data to identify signature aspects of the homicides, hopefully pointing to a single suspect.

800/634-4097

Anyone can request a copy of their own criminal record from the FBI through this office. The procedure for doing so is somewhat cumbersome, though.

202/324-5454

>Explosives Unit - Bomb Data Center

202/324-2696

FBI Academy, Quantico, Virginia

703/640-6131

FBI Academy, Forensic Science Re-search Unit

703/640-1445

Forensic Science Training Unit

703/640-1181

The FBI Law Enforcement Bulletin (publication)

703/640-1193

FBI Crime Lab, Office of the Direc-tor

202/324-4410

>Crime Lab, Hair & Fibers Unit

202/324-43440

The FBI Crime Lab, Documents Section analyses documents from computers, type-writers, check writers, rubber stamps, and photocopiers. Internal reference files in-clude *The Bank Robbery Note File, The Anonymous/Extortion Letter File*, and *The Office Equipment File*.

202/324-4452

Crime Lab, Scientific Analysis	202/324-4416
Crime Lab, Fingerprints	202/324-2163
Crime Lab, Special Projects	202/324-4220

Also see...COMBINED DNA INDEX SYSTEM.

Domestic Terrorism Unit

202/324-4656

The Criminalistics Laboratory Infor-mation System is a computer database of the FBI Crime Lab that identifies the weapon type used to fire a re-covered bullet or casing.

202/324-4410

The Forensic Science Information Resource System is a computerized

database of forensic evidence, including
tire tracks, shoe prints and ballistics.   202/324-4384

The *FBI's National Computer Crime
Squad* investigates intrusion into governmental, financial, and medical computers. It also has jurisdiction over
intrusion into the phone systems, pri-
vacy violations, and pirated software.   202/324-9164

FBI Field Offices:

Albany, NY	518/465-7551
Albuquerque, NM	505/224-2000
Anchorage, AK	907/258-5322
Atlanta, GA	404/679-9000
Baltimore, MD	410/265-8080
Birmingham, AL	205/252-7705
Boston, MA	617/742-5533
Buffalo, NY	716/856-7800
Charlotte, NC	704/377-9200
Chicago, IL	312/431-1333
Cincinnati, OH	513/421-4310
Cleveland, OH	216/522-1400
Columbia, SC	803/254-3011
Dallas, TX	214/720-2200
Denver, CO	303/629-7171
Detroit, MI	313/965-2323
El Paso, TX	915/533-7451
Honolulu, HI	808/521-1411
Houston, TX	713/868-2266
Indianapolis, IN	317/639-3301
Jackson, MS	601/948-5000
Jacksonville, FL	904/721-1211
Kansas City, MO	816/221-6100
Knoxville, TN	423/544-0751
Las Vegas, NV	702/385-1281
Little Rock, AR	501/221-9100
Los Angeles, CA	310/477-6565
Louisville, KY	502/583-3941
Memphis, TN	901/747-4300
North Miami Beach, FL	305/944-9101
Milwaukee, WI	414/276-4684
Minneapolis, MN	612/376-3200
Mobile, AL	334/438-3674
Newark, NJ	201/622-5613
New Haven, CT	203/777-6311
New Orleans, LA	504/522-4671
New York, NY	212/384-1000
Norfolk, VA	804/455-0100
Oklahoma City, OK	405/842-7471
Omaha, NE	402/493-8688
Philadelphia, PA	215/829-2700
Phoenix, AZ	602/279-5511
Pittsburgh, PA	412/471-2000
Portland, OR	503/224-4181

Richmond, VA	804/261-1044
Sacramento, CA	916/481-9110
St. Louis, MO	314/241-5357
Salt Lake City, UT	801/579-1400
San Antonio, TX	210/225-6741
San Diego, CA	619/565-1255
San Francisco, CA	415/553-7400
San Juan, PR	809/754-6000
Seattle, WA	206/622-0460
Springfield, IL	217/522-9675
Tampa, FL	813/273-4566
Washington, DC	202/252-7801

>*FBI Legal Attache, American Embassy,*
Moscow, Russia   011-7-095-252-2459

FEDERAL CONTRACTS
The *Governmentwide Information Systems Division* maintains a database of
all federal procurements over ten thousand dollars since 1979.   202/401-1529

Also see...*THE EXCLUDED PARTY INDEX* for information on parties
banned from participating as vendors or contractors for federal programs.

FEDERAL DISTRICT COURTS
This is a non-exhaustive list of key U.S. District Courts. Contact the court nearest
your search area to determine its jurisdiction.

Alabama, Northern	205/731-1701
Alabama, Middle	334/223-7308
Alabama, Southern	334/690-2371
Alaska	907/271-5568
Arizona, Phoenix Div.	602/514-7101
Arizona, Tucson Div.	520/620-7200
Arkansas, Eastern	501/324-5351
Arkansas, Western	501/862-1202
California, Northern	415/556-3031
California, Eastern	916/551-2615
California, Central	213/894-5261
California, Southern	619/557-5600
Colorado	303/844-3157
Connecticut	203/773-2140
Delaware	302/573-6170
District of Columbia	202/273-0555
Florida, Northern	904/942-8826
Florida, Central	904/232-2320
Florida, Southern	305/536-4131
Georgia, Northern	404/331-6886
Georgia, Central	912/752-3497
Georgia, Southern	912/652-4281
Hawaii	808/541-1300
Idaho	208/334-1361

Illinois, Northern	312/435-5684
Illinois, Central	217/492-4020
Illinois, Southern	618/482-9371
Indiana, Northern	219/236-8260
Indiana, Southern	317/226-6670
Iowa, Northern	319/364-2447
Iowa, Southern	515/284-6284
Kansas	316/269-6491
Kentucky, Eastern	606/233-2503
Kentucky, Western	502/582-5156
Louisiana, Eastern	504/589-4471
Louisiana, Central	504/389-3950
Louisiana, Western	318/676-4273
Maine	207/780-3356
Maryland	301/962-2600
Massachusetts	617/223-9152
Michigan, Eastern	313/226-7060
Michigan, Western	616/456-2381
Minnesota	612/348-1821
Mississippi, Northern	601/234-1971
Mississippi, Southern	601/965-4439
Missouri, Eastern	314/539-2315
Missouri, Western	816/426-2811
Montana	406/657-6366
Nebraska	402/221-4761
Nevada	702/455-4011
New Hampshire	603/225-1423
New Jersey	201/645-3730
New Mexico	505/766-2851
New York, Northern	518/472-5651
New York, Southern	212/791-0108
New York, Eastern	718/330-7671
New York, Western	716/846-4211
North Carolina, Eastern	919/856-4370
North Carolina, Central	919/333-5347
North Carolina, Western	704/255-4702
North Dakota	701/222-6690
Ohio, Northern	216/522-4356
Ohio, Southern	614/469-5835
Oklahoma, Northern	918/581-7796
Oklahoma, Eastern	918/687-2471
Oklahoma, Western	405/231-4792
Oregon	503/326-5412
Pennsylvania, Eastern	215/597-7704
Pennsylvania, Central	717/347-0205
Pennsylvania, Western	412/644-3528
Puerto Rico	809/766-6484
Rhode Island	401/528-5100
South Carolina	803/765-5816
South Dakota	605/330-4447
Tennessee, Eastern	615/545-4228
Tennessee, Central	615/736-5498
Tennessee, Western	901/544-3315
Texas, Northern	214/767-0787
Texas, Southern	713/250-5500
Texas, Eastern	903/592-8195

Texas, Western	512/229-6550
Utah	801/524-5160
Vermont	802/951-6301
Virginia, Eastern	703/557-5131
Virginia, Western	703/982-4661
Washington, Eastern	509/353-2150
Washington, Western	206/553-5598
West Virginia, Northern	304/636-1445
West Virginia, Southern	304/342-5154
Wisconsin, Eastern	414/297-3372
Wisconsin, Western	608/264-5156
Wyoming	307/772-2145
Guam (territorial court)	671/472-7411
Virgin Islands (territorial court)	809/774-8310

**FEDERAL EMERGENCY MAN-
AGEMENT AGENCY (FEMA)**
Federal agency that responds to nat-
ural and manmade disasters.   800/462-9029

>FEDERAL EXTRADITION AGENCY
FEA is a private company, specializing
in nationwide prisoner transport.   800/518-7171

FEDERAL FUGITIVES
Contact the *Communications Center*
of the *U.S. Marshals Service* to report
federal fugitives from justice.   202/307-9100

**FEDERAL GOVERNMENT
FRAUD HOTLINE**
*Fraud Prevention, General Account-
ing Office*   800/424-5454
                                               202/633-6987

**FEDERAL INFORMATION CEN-
TER**
The *Federal Information Center* is
the general information operator for
the entire U.S. government. The center maintains an impressive computerized database of federal government
agencies, departments, sections and
units. The information specialists are
well trained and knowledgeable. The
center is run by Biospherics, Inc. a
subcontractor to the U.S. Government. They handle over two and one
half million calls a year. > Tip: The
center's database will be available on
CD ROM in the near future through the
Government Printing Office.   800/688-9889
>TTY (For hearing impaired)   800/326-2996

FEDERAL LAW ENFORCE- MENT TRAINING CENTER

Sixty three separate federal agencies with law enforcement status train at the *Federal Law Enforcement Training Center* in Smyrna, Georgia.

800/74-FLETC
912/267-2100

>FEDERAL LICENSE PLATE CHECK

License plates aren't federal – they're issued by states! Right? Yes…with some exceptions, such as consulate plates. But there's a large number of state issued license plates that contain a federal code: amateur radio and land mobile call signs. The call signs are issued by the *Federal Communication Commission* and people who receive them typically will have either a license plate made with the call sign, or, their call sign will be on their license plate holder. There's not a set configuration for the call signs, but here's a typical amateur radio call sign, which I recently saw on a license plate – KD6JWI. Here's a land mobile call sign which I recently saw on a license plate holder – KMA367. (This call sign turned out to be registered to the City of Los Angeles. This was a city worker's car I had seen.) Once you learn to recognize these numbers, you'll be noticing them more and more. By calling the Federal Communications Commission, you can learn the name, address and date of birth of who the call sign is registered to.

888/CALL FCC

>FEDERAL PARENT LOCATOR SERVICE

The Federal Parent Locator Service (FPLS) is a federal program designed to help locate missing parents in child support, child custody, and parental kidnapping cases. Run by the *Office of Child Support Enforcement* (U.S. Department of Health and Human Services), the program relies upon the computerized records of the IRS, Social Security Administration, Department of Defense, and state employment security agencies to find a current address for the wanted parent. The agency does not accept requests for assistance from the general public. Rather, the request must come from a state child enforcement official, law enforcement, or a state court judge in an action to enforce a child custody order. Information obtained from *FPLS* is then released back to the authorized official, NOT to the parent requesting assistance.

202/401-9267

Also see...CHILD SUPPORT EN-FORCEMENT.

FEDERAL RECORD CENTERS
Ultimately federal criminal, civil, and bankruptcy files end up in one of 13 *Federal Record Centers*:

Anchorage (covers Alaska) — 907/271-2441

Atlanta (covers Alabama, Florida, Georgia, Kentucky, Mississippi, North Carolina, South Carolina, Tennessee) — 404/763-7477

Boston (covers Connecticut, Maine, Massachusetts, New Hampshire, Rhode Island, Vermont) — 617/647-8104

Chicago (covers Illinois, Indiana, Michigan, Minnesota, Ohio, Wisconsin) — 312/581-7816

Denver (covers Colorado, Montana, New Mexico, North Dakota, South Dakota, Utah, Wyoming) — 303/236-0804

Fort Worth (covers Arkansas, Louisiana, Oklahoma, Texas) — 817/334-5515

Kansas City (covers Iowa, Kansas, Missouri, Nebraska) — 816/926-7272

Los Angeles (covers Arizona, Clark County, Nevada, 11 southern California counties) — 714/360-2626

New York (covers New Jersey, New York, Puerto Rico, Virgin Islands) — 201/823-7242

Philadelphia (covers Delaware, Maryland, Pennsylvania, Virginia, West Virginia) — 215/671-8241

San Francisco (covers California, except 11 Southern California counties, Nevada, except Clark County,

| Hawaii, Pacific Ocean territories) | 415/876-9001 |

| *Seattle* (covers some of Alaska, Idaho, Oregon, Washington) | 206/526-6501 |

| *Washington, D.C.* | 301/457-7010 |

FEDERAL RESEARCH - IN PROGRESS (FEDRIP)

FEDRIP database contains early information on over 150,000 federal health, scientific, and technical research projects currently in progress. These companies provide access to the *FEDRIP* database:

Best & Company	410/563-2378
Dialog/Data-Star	800/221-7754
Knowledge Express	215/293-9712

>FEDERAL TRADE COMMISSION

Federal agency seeks to enforce fair business practices through civil actions. Areas of interest include telemarketing scams, credit bureau abuse, and other consumer related matters.

| *FTC Headquarters* | 202/326-2222 |

Regional Offices:
Atlanta	404/656-1399
Boston	617/424-5960
Chicago	312/353-4423
Cleveland	216/263-3410
Dallas	214/979-0213
Denver	303/844-2271
Los Angeles	310/235-4000
New York	212/264-1207
San Francisco	415/356-5270
Seattle	260/220-6363

FEDERAL WITNESS PROTECTION PROGRAM

Department of Justice, Witness Protection Office 202/514-3684

FINANCIAL CRIMES ENFORCEMENT NETWORK

Financial Crimes Enforcement Network ("FinCEN") is a Department of Treasury division charged with assisting authorized law enforcement agencies in the investigation of financial crime, especially drug money laundering. *FinCEN's* agents and computer analysts rely heavily upon computer databases to identify criminal activity, including the Treasury's Financial Database, containing reports filed under the Bank Secrecy Act, identifying currency transactions over $10,000.

703/905-6096
800/SOS-BUCK

FINANCIAL INVESTIGATIONS
Also see...*IRS FORM 4506.*

Also see...*NEVADA CORPORATIONS..*

Also see...*BANKRUPTCY COURTS.*

Also see...*PACER.*

Also see...*REAL PROPERTY RECORDS.*

Also see...*BUSINESS BACKGROUND INVESTIGATIONS.*

Also see...*CORPORATIONS.*

>FIND/SVP PUBLISHING
FIND/SVP may your first stop if you are conducting a market intelligence or technical investigation. Every two months they publish a lengthy catalog of reports, market surveys, and studies with such technical titles as "The Bottled Water Market", "East Asian Business Intelligence", and "The U.S. Casino Gaming Market". Also included are many books and reports on conducting competitor intelligence. (Website: *http://www.findsvp.com*)

800/346-3787

FIREARM FORENSICS
The Bureau of Alcohol, Tobacco, and Firearm's National Tracing Center aids law enforcement agencies by tracing the history of firearms from manufacture through current ownership.

304/274-4100

The Criminalistics Laboratory Information System is a computer database of the FBI Crime Lab that identifies the weapon type used to fire a recovered bullet or casing.

202/324-4410

Forensic Science Consulting Group is a privately owned crime lab whose specialties includes ballistics.

760/436-7714

FIREARM TRAINING
The *Smith & Wesson Academy* offers firearm training and certification.   800/331-0852

FIRE INCIDENT REPORTING SYSTEM
The *U.S. Fire Administration* maintains a nationwide database of fire incidents, as submitted by participating local fire agencies. It's known as the Fire Incident Reporting System.

301/447-1349
301/447-1024

FLORIDA ACCIDENT HISTORIES
International Research Bureau maintains a database of every person involved in a Florida motor vehicle accident (as driver, passenger or pedestrian) from 1983 through the present.   904/942-2500

FOOD TAMPERING
The FDA Forensic Chemistry Center investigates food tampering cases and unauthorized/counterfeit drugs.   513/684-3501

Forensic psychiatrist *Dr. Park Dietz* is a recognized expert in food tampering cases, including the Chicago Tylenol murders.   714/760-0422

FOREIGN AGENT REGISTRATION
Agents of foreign countries are required to register with the *Dept. of Justice, Internal Security Section.*   202/514-1216

FOREIGN COMPANY CREDIT REPORTS
For $100 per report, this *U.S. Dept. of Commerce* unit will provide credit report and background info on foreign companies. Ask for *World Trade Data Reports.*   202/482-4204

Graydon America offers business credit reports on overseas companies.   800/466-3163

The *Export-Import Bank of the United States* will provide credit data on foreign companies to whom it has extended credit. It can also provide loan repayment statistics for countries as a whole, as well.   202/565-3960

**FOREIGN COUNTRIES - INFOR-
MATION**
The U.S. State Department has a
Country Officer assigned to every foreign country. The Country Officers are
knowledgeable of their assigned count-
ry's affairs and institutions.   202/647-4000

FOREIGN INVESTIGATIONS
*The Regency International Directory
of Private Investigators* is 466 pages
long and is filled with listings and ads
for investigators in just about every
corner of the globe. Published out of
England, it can be purchased in the U.S.
through Thomas Publications for $95.00
plus S&H.   512/420-9292

>Are you conducting a criminal investi-
gation, in cooperation with an authorized
law enforcement agency? Then you need
to know about the *U.S. National Central
Bureau*, the American interface of Interpol.
When American law enforcement needs
assistance in foreign lands, the request is
routed through USNCB. Are you investigating a case of international child abduction? Is there an authorized law enforcement agency active in the case as well?
(USNCB is prohibited from processing
requests from non-law enforcement persons or organizations.) Why not have
them make an assistance request through
USNCB/Interpol to have field investigation
conducted abroad?   202/616-9000

The U.S. State Department offers a hotline
with travel warnings about areas that are
considered a risk to Americans.   202/647-5225

Pinkerton Risk Assessment Services monitors political, terrorist and other threats in
foreign lands and publishes a daily bulletin. 703/525-6111

The Centers for Disease Control offer a
travel advisory hotline for assessing health
threats to travelers in foreign countries.   404/332-4559

>Will the call of duty be taking you to
one of the world's war zones, "forbidden
areas", or criminal regions? *The World's
Most Dangerous Places* is an intensely
interesting and fact jammed book about
the 85 worst places on our planet — and
how to get in and out of them alive. The
book also contains some very interesting

reference material, including contact addresses for terrorist groups, such as Hezbollah, the shadowy Middle Eastern terrorist organization. My favorite chapter is on the do's and don'ts of bribing foreign officials. Thoughtfully included is current price information on buying your way out of trouble abroad. (Common traffic tickets, $5 - $10; Accidents with a fatality involved, $2,000 - $6,000.) The book sells for $20, and is updated annually. Published by *Fielding*, the book can be found at most major bookstores.

Also see...*INTERNATIONAL DIRECTORY ASSISTANCE.*

Also see...*MEXICAN INVESTIGATIONS...CANADIAN INVESTIGATIONS...ENGLAND INVESTIGATIONS.*

Also see...*EMBASSIES.*

FOREIGN LAW
The Library of Congress, Law Library, maintains two foreign law divisons:

Eastern Law includes Poland, Russia, Turkey, Iran, Iraq, the Middle East, South Africa, China, the Far East, and others — 202/707-5085

Western Law includes Britain, Canada, Australia, Europe, India, Pakistan, Mexico, South America and others — 202/707-5077

FOREIGN PUBLICATIONS
DataTimes offers access to data from over 1000 foreign news sources. Current fee is $39 per month for unlimited searching of headlines, plus a charge of $2.95 per article printed. If you just need to access this on a spot basis and don't want to pay the monthly fee, see *INFOACCESS.* — 800/642-2535

FORENSIC ACCOUNTANTS
Forensic accountants detect fraud, theft, and motive through investigation of financial records and documents.

>*Arthur Andersen Business Fraud Risk Services* maintains offices

throughout the U.S. and overseas
manned with forensic accounts.
Call their headquarters for a local
referral.   312/507-9937

FORENSIC ENTOMOLOGY
Forensic entomology is the study of
what bugs do to dead bodies and
what that tells us about time, place,
and method of death.

M. Lee Goff   808/956-6741

Rob Hall   573/882-8254

Richard W. Merritt, Ph.D.   517/355-8309

Gail S. Anderson, Ph.D.   604/291-4284

FORENSIC SCIENCE CON-SULTING GROUP
Forensic Science Consulting Group is
a privately run crime lab whose specialties includes crime scene anaylisis, ballistics, fingerprints and trace
evidence anaylisis.   760/436-7714

FORENSIC SCIENCE ORGANI-ZATIONS
Most, if not all, of the following
groups can provide referral to a locally based expert in their field:

*American Academy of Forensic Sci-
ences* is a professional organization
that offers an expert referral service.
Also maintains a reference library.   719/636-1100

*American Association of Questioned
Document Examiners*   404/244-2500

*American Board of Forensic Docu-
ment Examiners*   713/784-9537

*American Board of Forensic Odon-
tology*   719/636-1100

*American College of Forensic Exam-
iners*   417/881-3818

Forensic anthropology is the science
of obtaining information from human
remains. Contact The *American Board
of Forensic Anthropology*.   207/866-7865

American Forensic Association   715/425-3198

Mass spectometry is the identification of substances based on the mass of ionized molecules. For more information, contact the *American Society for Mass Spectrometry.*   505/989-4517

For the *Midwestern Association of Forensic Scientists,* contact Anthony Tambasco   419/755-9732

For the *Northeastern Association of Forensic Scientists* contact Kirby Martir   914/377-7762 (fax)

For the Northwest Association of Forensic Scientists contact Roger A. Ely, membership chairman.   415/744-7051 ext.29

American Society of Crime Lab Directors   813/341-4409

New Jersey Association of Forensic Scientists   609/882-2000

International Association for Identification   510/865-2174

For the *International Association of Blood Stain Pattern Analysts,* contact Norm Reeves.   609/478-4085

FORENSIC TOXICOLOGY
See...*CRIME LABS - PRIVATE*

FOREST FIRE REPORTS
U.S. Aviation and Fire Management tracks forest fires currently burning in the U.S.   202/205-1483

FRAUD SECTION, DEPT. OF JUSTICE
Focuses on white collar crime involving government programs.　　　202/514-7023

FREEDOM OF INFORMATION ACT RETRIEVALS
These companies specialize in assisting Freedom of Information Act requests in Washington, D.C.
Washington Researchers　　　202/333-3499
FOIA Clearinghouse　　　202/785-3704

The Reporters Committee for Freedom of the Press offers a hotline and publications to assist journalists in obtaining government records through the Freedom of Information Act.　　　703/807-2100

>GANG INVESTIGATIONS
The scourge of modern day street gangs has led to a small but growing number of books that might be useful in gang investigations.

Gang Slanging by Russell Flores contains over 5,400 gang words and phrases from around the country ($16.95).　　　800/498-0911

The Street Gang Identification Manual, identifies gang trademarks, insignias, tattoos, graffiti and hand signs. Over 400 pages. Sells for around $55.　　　800/295-4264

Former Nevada State Prison gang intelligence officer Bill Valentine's book *Gang Intelligence Manual* contains both gang identifiers and behind the scenes information on gang inner-workings ($25.00)　　　800/392-2400

Also see...*CHICAGO CRIME COMMISSION.*

GENEALOGY RESEARCH
>*AGLL Genealogical Services* will certainly be a good starting point for family history investigations. They publish extensive catalogs on books and software to aid in genealogical investigations. Sample computerized titles available include Utah Death Index 1898-1905 and How to Research American Indian Bloodlines. (Website: *www.agll.com*)　　　800/760-AGLL

Harvey E. Morse, P.A. specializes in international genealogical research — 904/322-9999

There are roughly 1600 *Family History Centers* throughout the U.S. They're funded by The Church of Jesus Christ of Latter-Day Saints (aka the Mormons) and are staffed by volunteers. Several computerized databases are available, free of charge, for genealogical research. Non members of the church are always welcome. Databases available include the *Social Security Administration Master Death Index*; a *Military Records* index of pre-Korean war service; and a third called the *International Genealogical Index*. Due to staff shortage, phone look ups are discouraged. To find your nearest *Family History Center*, call this number: — 800/346-6044

The Immigrant Genealogical Society — 818/848-3122

International Genealogical Search, Inc. specializes in locating missing heirs — 800/663-2255

>GENERAL ACCOUNTING OFFICE (GAO)
The *GAO* serves as the non-criminal investigative branch for the federal government. Ever hear a congressman talking in depth on a complex subject like computer security at the Defense Depatment? There's a good chance that what you're hearing is a regurgitation of a *GAO* report.

GAO, Main Number — 202/512-3000
Inspector General, GAO — 800/424-5454
GAO Publications — 202/512-6000

GEOGRAPHIC NAMES DATABASE
The *United States Geological Survey* has a database called the *Geographic Names Data System* (aka National Geographic Names Database), which stores the names of over two million places in the United States. If you have the name of a place, but don't know the state or region, they'll find it for you. — 703/648-4550

GEORGIA DRIVER'S STATUS
The status of a Georgia driver's license can be checked for free by

calling the state's *Automated Driver's Status Line:* 404/657-9300

GOVERNMENT PRINTING OFFICE (GPO)
Thousands of government funded publications are available through the *GPO.* 202/512-1800

U.S. Fax Watch, a program of the Government Printing Office, offers popular documents and information about available government documents and CD ROMS by phone. Information available includes popular editions of the Federal Register, the Code of Federal Regulations, and listings of government information indexed by 200 subject listings. 202/512-1716

Atlanta	404/347-1900
Birmingham	205/731-1056
Boston	617/720-4180
Chicago	312/353-5133
Cleveland	216/522-4922
Columbus	614/469-6956
Dallas	214/767-0076
Denver	303/844-3964
Detroit	313/226-7816
Houston	713/228-1187
Jacksonville	904/353-0569
Kansas City (open 7 days)	816/765-2256
Laurel, MD	301/953-7974
Los Angeles	213/239-9844
Milwaukee	414/297-1304
New York	212/264-3825
Philadelphia	215/636-1900
Pittsburgh	412/644-2721
Portland	503/221-6217
Pueblo, CO	719/544-3142
San Francisco	415/252-5334
Seattle	206/553-4270
Washington, D.C	202/653-5075

GUIDE TO BACKGROUND INVESTIGATIONS, THE
I have many books in my investigative library. However, there are only two that I keep *on* my desk. You're reading one. The other is *The Guide to Background Investigations.*

The Seventh Edition in now out with lots of new and updated information on where to get information from court house records to workers' compensation records to driving records and much more. The new volume is over 1,300 pages thick and has ordering information from over 15,000 public record sources. The book sells for $129.50 — but don't be put off by the price. It will be the cornerstone of your library and will more than pay for itself in time saved.   800/247-8713

HATE GROUP INVESTIGATIONS

The Simon Wiesenthal Center will provide information on various forms of racial intolerance.   310/553-8403

Also see...SOUTHERN POVERTY LAW CENTER for information on Klanwatch..

Also see...MILITIA GROUPS.

HAWAIIAN ATTORNEY SERVICE

Docu Search Hawaii will retrieve court documents from various courts in the Hawaiian Islands.   808/523-1200

HAWAIIAN INVESTIGATORS

Wood & Tait is the largest private investigation firm in Hawaii with offices on four islands.

800/774-8585
808/885-5090

HIDDEN CAMERAS

ISIS Investigations, Inc. manufactures and sells its own pager hidden camera systems to both law enforcement agencies and private sector investigators. The system features a hidden micro-chip camera inside a real pager. The camera hooks up through one simple connection to a state-of-the-art Sony EVO 220 video recorder that is so small, it can be hidden under one's clothing in a body sling. There's a single on/off switch for recording. When undercover, a complicated video system is the last thing an investigator needs. The simplicity and ease of use of this system alone makes the system worth the investment. Sells for around $2,500. ISIS also custom builds other hidden camera set ups, too.   903/533-1711

CCTV Corp. has put together a clever catalog of hidden cameras. One is a working telephone, called the "phone cam", which sends a video signal through a phone line. Others come in smoke detectors, wall mounted pictures and thermostats.

800/221-2240
201/489-9595

One of the most unique...and frankly... obscure offerings comes from *Dave Parry*, who specializes in custom building concealment devices for surveillance gear. His primary offerings are psuedo trees and rocks with compartments to hold electronics.

215/657-1909

Electronic Security Products, Inc. offers "video sunglasses" for top secret taping.

800/559-4377

CrimEye, Inc. offers a catalog of hidden cameras, time lapse recorders, and video transmitters.

800/835-1661

First Witness Video Surveillance Systems offers an impressive catalog of hidden camera systems.One looks like a VCR, but a hidden camera mounted in the control panel sees and captures everything nearby. They also sell time lapse video recorders.

800/880-1521

>HOME PRICE SEARCH
Home Price Search operates 24 hours a day, 7 days a week and makes real estate sale information available from throughout much of the United States by touchtone phone. Information available includes when the property was last sold and for how much. An entire street can also be checked to learn what homes sold have sold when, and for how much. You'll need your credit card to access the system. (The cost is $10 for ten minutes of searching.) At no additional charge, you can also receive a fax print out of the data. Sales data begins around five years ago and is current up through approximately 6 weeks ago.

How can this be useful to a PI? For a financial investigation, obtaining sales data for an entire street might serve as an inexpensive comparable worth analysis. Another use might be for an investigator out on a surveillance. Ever arrive at an address, only to find the house vacated...or inhabited by persons who don't look like they should be there? A short cell phone call to *Home Price Search* might tell you that the home was sold two months ago, confirming your suspicion that you're at a bad address.

800/775-1212

>HOMICIDE INVESTIGATION
For most private investigators, homicide investigations are far and few between. When a homicide case does come in, the investigator may not be fully skilled and experienced in this type of investigation. One option is to call in an expert who has spent years working homicide cases for assistance. Former LAPD homicide detective *Tom Lange* became a household name during the OJ Simpson murder trial. However, few people know that he's held a private investigator's license in California since 1980. Now retired from the LAPD, *Tom Lange* is available as a consultant and expert witness in homicide cases.
F.D. Lange Private Investigations & Consulting

805/526-2305

Also see...*DEATH INVESTIGATION*.

HOSTAGE NEGOTIATORS
Situational Crisis Management consults on hostage negotiations, barricaded subjects and potential suicides.

916/663-4192

>HOW TO GET ANYTHING ON ANYBODY - THE NEWSLETTER
Lee Lapin is back at it again — and not one of us is safe. You may know him as the author of *The Whole Spy Catalog* and *How to Get Anything on Anyone (Books I and II)*. Now he's back 10 times a year with a newsletter disseminating information that will send shivers up the spine of privacy rights advocates. Mr. Lapin tells the ins and outs of everything from electronic surveillance, to lock picking to acquiring confidential financial records. Much of this is (thankfully) outside the scope of your average law abiding investigator. But its good stuff to know and a great read. Recommended. (Subscription price is $89 per year.)

650/513-5549

HUMAN REMAINS
Forensic anthropology is the science of obtaining information from human remains. Contact the *American Board of Forensic Anthropology*.　　207/866-7865

Forensic odontologists identify the dead through dental examination. Contact the *American Board of Forensic Odontology* for a local referral.　　719/636-1100

Also see...*FORENSIC ENTOMOLOGY*.

Also see...*NECROSEARCH*.

>I.D. CHECKING GUIDE
One way to determine the authenticity of an out-of-state drivers license is with *The I.D.Checking Guide*. You'll find a replica of each states license along with other pertinent details. Cost is $18.95.　　800/227-8827

IMMIGRATION & NATURALIZATION SERVICE, U.S.
General Info　　202/514-1900

Intelligence Division　　202/514-4402

INDEX SYSTEM, THE
Ever wonder how the insurance company keeps track of persons making injury claims — so that they don't go to 10 different insurance companies with the same injury? The primary way this and other fraud attempts are foiled is through a mega database called *The Index System*. Each year roughly 1,600 insurance companies send in data on 20 million injury claims. Access to the database is limited to insurance and related companies.
AISG, Marketing　　212/669-0406
The Index System, Customer Support　　732/388-0332

INFOACCESS
InfoAccess is a handy source of information at a great price. Their monthly subscription charge is just $6.95, although certain premium services cost more. You'll get free access to a national directory assistance service that offers pluses you don't get through Ma Bell. Their operators can look up phone and address information on either a busi-

ness or person — even if all you have is
a name, and no idea where the firm or
person is located. Reverse look ups are
also offered. For just $3 per report, you
can order Company Profiles. These provide
a cheap snap shot of any given business,
including its SIC code, number of
employees, and key personnel. Also
available are Business Credit Reports
(TRW) for $25 each, and Business
News Network, which is a search of the
impressive Datatimes database of 5,000
publications, for $2 per citation and $6
per article.   800/808-INFO

INPHOTO SURVEILLANCE
Inphoto Surveillance claims to be the
nation's largest surveillance company
with investigators in city's both nationwide and in Latin America, the
Caribbean and elsewhere abroad.
Their primary specialty is investigation of bodily injury claims for insur-
ance companies   800/822-8220

INSIDER TRADING
The *Division of Enforcement, Securities
& Exchange Commission* investigates
illegal insider trading in the financial
markets.   202/942-4000

**>INSURANCE INFORMATION EX-
CHANGE**
Private information company offers computerized driver's license information on
a nationwide basis. Fast, easy, inexpen-
sive.   800/530-9962

INSURANCE INVESTIGATIONS
>Producer Database is the first national
database of licensing information on
insurance agents and brokers, including
disciplinary information from state licensing authorities. See *PRODUCER
DATABASE* for more details.   913/599-8085

>The *National Association of Fraud
Control Units* is a national organization for state government anti-insurance
fraud agencies.   202/434-8020

*Also see...CLAIMS INTELLIGENCE
REPORT.*

Coalition Against Insurance Fraud   202/393-7330

ClaimSchool Inc. publishes several books on the detection and investigation of suspected fraudulent insurance claims, including *Uncover the Truth!* which focuses on interview techniques. They also publish *Zalma's Insurance Fraud Letter,* which is devoted to educating insurance types on how to defeat fraudulent claims. The mastermind behind *ClaimSchool* is legendary Los Angeles fraud fighter and attorney Barry Zalma.   310/390-4455

National Association of Independent Insurance Adjusters   312/853-0808

The National Insurance Crime Bureau (NICB) is an insurance industry funded investigative agency formed to combat insurance fraud. Although it is a private agency without law enforcement status, most of its agents are former law enforcement officers.   708/430-2430

The *NICB* also maintains a hotline for reporting insurance fraud.   800/TEL-NICB

Inphoto Surveillance claims to be the nation's largest surveillance company with investigators in city's both nationwide and in Latin America, the Caribbean and elsewhere abroad. Their primary specialty is investigation of bodily injury claims.   800/822-8220

The John Cooke Insurance Fraud Report keeps insurance fraud investigators up to date on the latest scams, legal developments, resources and more.   714/289-7777

Also see...*PROPERTY LOSS INSURANCE REGISTRY.*

Also see...*THE INDEX SYSTEM.*

>INTEGRATED DATABASE SOFT-WARE

IDS has been used by collection agencies, skip trace firms, and a select few PI's in the know for conducting dirt cheap locates. *IDS* makes available a small number of the most commonly used bread and butter databases for conducting locates. Social Security traces are $2.25 each, bankruptcy checks, $1.00, and single property ownership searches are just $3.00 a match. There is no monthly minimum fee or sign up fee. The data is accessible by either a dial up modem (at a charge of $6.50 per hour), or via the telnet (if you have an ISP for the Internet, instead of AOL you probably already have telnet) for *free*. There's one catch, though: The graphics look like a throw back to a 1960's government computer program. If you're spoiled by crisp, modern Windows style graphics, you might find the system's graphical interface to be an unpleasant eye strainer.   630/530-9962

INTERACTIVE INFORMATION SYSTEMS (IIS)

IIS is a well kept secret of both private investigators and state and federal law enforcement agencies. Services available include 800ID "trap lines", "sting cards" and a "Blindline" which allows its user to make untraceable calls. Need a temporary 800 line for a reward offer? They'll handle that, too.   800/495-0888

INTERNAL REVENUE SERVICE
General Information   800/829-1040

>Criminal Investigations, Headquarters   202/622-3200

>The *Internal Revenue Service* employs nearly 3,200 Special Agents nationwide. Here's their field offices:

Alabama	205/912-5563
Alaska	907/271-6315
Arizona	602/207-8944
Arkansas	501/324-6266
California	714/360-2084
	213/894-2670
	916/974-5294
	415/522-6017
	408/494-7900
Colorado	303/446-1800

Connecticut	203/240-4233
Delaware	302/791-4519
District of Columbia	202/874-0155
Florida	305/423-7280
	904/232-2963
Hawaii	808/541-1151
Idaho	208/334-1000
Illinois	312/886-4500
	217/527-6091
Indiana	317/226-7788
Iowa	515/284-4445
Kansas	316/352-7670
Kentucky	502/582-5341
Louisiana	504/558-3333
Maine	603/433-0561
Maryland	410/962-3173
Massachusetts	617/565-1620
Michigan	313/226-7220
Minnesota	612/290-3466
Mississippi	601/965-5099
Missouri	314/539-2018
Montana	406/441-1038
Nebraska	402/221-3596
Nevada	702/455-1103
New Hampshire	603/433-0561
New Jersey	201/645-2146
New Mexico	505/837-9025
New York	212/436-1033
	518/431-4668
	718/488-2008
	716/551-5461
North Carolina	910/378-2199
North Dakota	701/239-5143
Ohio	513/684-2528
	216/522-3231
Oklahoma	405/297-4000
Oregon	503/326-3201
Pennsylvania	215/597-2250
	412/644-5678
Rhode Island	401/823-1796
South Carolina	803/253-3712
South Dakota	605/330-4449
Tennessee	615/736-5449
Texas	512/499-5206
	214/767-1076
	713/653-3620
Utah	801/524-5900
Vermont	802/860-2017
Virginia	804/771-2252
Washington	206/220-6025
West Virginia	304/420-6634
Wisconsin	414/297-3904
	715/836-8741
	608/829-5806
Wyoming	307/633-0900

>*IRS Internal Security* maintains watch over IRS employees who might be tempted by bribery, fraud or other shortcomings.

202/622-4600

>Did you know that the *Internal Revenue Service* has a reward program for snitching on tax cheats? See...*REWARDS OFFERED*.

>Direct Freedom of Information Act requests to: *Internal Revenue Service, Freedom of Information Request, PO Box 795 - Ben Franklin Station, Washington, DC 20044.*

For information on obtaining the tax returns of tax exempt organizations, see...*CHARITABLE ORGANIZATIONS*.

>Also see....*IRS FORM 4506*.

>Also see...*U.S. TAX COURT*.

>**INTERNATIONAL DIRECTORY ASSISTANCE**
Do you need to locate a business or person in a foreign land? For just $6.95 per look up, *International Directory Assistance* will provide published address and phone number information in any one of 42 foreign lands.If you haven't used *International Directory Assistance* before, you'd probably imagine that after dialing double zero, one ends up getting patched through to foreign based operators who speak little or no English. Not true! The operators are American and have access to the published phone numbers of 42 countries. Making a call to them is as effortless as calling your local directory assistance.

00

>**INTERNET - RESOURCES**
Private investigator's have taken to the Internet, hungry for information, resources, and other PI's to network with.

There are hundreds of websites of interest to PI's, several "mailing lists" and one newsgroup. Sources of information avail- on the Internet would be a book in itself. Here's a few of the best places for an investigator to be in Cyberspace:

Pro-Inv is a list-serve that over 1,000 PI's now belong to and share information with each other through. (The list was originally started by PI's LaMont Bankson and Phil Agrue, from Phoenix and Portland, respectively.) Once a day, a digest of "posts" sent in by individual members is broadcast to every member on the list. To join, send an e-mail message to *majordomo @teleport.com*. In the body of the message type: *subscribe proinv-l (your email address)* (That's an "L" not a "one" after proinv.)

Although there are hundreds of websites by or for private investigators, here are two of the best:

The National Association of Investigative Specialists' website (*http://www.pimall/ nais*) is a monument in cyberspace to the boundless energy and enthusiasm of *NAIS* and *Thomas Investigative Publications* impresario, Ralph Thomas. There's an amazing amount of information for PI's here. You'll never get all the way through the site in one sitting. You'll want to keep returning to it, too, as the site is continually updated. Much of it is commercial in nature, aimed at selling books, videos, gear and other products for investigators. You'll also find free articles written by PI's for PI's.

Many individual private investigation agencies have put up a website to promote their services. Many add "link" pages to their sites to attract additional traffic. Of these, there's one that truly stands out for the sheer number of "links" it has provided to websites that might contain information useful to investigators. Run by *Corporate Investigative Services* out of Huntsville, Alabama, the site can be found at *www. hsv.tis.net/~pvteye/source.html*. Check it out!

>INTERNIC
Need to know who is the registered owner of an Internet domain name? (Example: www.crimetime.com) On you computer, go to *http://rs.internic.net* or call the *Internic*, the organization that registers the names.   703/742-4777

Also see the appendix of this book where INTERNET ABBREVIATIONS further identifies information con-

tained in Internet addresses.

INTERPOL
>Short for the International Criminal
Police Organization, *INTERPOL*
brokers the cooperation of police
agencies in 177 countries. It's the
only international police organization.
Headquartered in Lyon, France. 011-33 044 72 44 70 00

When American law enforcement
needs assistance in foreign lands,
the request is routed through the
U.S. National Central Bureau,
the American interface of INTER-
POL. (*USNCB* is prohibited from
processing requests from non-law
enforcement persons or organizations.) 202/616-9000

INTERPRETERS - BY PHONE
AT&T Language Line offers interpreters by phone in dozens of languages.
You call them, they connect you to
an interpreter, then to the subject of
your interview. Payment accepted by
credit card 800/843-8420

>INTERSTATE IDENTIFICATION INDEX
The *Interstate Identification Index* is the
largest file in NCIC, the FBI's nationwide criminal history system. Also commonly referred to as *"Triple I"*. See *CRIM-
INAL RECORDS* for more details.

INVESTIGATIVE REPORTERS & EDITORS
Professional group, largely concerned
with the usage of computerized information for reporting 573/882-2042

>INVESTIGATOR GAZETTE, THE
Neat little newsletter put out by Florida
PI, author, and self-described "Infomaniac",
CJ Bronstrup. Contains lots of insider tips
as well as advertising for many skip tracing,
asset, and other searches which are offered
by CJ. ($24.00 per year) 352/666-4371

INVESTIGATOR'S INSURANCE
*Alliance Management & In-
surance Services* offers insurance
coverage for private investigators 800/843-8550
619/471-7116

Costanza Insurance Agency also offers insurance coverage to investigation agencies

800/346-0942

>*El Dorado Insurance Agency* offers policies specifically designed for both PI's and Polygraph Examiners.

800/221-3386
713/521-9251

>*U.S. Risk Underwriters* specializes in professional liability insurance for PI's.

800/232-5830
214/265-7090

INVESTIGATOR'S OPEN NETWORK (ION)

Investigator's Open Network is a well established private investigator's referral service with members throughout America and in many countries abroad. Membership allows a PI to both give assignments to and receive assignments from out of town investigators. If you're not a member, you can still depend on ION when you're in need of an out of town investigator. They'll assign the investigation to a member investigation firm nearest the assignment.

800/338-3463

INVISIBLE INK

Sirchie Fingerprint Laboratories, Inc. manufactures invisible ink for marking paper money. When put under ultra violet light, the ink becomes visible. Used for documenting the money trail in illegal drug transactions, among other things.

800/356-7311
919/781-3120

>**IRS FORM 4506**

Did you know that the Internal Revenue Service will release a person's tax return to a third party? They will — with the signed authorization of the tax filer on a completed *Form 4506*. Why have *Form 4506* handy at your interviews, statements. and depositions? One reason is because many subjects may promise to deliver a prior year's tax returns, only to later renege, or to produce fraudulent documents. With *Form 4506*, the return does directly from the IRS to the third party named on the form. There's a $23 charge for each tax period received. Also included are copies of attachments, including W-2 forms. Don't wait untill you need this form to request it. Call this IRS number now and request *Form 4506*, then keep it in your briefcase.

800/829-3676

Form 4506 can also be downloaded directly off the Internet from the IRS website. Go to *www.irs.ustreas.gov/ forms_pubs/forms.html* and scroll down the list of forms to 4506.

>JANE'S INFORMATION GROUP, LTD.

Sixty Minutes has described *Jane's* as a private Central Intelligence Agency. *Jane's Information Group* collects and publishes information on the military capabilities of most of the world's nations. Their books, magazines and CD ROMS are a good starting point for obtaining information on virtually any military weapon or armed forces. They also offer foreign report subscriptions to track developments in foreign markets. *Jane's World Armies* surveys the capabilities, weaponry, budget and structure of the world's armies.

703/683-3700

JEWELERS BOARD OF TRADE

Jewelers Board of Trade is a jewelry trade organization that maintains a database of background information on persons in the jewelry business. Access to the database is restricted to subscribers.

213/627-4238

JOHN COOKE FRAUD REPORT

Not available to the general public, *The John Cooke Fraud Report* is offered in two editions: one focuses on insurance fraud, the other on financial fraud. Both are packed with great reading on how scams work, and how they're exposed. The paper is owned and operated by professional investigators and their insider's knowledge shows. Archives are available on a CD ROM ($129) which is searchable by topic or author.

714/289-7777

>JOHN E. REID & ASSOCIATES
John E. Reid & Associates has made a science of detecting deception. They've studied thousands of investigative interviews and have developed a profile of how guilty subjects unconsciously might indicate their guilt through physical and verbal behavior and through their answers to a carefully selected list of control questions. This system is both fascinating and very useful. It's available through seminars, and in published books, such as *Criminal Interrogation and Confessions*.

800/255-5747
312/876-1600

JUDGES - BACKGROUND INFORMATION
Verdict Research maintains a database profiling the prior decisions of individual judges.

619/487-1579

JUDGMENT PURCHASE CORPORATION
This is a private company that advances money against judgments on appeal.

800/572-1986

JURY VERDICT RESEARCH
Jury Verdict Research has profiled over 100,000 personal injury cases verdicts and settlements on CD ROM.

800/341-7874

Or try *VerdictSearch*

800/832-1900
516/581-1930

JUSTICE DEPARTMENT - U.S.
Main #

202/514-2000

KINKO'S COPIES
Call this number 24 hours a day to find the nearest Kinko's. They have fax machines, copy machines, computers and more available, 24 hours a day.

800/2-KINKOS

K/L

>KNOW X
Know X is a database provider, owned
by Information America, that offers
public record information for sale over
the Internet (*www.knowx.com*). Their
current menu of databases is quite
limited. *Know X* doesn't advertise a
phone number. Their e-mail address is: *support@knowx.com*

LABOR UNIONS
*Disclosure Room, Office of Labor-
Management Standards Enforcement,
U.S. Dept. of Labor* maintains background information on labor unions,
their officials, by-laws, and financial
reports.   202/219-7393

LAS VEGAS, NV
Divorce Records   702/455-4413
Marriage Licenses   702/455-3156
Police Department   702/795-3111

LAW ENFORCEMENT - AT SEA
*U.S. Coast Guard, Law Enforcement
and Defense Operations*   202/267-0977

**>LAW ENFORCEMENT DIREC-
TORIES**
*See...NATIONAL DIRECTORY OF
LAW ENFORCEMENT ADMINI-
STRATORS.*

LAW LIBRARY
The single largest law in the world is
the *Library of Congress, Law Library.*   202/707-5065

*>Library, Supreme Court of the United
States*   202/479-3177

*The Library of Congress, Law Li-
brary,* maintains two foreign law divisons:
Eastern Law   202/707-5085
Western Law   202/707-5077

**LAW SCHOOL ACCREDITA-
TION**
The *American Bar Association* re-
cognizes 176 law schools. Call this
number to determine if a given law
school has *ABA* accreditation.   312/988-5000

LAWSUIT LOCATOR SERVICE
Searchers specializes in locating lawsuits -- anywhere in America. Give
them the name of the case and they

will find it.   612/687-7740

LAWTECH PUBLISHING CO.
Publisher of Qwik Codes, the field
editions of the California Penal and
Vehicle Codes, among other law en-
forcement publications.   800/498-0911
                                                   714/498-4815

LEGAL MALPRACTICE
Expert Witness/Consultant   310/LEG-MALP

Westlaw maintains a database known
as the *Professional Malpractice Li-
brary.*   800/937-8529

LEGAL RESEARCH CENTER
Legal Research Center is a private
company that researches court deci-
sions.   800/776-9377

LEXIS-NEXIS
Lexis-Nexis is a massive provider of
computerized information, a favorite
child of the legal profession. Few PI's
use the service, because the core information PI's use most can be found
more cheaply elsewhere. Nevertheless,
Lexis-Nexis boasts 1,100 sources of
information. Much of this, though,
is geared toward the needs of lawyers,
not PI's. Included is a vast archive
of case law, constantly updated state
and federal statutes, and state insurance regulations. Also available are
numerous public record databases,
plus some interesting specialty databases. *M-Find* is a locator database of
US Military personnel. Another database features FEIN (Federal Employer
Identification Numbers).   800/227-4908

Now, if you don't want to subscribe
to *Lexis-Nexis*, but would like to make
spot buys from their many databases,
consider *Lexis-Nexis Express*. Non-
subscribers can use the aid of staff
Lexis-Nexis researchers to buy information ala carte. Payment accepted by
credit card.   800/843-6476

LIBRARIES
>*American Library Association*   312/944-6780

>*NASA headquarters Library* is a
good starting point for space and

flight related inquiries.	202/358-0168
Library of Congress	202/707-5000
>Library of Congress, Telephone Reference Service	202/707-5522
>Library, Supreme Court of The United States	202/479-3177
>Special Libraries Association can refer you to a library in one of many specialty areas.	202/234-4700
Library of Congress, Law Library	202/287-5065
UCLA Maps & Gov't Info	310/825-3135
USC Criminal Justice Library	213/740-1768
The Academy of Motion Picture Arts & Sciences library contains a wealth of information on movie credits.	310/247-3000
Environmental Protection Agency, Library	202/260-5922

LLOYD'S MARITIME INFORMATION SERVICES, INC.
Lloyd's Maritime maintains a database on over 79,000 ocean going vessels. Information includes ship ownership, casualties, and ship movements.

800/423-8672
203/359-8383

MAPS - TOPOGRAPHIC
The U.S. Geological Survey maintains topographic maps of the entire United States:

East of Mississippi	703/557-2751
West of Mississippi	303/236-7477
Alaska	907/456-0244

Or try the central USGS information clearinghouse, called the *Earth Science Information Center:*   800/USA-MAPS

MARINE INDEX BUREAU
The Marine Index Bureau maintains a database of injury claims made by maritime personnel.

800/929-0654
609/882-8909

MARINES - PERSONNEL LOCATOR

To locate active members of the *U.S. Marine Corp.*   703/784-3942

MARITIME INFORMATION SYSTEM

The Maritime Information System is a CD ROM containing several databases culled from Coast Guard files, and other sources. Included is a database of boating accidents, another database of vessel recall and defect notices, another database of federally registered boat owners and more. The CD ROM sells for around $295. Just need to do a look up or two? *The Maritime Information System* can also be accessed on a pay per look up basis over the Internet at *www.boatman. com/maritime/*   619/226-1895

Also see... *MERCHANT VESSEL DATABASE.*

MEDICAL DEVICES

The Food & Drug Administration, Center for Devices and Radiological Health regulates medical devices.   800/638-2041

MEDICAL DOCTORS

AMA Physician Select is a database of the *American Medical Association* that contains address, biographical, and disciplinary information on every physician in the United States.   312/464-5000

>AMA Physician Select can also be found on the Internet at *www.ama-assn. org*

>To learn if a doctor is registered on the *Drug Enforcement Administration's National Controlled Substance Registrations* list, get online with:
Database Technologies   800/279-7710

Questionable Doctors, published annually, lists doctors, dentists, and chiropractors who have been disciplined by various licensing agencies.   202/588-1000

If you don't want to invest in the price of Questionable Doctors, contact *Tracers Worldwide Services* who will do look ups in *Questionable Doctors* on a pay per use basis.   800/233-9766

>*Medi-Net* combines data from various
sources into a unified, detailed report
on any given physician. Their fee is
$15 per report. For more details, call
them directly or visit their website,
http://www.askmedi.com   888/275-6334

>*The Federation of State Medical
Boards of the United States, Inc.* is
the nationwide organization for state
medical licensing authorities.   817/868-4006

*The American Board of Psychiatry &
Neurology* board certifies psychia-
trists and neurologists.   847/945-7900

The American Board of Specialties
board certifies M.D.'s in several areas
of expertise. Certification status can
be verified through this number.   800/776-2378

>*Physician and Surgeon's Profiles* are
available to subscribers of *Info Access*
for $10 each. The reports contain the
same biographical information that can
be received for free through *AMA Physician Select* PLUS offers such unique information as special interests (like golf
and skiing), volume of patients per week,
and HMO's that he or she is affiliated
with.) See...*INFOACCESS.*

Fee Facts is a reference publication
on chiropractic fees. Published by
Data Management Ventures, Inc.   404/955-9494

>Discipline history, license status, and
key biographical facts can be found
on medical doctors through their
state's disciplinary or "medical
examiners" board:

Alabama	334/242-4153
Alaska	907/269-8179
Arizona	602/225-3751
Arkansas	501/296-1802
California	916/263-2388
Colorado	303/894-7690
Connecticut	203/566-1011
Delaware	302/739-4522
District of Columbia	202/727-5365
Florida	904/488-0595
Georgia	404/656-3913
Hawaii	808/586-3000
Idaho	208/334-2822
Illinois	217/785-0800

Indiana	317/232-2960
Iowa	515/281-5171
Kansas	913/296-7413
Kentucky	502/429-8046
Louisiana	504/524-6763
Maine	207/287-3601
Maryland	410/764-4777
Massachusetts	617/727-3086
Michigan	517/373-0680
Minnesota	612/642-0538
Mississippi	601/354-6645
Missouri	314/751-0098
Montana	406/444-4284
Nebraska	402/471-2115
Nevada	702/688-2559
New Hampshire	603/271-1203
New Jersey	609/826-7100
New Mexico	505/827-5022
New York	518/474-8357
North Carolina	919/828-1212
North Dakota	701/223-9485
Ohio	614/466-3934
Oklahoma	405/848-6841
Oregon	503/229-5770
Pennsylvania	717/787-2381
Rhode Island	401/277-3855
South Carolina	803/737-9300
South Dakota	605/334-8343
Tennessee	615/367-6231
Texas	512/305-7010
Utah	801/530-6623
Vermont	802/828-2673
Virginia	804/662-9908
Washington	360/753-2287
West Virginia	304/558-2921
Wisconsin	608/226-8794
Wyoming	307/778-2069

Also see...*NATIONAL PRACTITIONERS DATA BANK.*

MEDICAL EXAMINERS
See...*CORONERS.*

MEDICAL INFORMATION BUR-EAU
Mega database of confidential medical information on millions of Americans. Available only to member insurance companies. However, an individual can request a copy of their own
file: 617/426-3660
>In Canada, call: 416/597-0590

MEDICAL REFERENCE INFORMATION
The National Library of Medicine
is the largest medical library in the
world, located in Bethesda, Maryland.　888/FINDNLM
Health Professional Inquiries　301/594-5983
Public Information　301/496-6308

Medline is a mega database of
nearly 9 million articles from
medical journals dating back to
1966. It's searchable, for free, over
the Internet at *www.nlm.nih.gov*

MERCHANT VESSEL DATABASE
Need to identify ownership or other
information on a documented merchant
vessel of the United States? Try the
Merchant Vessel Database.　619/226-1895

MERLIN INFORMATION SERVICES
Merlin Information Services has carved
out its own growing niche in data land
through a library of public record CD
ROMS. They take much of the same
information that the online providers
offer on a pay-by-search basis and
package it into a CD ROM. You just
pop the disc into your computer and
do unlimited searching for just the
initial cost of the disc. If your company does a sufficient volume of
searches, you'll find Merlin's cost per
search to be very attractive. For more
details, see...*DATABASE PROVIDERS.*　800/367-6646

>METROMAIL
There's been a lot of misinformation
published about *Metromail* and the
availability of its products to investigators. *Metromail* maintains a huge
file on the consumer habits of millions
of Americans. The information comes
from survey forms, product registration
forms, subscriptions, and elsewhere.
(The information is then regurgitated
into mailing lists for targeting specific
groups.) Sorry, none of this is available
to private investigators. There is only
one *Metromail* product available to PI's,
called *Metronet National Look Up Service*. See the section below for full details.

METRONET
Metronet's National Look Up Service

offers a limited menu of searches by phone. Searches available include nationwide surname scans, reverse directory look ups and neighbor information. No Social Security Number based information is included in any *Metronet* product. The charge is $3 for the first minute and $2 for each additional.   900/288-3020

MEXICAN INVESTIGATIONS
Gaslamp Quarter Investigations, located in San Diego, offers south of the border investigations in Mexico, and throughout Latin America. In countries where information doesn't always flow freely, you'll want to rely upon a company like *Gaslamp* .   619/239-6991

Located in Tucson, Arizona, *Pan American Investigations* also specializes in investigations south of the border.   520/297-9318

>If you don't actually need to cross the border, but need public or private record information, contact New Jersey based information broker, *Dig Dirt, Inc.* They offer a unique menu of Mexican related searches, including company credit reports and criminal histories.   888/833-DIRT

MILITARY PERSONNEL
The National Personnel Records Center maintains the personnel files of all retired U.S. Military personnel. However, 18 million Army service records were destroyed in a ferocious fire in 1973. The destroyed records comprised 80% of all army personnel records between 1912 - 1959.   314/263-3901

>*Also see...AMERICAN WAR LIBRARY.*

Need professional help obtaining military records, or locating a current or former member of the military? *Military Information Enterprises, Inc.* specializes in obtaining them. They know all of the ins and outs of the system. Co-owner of the company is Col. Richard Johnson, a recognized expert in the field and author of the book, "How to Locate Anyone Who Is or Has Been in the Military" .   800/937-2133

>There's an interesting new source on the Internet for locating current members of the US military. *Military City Online* (www.militarycity.com) has a database for locating the current whereabouts of active servicemen and women. You'll need to subscribe to the website to access the database — but don't worry — the subscription cost is low. It's just $4 per month, or $36 per year.

CSRA offers a proprietary database for locating active military personnel, Coast Guard not included.
800/327-2772
714/653-2101

>Through official sources, start your search here for active members. Be forewarned, information given out is usually limited to family members:

Navy Personnel Locator, worldwide: 703/614-3155
Navy Reservists 800/535-2699

U.S. Marine Corp. locator 703/784-3942

Army Personnel Locator 703/325-3732

Air Force 210/652-5774
210/652-6377

An index of military records through the Korean war are available on computer at most of the 1600 Church of Jesus Christ of Latter Day Saints' *Family History Centers*. Free. Call this number to find your nearest one: 800/346-6044

MILITARY - U.S.
The *Pentagon* 703/545-6700

The *Pentagon locator* finds Pentagon employees. (This number is not for locating military personnel.) 703/545-6700

The *Department of Defense, Defense Investigative Service* 703/325-5308

The *Defense Prisoners Military Operations Center* tracks U.S. POW's and MIA's for all branches of the armed services. 703/602-2202

Defense Fraud Hotline is for both reporting fraud and waste within the Department of Defense and for reporting

defense contractor security violations.	800/424-9098
	202/693-5080
U.S. Army Criminal Investigation Command	703/756-1232
Department of Defense, Amnesty Programs	202/697-3387
Department of Defense, Deserter Programs	202/697-3387
Department of Defense, Conscientious Objectors	202/697-9525
Korean War POW records	202/523-3223

Also see...JANE'S INFORMATION GROUP.

>MILITIA GROUPS

Time Magazine estimated that militia groups, "patriot" organizations and white supremacist groups together have twelve million followers. While this may be an exaggeration, after the bombing of the Oklahoma City Federal building and subsequent conviction of Timothy McVeigh, no one can deny their existence. *The Southern Poverty Law Center's Militia Task Force* began identifying Militia members and organizations six months *before* the bombing in Oklahoma City. After Oklahoma City, one of the first places the FBI turned to for information on militia groups was the *Southern Poverty Law Center*. Their website (*www.splcenter. org/klanwatch/kw-1.html*) names names of militia members and organizations in a growing, publicly available database.   334/264-0286

MISSING PERSONS

Central Registry of the Missing distributes publications with profiles of missing persons to law enforcement agencies and other interested parties.   201/288-4445

Missing Persons International   805/252-3352

The State of Florida operates its *Missing Children Information Clearinghouse* hotline to assist in locating missing children.   888/FL-MISSING

There are many organizations set up to aid in the search for missing children. Only one has quasi-governmental status which includes partial access to NCIC and other usually law enforcement only sources of information. For full details, see...*NATIONAL CENTER FOR MISSING AND EXPLOITED CHILDREN.*

National Runaway Hotline:
Nationwide   800/621-4000
Illinois   800/972-6004

The Department of State, Overseas Citizen Services, helps locate U.S. Citizens missing in foreign lands.   202/647-5226

The U.S. Department of State also operates the *International Parental Child Abduction* unit.   202/647-2688

The *FBI* does not search for missing persons. However, at the request of other law enforcement agencies they will post a stop notice on NCIC.   202/324-3000

The *Social Security Administration* will assist in locating a missing person -- if it's for humanitarian purposes. A letter to the missing person needs to be sent to the SSA in a stamped, unsealed, blank envelope. Include with this as much of the following information as possible: The missing person's full legal name; name of his/her parents; social security number; date of birth; place of birth; and last known address. The SSA office does not have a published telephone number. Direct requests to: *Social Security Administration, att: Missing Persons, 300 N. Green Street, Baltimore, MD 21201.*

>The *Internal Revenue Service* offers a similar service. Send your request to: *Internal Revenue Service, Office of Disclosure Operations, 1111 Constitution Avenue NW, Washington, DC 20224.*

>**MISTRAL SECURITY**
Mistral Security makes a handy collection of presumptive field tests for various drug substances, explosives, and

fingerprints. Packaged in aerosol cans, the tests are sprayed on suspect materials to identify chemical agents present. One, *Ferrotrace*, is sprayed on a suspect's hands to determine if a weapon has been recently handled. *Nin Plus* exposes latent fingerprints on porous surfaces, such as checks and paper currency. *Expray* detects trace amounts of explosives and can be used, among other things, on suspected letter or package bombs. Individual spray cans cost roughly $20 - $30 each. Also available in kits, which contain several different tests.   800/9MISTRAL

MOTOR VEHICLE RECORDS
See...DRIVER'S LICENSE INFORMATION.

See...AGENCY RECORDS.

MUTILATED U.S. CURRENCY
Partially mutilated, burned, mildewed or otherwise destroyed money can be submitted to the *Department of Treasury* for redemption:

Mutilated Paper Money	202/874-2361
Mutilated Coins	202/874-6440

MVR's
See...*DRIVER'S LICENSE INFORMATION.*

MVR DECODER DIGEST
MVR (Motor Vehicle Record) *Decoder Digest* is a reference publication that decodes vehicle code section numbers in all fifty states. Also decodes VIN's (Vehicle Identification Number). Published by BRB Publications   800/929-3764

>NAMEBASE
Namebase is a unique database of over 96,567 persons who have been named in at least one of hundreds of investigative journalism books. If the subject of your investigation travels in the upper circles of business, organized crime, politics, unions or the military, you should check *Namebase* to learn of possible past associations and activities. You can't access *Namebase* without a

computer. If you have a computer, you can search the database for a name by getting off the Internet at *http://www.pir.org*. Doing a name search is self-explanatory. If you get a hit, the name of the book and what pages the name appears on will come up on the screen. That's as far as you'll get for free. For a $30 membership, plus photocopy and fax costs, *Namebase* will copy the citations your searched name appears in and fax or mail the results to you. Obviously, this saves one the hassle of having to find and purchase the entire book. Many investigative journalists know about and use Namebase. Far fewer private investigators do.
Public Information Research   210/509-3160

NAPPS
See...*NATIONAL ASSOCIATION OF PROFESSIONAL PROCESS SERVERS.*

>NATIONAL ANTI-PIRACY ASSOCIATION
NAPA is a privately owned company that specializes in the investigation of pirated pay-per-view programming. They hire investigators, on a commission basis, to ID commercial establishments who are showing the programming without authorization. Interested? Call *NAPA* and request their information packet.   888/USA-NAPA

>NATIONAL ASSOCIATION OF BUNCO INVESTIGATORS
They are known by many names, including swindlers, travelers, and gypsies. They prey upon the elderly, unsophisticated, and unsuspecting with such schemes as *The Pigeon Drop*, *The Bank Examiner*, and *The Three Card Monte*. Thankfully, the movements and activities of many of these "Bunco" artists are tracked through a private organization called *The National Association of Bunco Investigators*, which includes both street level law enforcement officers and private sector investigators among its members. The organization's monthly bulletin alone makes the price of membership ($50 per year) well worth it. It's jammed with photographs and other specifics

on these traveling con artists that
should be of interest to not only bunco
investigators, but also to insurance
fraud investigators, casino investigators, and other type of investigators
who might come into contact with
these types.   410/752-8150

NATIONAL ASSOCIATION OF INVESTIGATIVE SPECIALISTS (NAIS)

The *NAIS* is a trade group for private investigators, with goals of
networking, continuing education,
and the development of new investigative techniques. Members
enjoy conferences, newsletter, web
site, membership directory and more.
($85 for a two year subscription.)   512/420-9292

>NATIONAL ASSOCIATION OF LEGAL INVESTIGATORS

*The National Association of Legal
Investigators* is one of the largest
and most respected national organizations for investigators. Be forewarned, though, membership is limited
to investigators who devote a majority
of time to conducting investigations
for plaintiffs (in civil cases), or for the
defense (in criminal cases).   800/266-6254

NATIONAL ASSOCIATION OF PROFESSIONAL PROCESS SERVERS (NAPPS)

NAPPS is a nationwide network of process servers and public record retrievers.
However, many PI's also belong. The
organization's membership directory
is a handy place to find help when a run
to an out-of-town courthouse is needed. (If
you're a member, you'll get a book version of the directory for free. If not, the
same information can be found for free on
the Internet at *www.napps.org.*)   800/477-8211

NATIONAL ASSOCIATION OF SECURITIES DEALERS (NASD)

Self policing organization for stock
broker types. The hotline number will
provide discipline histories for securities
brokers-dealers.

License Status   301/590-6500
Hotline Info   800/289-9999

NATIONAL AUDIO/VIDEO FORENSIC LABORATORY
Private lab specializing in the forensic analysis and enhancement of audio, video, and photographs. 818/989-0990

NATIONAL BIKE REGISTRY
National Bike Registry seeks to combat bicycle theft through registration. 800/848-BIKE

>NATIONAL CENTER FOR MISSING & EXPLOITED CHILDREN
There are many organizations set up to aid in the search for missing children. Only one has quasi-governmental status which includes partial access to NCIC and other usually law enforcement only resources. *The National Center for Missing and Exploited Children* is active in not only the recovery of abducted children, but also in the prevention of various types of sexual exploitation. Assistance offered to law enforcement includes photograph and poster preparation, technical case assistance and forensic services. *NCMEC* collaborates with the U.S. Secret Service's Forensic Division to provide handwriting, polygraph, fingerprint and other technical forensic assistance.

800/THE-LOST
703/235-3900

>NATIONAL COUNCIL OF INVESTIGATIVE AND SECURITY SERVICES
NCISS is the primary...and sometimes *only* ...voice in national matters that might affect the private investigation industry. When new legislation is introduced in Washington that seeks to trim back our right to investigate, *NCISS* has often been there to fight back. 800/640-4772

NATIONAL CRIME INFORMATION CENTER (NCIC)
See...*CRIMINAL RECORDS*.

For information on where NCIC is headed in the future, see...*NCIC 2000*.

NATIONAL CRIMINAL JUSTICE REFERENCE SERVICE
National Criminal Justice Reference Service is the National Institute of Justice's massive repository of over 130,00 documents, publication and books. Information Specialists are

available to consult by phone on crime and justice related research matters. This is a department of the U.S. Department of Justice. — 800/851-3420

Juvenile Justice Clearinghouse — 800/638-8736
Bureau of Justice Statistics Clear-inghouse — 800/732-3277
National Victims Resource Center — 800/627-6872
Bureau of Justice Assistance Clear-inghouse — 800/688-4252

NATIONAL DIRECTORY OF ADDRESSES & TELEPHONE NUMBERS
Publication contains contact numbers for thousands of business, government, educational and cultural institutions in the United States. Over 1,640 pages long. $69.95 each. — 800/848-8000

>A similar but expanded product called the *Business Phone Book U.S.A.* sells for $140 — 800/234-1340

>NATIONAL DIRECTORY OF LAW ENFORCEMENT ADMINISTRATORS
This is the best directory of law enforcement agencies we have been able to locate. It is comprehensive in scope and identifies local police departments, sheriff departments, state police agencies, correctional agencies, federal law enforcement agencies and even contacts for local police in key cities abroad. There are over 32,000 agencies listed in all. The only knock on it is that many of the agency contact phone numbers are to administrative offices, not to the general agency number. Sells for $80, including S&H. — 800/647-7579

>NATIONAL DRIVER REGISTER
The *National Driver Register* is a computerized database of information on the most dangerous drivers in America. Typically, they've had their licenses suspended or revoked for serious violations including driving while impaired on alcohol or drugs. Administered by the NHTSA, the purpose of this federal program is to keep problem drivers who have had their licenses yanked in one state from getting a new one in another state. The database is restricted to persons wanting their own informa-

tion, prospective employers (with a
signed release from the applicant), the
FAA, the FRA (Federal Railroad Administration), US Coast Guard, State
and federal driver's license officials,
and federal accident investigators. 202/366-4800

NATIONAL FIRE INCIDENT
REPORTING SYSTEM
The *Office of Fire Data Analysis,
Federal Emergency Management
Agency*, maintains a statistical database on over one million fire incidents,
as supplied by participating local and
state agencies. 301/447-1349

NATIONAL FISH & WILDLIFE
FORENSIC LAB
*The U.S. Department of Fish &
Game's National Fish & Wildlife Forensic Lab* has been called the first full
service wildlife crime lab in the world. 541/482-4191

NATIONAL INSTITUTE FOR
COMPUTER-ASSISTED RE-
PORTING (NICAR)
NICAR is a joint project of Investigative Reporters and Editors and the
University of Missouri School of
Journalism, aimed at furthering the
journalistic usage of computer
assisted reporting. Includes newsletter, seminars, website, and e-mail
list. 573/882-0684

NATIONAL INSTITUTE OF PRI-
SONS, THE
Corrections Information Center 303/444-1101

NATIONAL INSURANCE
CRIME BUREAU (NICB)
*The National Insurance Crime Bur-
eau (NICB)* is an insurance industry
funded investigative agency formed to
combat insurance fraud. Although it
is a private agency without law enforcement status, most of its 206 agents
are former law enforcement officers.

National Headquarters 708/430-2430

>International Operations 214/484-1400

>Regional Offices:

Eastern:	
Atlanta	404/325-3993
New England	860/870-0675
New York	516/921-0200
Central	708/430-5100
Western	818/335-9499

The *NICB* also maintains a hotline
for reporting insurance fraud   800/TEL-NICB

>*The National Insurance Crime
Bureau* has expanded its reach
to include powerful databases for
the purpose of busting insurance
scammers:

>*ClaimXchange* is a basic database,
which allows investigators to submit
current insurance claims and compares
them to existing claims.

>*NICB EyeQ* digs even deeper, cross
indexing key information from a
current insurance claimant (like a
social security number) against a
fat database of 350 million plus
other records.

>*VINassist* works like a spell checker,
editing and decoding vehicle identification numbers.

>*NICB Infocenter* is an electronic
bulletin board where SIU's, claim
reps, law enforcement and others
exchange insurance claim related
information.   708/430-2430

**NATIONAL LAW ENFORCE-
MENT AND CORRECTIONS
TECHNOLOGY CENTER**
Program of the *U.S. Dept. of Justice*
focuses on new products and technologies for the advancement of law
enforcement.   800/248-2742

>**NATIONAL PERSONNEL
RECORDS CENTER**
Located in St. Louis, Missouri, the
National Personnel Records Center
is the primary repository and archive
for United States Government non-
military employee records.   314/425-5761

>NATIONAL PRACTITIONER DATA BANK

NPDB is the little known and even less understood nationwide database that maintains background information on virtually every doctor (and 39 other categories of health care providers) in the United States. Signed into law in 1986 by Ronald Reagan, the purpose of the Data Bank was to track problem doctors who were maiming patients through incompetence. By having a central repository for derogatory information, problem doctors who moved from state to state or institution to institution would be followed by their records. There are very tight restrictions on who can access the data. Security measures on the data itself are very high as well, including issuance of Entity Identification Numbers, access passwords, electronic mailbox numbers, and access codes.

Run by the Department of Health and Human Services, NPDB collects adverse information from medical licensing boards, hospitals, professional societies and medical malpractice payers. By federal law, access to the information is only allowable to authorized hospitals, their agents, practitioners requesting information on themselves, state medical licensing boards, and attorneys under very limited circumstances. (A plaintiff's attorney, or a plaintiff representing himself or herself who has filed a medical malpractice lawsuit in state or federal court can request access ONLY when evidence is submitted that a hospital failed to make a required query of the Data Bank. This evidence must be obtained through investigation or discovery, and cannot be determined through a Data Bank inquiry.)   800/767-6732

NATIONAL REFERENCE CENTER

The *National Reference Center* is a free program of the Library of Congress which maintains a huge database of experts and organizations on virtually any technical or scientific subject.   202/287-5670

NATIONAL TECHNICAL IN-FORMATION SERVICE (NTIS)
NTIS maintains a computerized database of over one million reports on a wide range of technical subjects.

800/553-NTIS
703/487-4650

>NATIONAL WHITE COLLAR CRIME CENTER
Funded by the U.S. Congress and administered by the U.S. Department of Justice, the *National White Collar Crime Center* fights economic crime through prevention, education, investigation, and prosecution. The organization is primarily to assist law enforcement agencies in conducting investigations of advance loan fee schemes, credit card fraud, computer fraud and other economic crimes. It also maintains a *Criminal Information Pointer* database that maintains information on persons and businesses suspected of economic criminal activity. The database is confidential and subjected to the same privacy provisions as NCIC.

804/323-3563

NAVY PERSONNEL LOCATOR
To locate *U.S. Navy personnel,*
worldwide

703/614-3155

Reservists

800/535-2699

NAZI WAR CRIMINALS
Office of Special Investigations, Criminal Division, Dept. of Justice investigates suspected Nazi war criminals believed to be living in the United States.

202/616-2492

For background information on the Holocaust, contact *The Simon Wiesenthal Center.*

310/553-8403

>NCIC 2000
The National Crime Information Center is in the process of a high tech rebirth. The new version, *NCIC 2000,* is scheduled to go online in 1999. New capabilities will include the transmission of mugshots, signature samples, and photos of stolen items. *NCIC 2000* will also provide fingerprint matching capability. Squad cars outfitted with a one finger live scan will be able to instantly check a subject's

fingerprint against the master *NCIC 2000* database. New files will also be added, including *Convicted Persons on Supervised Release. NCIC 2000* will operate out of the FBI's new facility in Clarksburg, West Virginia.

304/625-6200

>NECROSEARCH

Necrosearch is a non-profit organization of law enforcement investigators and scientists dedicated to finding clandestine gravesites through numerous scientific techniques, including botany, ground penetrating radar, and aerial imagery. *Necrosearch* has aided burial site searches in 20 states and 6 foreign countries. The group becomes involved in a case only at the request of law enforcement. They're also involved in basic research.

303/734-5187

>NEVADA CORPORATIONS

There's one state who's department of corporation has added value to investigators. Nevada has unique corporation laws that allow greater privacy, greater protection of assets, and greater protection of corporate officers from lawsuits than any other state. Put this in combination with no state income tax and Nevada has become a haven for persons looking to shelter assets through forming corporations in that state. Conducting a financial investigation? Never rule out Nevada corporations — regardless of where the subject is located. (You don't have to operate a business in Nevada for it to be a Nevada corporation.) Most of the major online database providers offer Nevada corporation searches. But, there's even a faster, cheaper, and more direct route to the information. The State of Nevada sells the information via a pay-per-call line. For just $3.50 per call, they'll search a person's name and determine if it is identified as the officer of a Nevada corporation.

900/535-3355

>NEWSPAPERS

Newspaper "morgues" or libraries have become more and more useful as sources of information, largely because their information has become computerized and is much easier to research. Typically, newspapers will charge $7 - $20 to research their database over the phone, although many times the look ups will be free. Sometimes a wealth of background information can be obtained for less than the cost of a decent lunch.

Here's a list of newspapers in big cities that may be useful:

Akron Beacon Journal	330/375-8111
Albuquerque Journal	505/823-3800
Arizona Republic (Phoenix)	602/271-8000
Arkansas Democrat Gazette (Little Rock)	501/378-3400
Atlanta Journal/Constitution	404/526-5151
Austin American-Statesman	512/445-3500
Baltimore Sun	410/332-6000
Boston Globe	617/929-2000
Buffalo News	716/849-3434
Charlotte Observer	704/358-5000
Chicago Tribune	312/222-3232
Cincinnati Enquirer	513/768-8600
Cleveland Plain Dealer	216/999-4500
Columbus (OH) Dispatch	614/461-5000
Daily Oklahoman	405/475-3311
Dallas Morning News	214/977-8222
Denver Post	303/820-1010
Des Moines Register	515/284-8000
Detroit Free Press	313/222-6600
Florida Times Union (Jacksonville)	904/359-4111
Fort Lauderdale Sun-Sentinel	305/356-4000
Fresno Bee	209/441-6111
Honolulu Star-Bulletin	808/525-8660
Indianapolis News/Star	317/633-1240
Kansas City Star	816/234-4300
Las Vegas Review-Journal	702/385-4241
Los Angeles Times	800/788-8804
Louisville Courier-Journal	502/582-4011
Memphis Commercial Appeal	901/529-2211
Miami Herald	305/350-2111
Milwaukee Journal Sentinel	414/224-2000
Minneapolis Star & Tribune	612/673-4000
Nashville Tennessean	615/259-8000
Newark Star-Ledger	201/877-4141
New Haven Register	203/789-5200
New York Post	212/815-8000
New York Times	212/556-1234
Oakland (CA) Tribune	510/208-6300
Orange County (CA) Register	714/835-1234
Philadelphia Inquirer	215/854-2000
Pittsburgh Post Gazette	412/263-1100
Portland Oregonian	503/221-8327
Raleigh (NC) News & Observer	919/829-4500
Richmond (VA) Times Dispatch	804/649-6000
Sacramento Bee	916/321-1000
St. Louis Post Dispatch	314/340-8000
Salt Lake Tribune	801/237-2045
San Antonio Express News	210/225-7411

San Diego Union-Tribune	619/299-3131
San Francisco Chronicle	415/777-1111
San Jose Mercury News	408/920-5000
Seattle Post-Intelligencer	206/448-8000
Tampa Tribune	813/259-7711
The Times-Picayune (New Orleans)	504/826-3279
USA Today	703/276-3400
Washington Post	202/334-6000

NEWS SOURCES

Many news organization will sell text formerly appearing in their publications. Databases are typically searchable by topic, name of individual, and date of publication.

>If you subscribe to *InfoAccess*, (you should — it's just $6.95 per month) you can use their News Network service. At no cost, they'll search the DataTime database of over 5,000 newspapers and magazines. You pay only for articles you choose to have printed out and faxed to your office. ($6 per article)   800/808-INFO

>*The Alternative Press Index*, published quarterly, offers a subject index to articles appearing in approximately 250 alternative, radical, and otherwise left wing publications.
Alternative Press Center   410/243-2471

Datatimes offers access to text previously appearing in over 5,000 publications and news sources, worldwide. Fee is $39 per month plus $2.95 per article printed. Headlines are free. If you don't want to subscribe, see *Info Access* for a pay-per-use alternative.   800/642-2525

Times on Demand offers full access, by phone, to back issues (dating back to 1985) of the *L.A.Times*. Their researchers can search by subject, or date and issue. Cost of a basic topic search, which produces a list of articles on a given subject is $10. Payment accepted by credit card.   800/788-8804

Dow Jones News Retrieval maintains an extensive database of business news   609/520-4088
    415/242-9120

Research Department is a private research company, excellent at retrieving
media coverage on a given subject or
individual.   800/953-INFO

>*Journal Graphics* has transcripts of
CNN and other broadcast programming.   800/825-5746

>*Burelle's Transcipts* also sells tran-
scripts of many television programs,
including most CBS News programm-
ing.   800/777-TEXT

>*The Associated Press*   212/621-1500
                                               800/821-4747
                                               202/736-1100

>*Reuters News Service*   212/859-1600

>*United Press International*   202/898-8000

Also see...*BROADCAST TRANSCRIPTS.*

Also see...*VIDEO MONITORING SER-
VICE OF AMERICA.*

Also see...*NAMEBASE.*

NEW YORK COURT RETRIEV-
ALS
Court-Fax specializes in retrievals
from the New York City courthouses: 800/486-3628
                                               212/608-8940

As does *Fidelifacts*:   800/678-0007
                                               212/425-1520

NICB
*See...NATIONAL INSURANCE CRIME
BUREAU.*

NIGHTVISION EQUIPMENT
Litton Electron Devices manufactures numerous nightvision
scopes and other devices.   602/968-4471

As does *ITT Nightvision*, whose products target the law enforcement
community.   800/448-8678

Hitek International also sells night-
vision equipment.   800/54-NIGHT
                                               415/363-1404

900# IDENTIFIER
Need to know who operates a 900#
Pay Per Call service? If it's carrier is
AT&T call: 800/642-2708

OCCUPATIONAL SAFETY &
HEALTH ADMINISTRATION
(OSHA)
General Information   800/321-6742

OSHA's *Office of Management of
Data Systems* maintains a database
of all OSHA workplace inspections
made since 1972. The database is
searchable by company name, but
not injured worker's.   202/219-7788

ODOMETER FRAUD
Odometer tampering is a federal off-
ense. Contact the *Odometer Fraud
Staff* of the *National Highway Traffic
Safety Commission.*   202/366-5263

>OFFICE OF FOREIGN ASSETS
CONTROL (OFAC)
OFAC is a little known Department of
the Treasury agency who's mission is
to quash the commerce between businesses and persons in the United States
and foreign narcotic traffickers, terrorists
and unfriendly nations, such as Libya.
OFAC maintains a list, known as
*Specially Designated Nationals and
Blocked Persons* containing all of the
above. Banks, insurance company and
all other businesses and persons are forbidden from doing business with these
parties. If the government finds out that
business has been transacted, either in-
tentionally or mistakenly, severe fines
are meted out. (The entire *OFAC* list
of "Specially Designated Nationals and
Blocked Persons" is included in *THE
EXCLUDED PARTY INDEX.*)
OFAC   202/622-2480
OFAC Compliance Hotline   800/540-OFAC
OFAC also has a bilingual hotline,
located in Miami, for issues related
to the Cuban embargo   305/536-6769

ORGANIZED CRIME
*Organized Crime & Racketeering
Section, Criminal Division, Depart-
ment of Justice*   202/514-3495

The *Chicago Crime Commission* is a not for profit organization that has been gathering information on mobsters since 1919.　　312/372-0101

Mid States Organized Crime Information Center　　417/883-4383

>PACER
Pacer is the computerized indexing system for much of the federal court system. Included are the indices of all but two bankruptcy courts, most federal civil and criminal courts, and eight of twelve appelate courts. You'll need a computer, modem, and communication software (like HyperTerminal). For just 60¢ per minute you can browse the indices and do name searches. Until very recently, the system was limited in that you had to search the PACER system one jurisdiction at a time. Now, nationwide searches of all available jurisdictions are available for the 60¢ per minute charge.　　800/676-6856

>PALADIN PRESS
Paladin Press has certainly earned its controversial reputation. Titles in this Boulder, Colorado publisher's extensive book and video catalog include "Homemade Grenade Launchers", "Secrets of a Super Hacker", "Rape Investigation Manual", "Marijuana Field Booby Traps", and "Hit Man, A Tactical Manual for Independent Contractors". Others subject areas include firearms, martial arts, self-defense, explosives, revenge, and action careers. *Paladin Press* is living proof that freedom of the press is alive and well in America. Their catalog can be obtained by sending two dollars to: *Paladin Press, P.O. Box 1307, Boulder, CO 80306.*
Order Department　　800/392-2400
Customer Service　　303/443-7250

PAROLE COMMISSION - U.S.
The *U.S. Parole Commission* controls parole of federal prisoners.　　301/492-5990

>PASSENGER VEHICLE IDENTIFICATION MANUAL
The *Passenger Vehicle Identification Manual* is a must for any investigator

working stolen vehicles. Published by the National Insurance Crime Bureau, this pocket sized book is a hardcore reference manual to understanding and decoding VINs (Vehicle Identification Numbers). Distribution of the book is restricted to professional investigators. Send your request on company letterhead, or with a business card, plus $6 to: *National Insurance Crime Bureau, 10330 South Roberts Rd, Palos Hills, IL 60465 ATTN: Operations Support Department.*

Also available is a similar edition, the *Commercial Vehicle Identification Manual,* devoted to commercial vehicles (primarily trucks). Also $6.

PATENT INFO
U.S. Patent & Trademark Office　　　800/786-9199

>Patents issued since 1971 can be found in a searchable database put up by IBM on the Internet It's located at *http://patent.womplex.ibm.com*

Questel-Orbit, Inc. is an online provider of patent and trademark filings information.　　　800/456-7248

L.A. Science & Patent Library will do a limited patent search by phone.　　　213/612-3270

Teklicon is a consulting firm specializing in high tech patent infringement matters.　　　415/965-2300

PENTAGON LOCATOR
The *Pentagon* locator finds Pentagon employees. (This number is <u>not</u> for locating military personnel.)　　　703/545-6700

PHONE BOOKS
>The Internet has many phone directories available on line, for free. One site features links to phone books in several dozen foreign lands. It's called *Telephone Directories on the Web* and is located at *www.contractjobs. com/tel*

>*Worldwide Books* specializes in finding phone books from around the world.　　　800/792-2665

>*The Directory Source* from US West can provide telephone books from any-

where in the United States. Not free.   800/422-8793

> *The Pacific Bell Directory Smart Resource Center* also sells phone books from throughout the country. Costs range from $6-$50 each and delivery time is around 2 weeks.   800/848-8000

> *The National Directory of Addresses & Telephone Numbers* contains contact numbers for thousands of business, government, educational and cultural institutions in the United States. Over 1,640 pages long. $69.95 each.   800/848-8000

The *Sherman Foundation Library* is a unique private library that houses an enormous collection of old phone books and city directories. Due to a staff shortage, they have a strictly limited policy on doing checks by phone   714/673-1880

However, local researcher *Victor Cook* is available to conduct on site research at a reasonable cost   714/675-5407

The *U.S. Dept. of Commerce* has a collection of foreign phone books and might do look ups over the phone if you ask in a very nice way.   202/482-5511

Also contact the business liaison office of any embassy listed in our *EMBASSY* section -- they usually have phone books from their home countries and often will often offer assistance by phone.

PHONEDISC POWERFINDER
Phonedisc Powerfinder offers most of the published phone numbers in the United States in a 6 CD ROM set, totally 115,000,000 listings. Easy to use, the discs also work as a reverse directory. You can enter a phone number, and get back an address; or, enter an address and get back a phone number. A single edition costs around $120. For around $170, you'll get an updated set of discs in six months.   800/284-8353

PHYSICIAN DISCIPLINARY BOARDS
See...*MEDICAL DOCTORS.*

PILR
See...*PROPERTY INSURANCE LOSS REGISTRY.*

P.I. MAGAZINE
Not familiar with *PI Magazine* yet?
Put just one piece of information to
use from this handy publication and
it will more than pay for itself. Each
issue contains useful information on
investigative techniques and resources.
Also included are marketing ideas for
PI's who are growing a new practice.
Subscription cost is $24 per year,
which includes four quarterly issues.
Single issue copies can be found at
many Barnes & Nobles Booksellers.   419/382-0967

PINKERTON RISK ASSESS-MENT SERVICES
Pinkerton Risk Assesment Services
monitors political, terrorist, and travel
threats in foreign lands. Publishes
daily bulletin.   703/525-6111

POISON - INFORMATION
The FDA maintains a database of
known poisonous substances:
Poison Control Branch   301/827-3223

>Also see...*CRIME LABS - PRIVATE*
for forensic toxicology sources.

Also see...*TOXIC CHEMICALS.*

POLICE REPORTS
Regional Report Services, Inc. specializes in retrieving police reports on
a nationwide basis.   800/934-9698

>POLITICIANS
The *Public Records Section, Federal
Election Commission,* maintains a
database of financial information dis-
closed by all federal candidates and
contributors since 1977.   800/424-9530

Project Vote Smart is a non-profit
voter information service that maintains
information on over 13,000 elected
officials, on both the federal and state
level. Information available includes
issue position, voting records, and
PAC funding.   800/622-7627

The Reporter's Resource Center is a special library staffed by trained researchers to assist political journalists in development of sources and factual information.   541/737-4000

The Reporter's Source Book is relied upon by political journalists and includes an extensive listing of special interest groups, experts and think tanks. Free for political reporters, but can also be accessed for free over the Internet at *http://www.vote-smart.org/about/ services/rrc/rsb/*   541/737-4000

Laird Wilcox Editorial & Research Service is relied upon by journalists for information on fringe political groups – of both the right and left.   913/829-0609

Need information on how to locate or contact nearly 10,000 members of the Washington press corp? Consider *Hudson's Washington News Media* ($185).   800/572-3451

CQ Washington Alert is an online information service specializing in congressional information -- from bills currently pending, to profiles of House/Senate members and more.   800/432-2250

To learn what bills are pending in Congress on any given topic, call the *Office of Legislative Information and Bill Status*. They'll do a free key-word search of their computerized database which contains information on all legislation pending in both the House and Senate.   202/225-1772

After the Bill Status Office has identified the House or Senate bill number, you'll want top obtain a hardcopy of the actual legislation. Call the *Legislative Resource Center*.   202/226-5200

POLYGRAPH
>*Ed Gelb* is considered by many to be one of the leading polygraph examiners in the world. It's been widely rumored that he administered a polygraph exami-nation to O.J. Simpson at the request of O.J.'s own attorneys. The results were never officially released. Gee, I wonder why.   213/932-0200

Need a polygraph examiner, but don't
know where to find one? *The American
Polygraph Association* will provide
referral to local members.

615/892-3992
800/272-8037

*National Training Center of Polygraph
Science*

212/755-5241

POSTAL INSPECTORS, U.S.
The *U.S. Postal Inspectors* investigate
the criminal usage of mail -- from
mail bombs to mail fraud:

National Headquarters — 202/268-4267

Complaint Line — 800/654-8896

Field Offices:
Atlanta Division	404/608-4500
Boston Division	617/464-8000
Buffalo Division	716/853-5300
Charlotte Division	704/329-9120
Chicago Division	312/765-4500
Cincinnati Division	513/684-5700
Cleveland Division	216/443-4000
Denver Division	303/313-5320
Detroit Division	313/226-8184
Ft. Worth Division	817/625-3411
Houston Division	713/238-4400
Kansas City Division	816/932-0400
Los Angeles Division	818/405-1200
Memphis Division	901/576-2137
Miami Division	305/436-7200
Newark Division	201/596-5400
New Orleans Division	504/589-1200
New York Division	212/330-3844
Oklahoma City	405/278-6291
Philadelphia Division	215/895-8450
Phoenix Division	602/223-3660
Pittsburgh Division	412/359-7900
Richmond Division	804/418-6100
St. Louis Division	314/539-9300
St. Paul Division	612/293-3200
San Diego Division	619/233-0610
San Francisco Division	415/778-5800
San Juan Division	809/749-7600
Seattle Division	206/442-6300
Tampa Division	813/281-5200
Washington, D.C. Division	202/636-2300

Also see...*REWARDS OFFERED* for
information on reward money posted
by the *USPS*.

POSTAL SERVICE
For inquiries relating to lost, stolen or
unclaimed Postal money orders, contact the *US Post Office, Money Order
Branch.* 800/868-2443

To verify the employment of a person
with the *U.S. Postal Service,* call
this number and when prompted by
the automated attendant, punch in
their social security number. 800/276-9850

Also see...*ZIP CODE INFORMATION.*

PRESIDENTIAL PARDONS
All requests for presidential pardons
are to be submitted to *Pardon Attorney, Department of Justice.* 202/616-6070

>PRISONER TRANSPORT
Federal Extradition Agency is a private
company specializing in prisoner transport. Nationwide. 800/518-7171

PRISONS
See...*STATE PRISONS.*

Also see...*BUREAU OF PRISONS.*

PRIVACY RIGHTS CLEARING-
HOUSE
Privacy Rights Clearinghouse main-
tains information relative to protec-
tion of personal privacy
California Only 800/773-7748
Outside California 619/298-3396

PRIVATE INVESTIGATION LI-
CENSES
Most states license private investigators. Several states offer no statewide
licensing - relying on either local
registration or no licensing at all.

Alabama	205/532-3316
Alaska	by local gov.
Arizona ·	602/223-2361
Arkansas	501/224-3101
California	916/322-7788
Colorado	by local gov.
Connecticut	203/238-6631
Delaware	302/736-5900
District of Columbia	202/939-8722
Florida	904/488-5381
Georgia	404/656-2282

Hawaii	808/548-7079
Idaho	by local gov.
Illinois	217/785-0800
Indiana	317/232-2980
Iowa	515/281-3211
Kansas	913/296-8200
Kentucky	by local gov.
Louisiana	504/275-8423
Maine	207/624-8775
Maryland	301/799-0191
Massachusetts	617/727-3693
Michigan	517/322-1964
Minnesota	612/642-0755
Mississippi	by local gov.
Missouri	by local gov.
Montana	404/444-3728
Nebraska	402/471-2554
Nevada	702/885-5000
New Hampshire	603/271-3575
New Jersey	609/882-2000
New Mexico	505/827-7323
New York	518/474-4429
North Carolina	919/779-1611
North Dakota	701/224-3404
Ohio	614/466-4130
Oklahoma	405/425-2775
Oregon	by local gov.
Pennsylvania	by local gov.
Puerto Rico	809/781-0227
Rhode Island	402/277-2000
South Carolina	903/737-9000
South Dakota	by local gov.
Tennessee	615/741-6382
Texas	512/463-5545
Utah	801/965-4484
Vermont	802/828-2191
Virginia	804/786-1132
Washington	360/664-9071
West Virginia	304/558-6000
Wisconsin	608/266-0829
Wyoming	by local gov.

>**PRODUCER DATABASE (PDB)**
Producer Database doesn't refer to slick
Mercedes drivin' movie makers. The
"Producers" are insurance agents and brokers. Created by an offshoot of the National Association of Insurance Com-
missioners, *PDB* is the first nationwide
database of licensing information on
these "producers". The purpose is to
verify license status and to track the
disciplinary records of questionable
insurance agents and brokers, even if
they cross state lines. Currently, the
records of 18 states are included, with

plans to add more soon. The information
is currently available over the Internet,
on a fee basis. There's a $500 set up fee,
plus an annual charge of $100 plus a
charge of $2 per look up.   913/599-8085

PRODUCT SAFETY
Consumer Product Safety Commis-
sion   800/638-2772

Consumer Product Safety Commis-
sion, National Inquiry Information
Clearinghouse maintains a database
on product related injuries   800/638-2772
                                        202/492-6424

Consumer Report Books   515/237-4903

Auto Safety Hotline, Dept. of Trans-
portation, maintains information on
auto safety related information, including auto recalls   800/424-9393

Underwriter's Laboratories can provide information on any product
marked "UL Approved"   708/272-8800

**PROFESSIONAL GROUPS - IN-
VESTIGATORS**

>*Alaska Investigator's Association*   907/373-5453

>*Alberta Association of Private*
Investigators   403/650-8684

American Polygraph Association   800/APA-8037

American Society for Industrial Se-
curity   703/522-5800

>*Arizona Association of Licensed*
Private Investigators   602/231-6837

>*Associated Detectives of Illinois*   847/352-9900

Associated Licensed Detectives of
New York State   212/962-4054

Association of British Investigators,
Ltd   011-44-0181 546 3368

Association of Certified Fraud Exam-
iners   800/245-3321
                                        512/478-9070

>*Association of Christian Investi-*

gators	210/342-0509
Association of Massachusetts Licensed Private Investigators	508/586-8057
Business Espionage Controls & Countermeasures Association	301/292-6430
California Association of Licensed Investigators	800/350-CALI 916/456-9908
>California Conference of Arson Investigators	714/283-2295
California Institute for Professional Investigators	800/400-CIPI
Coalition of Virginia Private Investigators & Security Association	703/360-4848
Council of International Investigators	800/759-8884
Evidence Photographers International Council	717/253-5450
>Florida Association of Licensed Investigators	888/845-FALI
>Global Investigators Network	708/579-1776
>Idaho Private Investigators Association	208/375-1906
Information Professionals Network (IPN)	415/364-6121
>Information Systems Security Association has a membership of persons who protect computerized information.	847/657-6746

>*Indiana Society of Professional Investigators* (formerly Indiana Association of Private Detectives)	812/334-8857
>*Intelnet* is a professional association of mostly former agents from the U.S. intelligence community, now working in the public sector	800/784-2020
>*International Society of Air Safety 'nvestigators*	703/430-9668
International Association of Arson Investigators	800/468-4224
International Association of Auto Theft Investigators	352/498-3446
>*International Association of Counterterrorism & Security Professionals*	703/243-0993
International Association of Credit Card Investigators	415/897-8800
International Association of Marine Investigators, Inc.	508/927-5110
International Association of Special Investigation Units	410/931-8100
International Bodyguard Association	901/837-1915
International Livestock Identification and Theft Investigators	303/294-0895
Investigator's Open Network (ION) is a private nationwide referral service.	800/338-3463
Iowa Association of Private Investigators	515/546-6353
Jewelers Security Alliance of the United States	212/687-0328
>*Kansas Association of Private Investigators*	913/362-0104
>*Licensed Private Detective Association of Massachusetts*	617/843-1100
Louisiana Private Investigators Association	504/275-0796
>*Maryland Investigators and Security Association*	800/414-6472

Michigan Council of Private Investigation, Inc.	800/266-MCPI
Minnesota Association of Private Investigators	800/894-9186 612/659-9551
>Mississippi Professional Investigators Association	601/841-1158
>Missouri Professional Investigators Association	573/562-1235
>Montana Association of Private Investigators & Security Operators	406/442-2790
>National Association of Bunco Investigators	410/752-8150
>National Association of Fraud Control Units	202/434-8020
>National Association of Fraud Investigators	904/274-5538
National Association of Investigative Specialists	512/420-9292
National Association of Legal Investigators	312/226-6300
National Association of Professional Process Servers	800/477-8211
>National Association of Railroad Safety Consultants and Investigators	615/255-6288
>National Constable Association	215/547-6400
National Council of Investigative and Security Services	800/640-4772
>National Finance Adjusters is an association of auto repossessors.	410/728-2800
>National Investigation Academy	818/883-6969
Nevada Investigator's Association	702/795-3317
New Hampshire League of Investigators	603/753-6734
>Northern Alabama Investigators Association	205/533-1413

Ohio Association of Investigative & Security Services	614/759-7435
Oklahoma Private Investigators Association	405/239-2241
>Oregon Association of Licensed Investigators	503/224-3531
>Pacific Northwest Association of Investigators, Inc.	206/624-3910
>Private Detective Association of New Jersey	973/808-2242
>Private Investigators Association of Utah	801/467-9500
Private Investigators Association of Virginia	703/960-2810
Professional Association of Wisconsin Licensed Investigators	414/529-2804
Professional Private Investigators Association of Colorado	303/430-4802
Society of Competitive Intelligence Professionals	703/739-0696
>Society of Private Detectives of Puerto Rico	787/745-1930
>South Carolina Association of Legal Investigators	864/963-0988
>Southeastern Association of Private Investigation	305/822-4842
Southern California Fraud Investigators Association	310/549-1314
>South Florida Investigators Association	800/477-5018
>Tennessee Professional Investigators Association	423/523-3939
>Texas Association of Accident Reconstruction Specialists	713/898-9673
Texas Association of Legal Investigators *TALI Newsletter*	713/827-8542 972/492-9097

>Time Finance Adjusters is another

auto repo trade group	800/874-0510
	904/274-4210
Women Investigators Association	800/603-3524
	818/340-6890
World Association of Detectives	800/962-0516

PROFESSIONAL GROUPS - LAW ENFORCEMENT

>California Gang Investigators Association	888/229-CGIA
>National District Attorney's Association	703/549-9222
>Florida Sex Crimes Investigators Association	954/917-7917
International Association of Bomb Technicians and Investigators	941/353-6843
International Narcotic Enforcement Officers Association	518/463-6232
National Association of Chiefs of Police	305/573-0070
International Police Congress	305/238-1147
International Association of Chiefs of Police	800/THE-IACP
National Sheriffs' Association	703/836-7827
United States Police K-9 Association	612/484-2537
International Association of Campus Law Enforcement	203/233-4531
National Police Officers Association of America	502/451-7550
Police Marksman Association	800/223-7869
American Federation of Police	305/573-0070
National Tactical Officers Association	800/279-9127
>National Organization of Black Law Enforcement Executives	703/658-1529
Women in Federal Law Enforcement	800/479-9685
	515/229-8739

PROPERTY INSURANCE LOSS REGISTRY (PILR)
The *Property Insurance Loss Registry (PILR)* is the insurance industry database of persons who have filed property loss claims, arising from such events as arson, theft, and natural calamity. More than 7 million claims are now in the database, with over 1.5 million new ones each year. Access to *PILR* is limited to insurance and related companies.

AISG, Marketing   212/669-0406
PILR, Customer Support   732/388-0157

>PUBLIC RECORD RESEARCH SYSTEM
Public Record Research System is a compendium of information contained in several public record directories published by BRB Publications. The program itself, which comes on CD ROM, is made by Merlin Information Services and includes contact information for federal, state and many local courts, as well as for many other catagories of public records. To use the system, simply indicate the area where you need information from, and a menu comes up showing contact information and release of information policy for government offices that hold public record in that particular area. Sells for $199.   800/367-6646

QUESTIONED DOCUMENT EXAMINATION
American Association of Questioned Document Examiners   404/244-2500

American Board of Forensic Document Examiners   713/784-9537

For equipment used in the analysis of questioned documents and handwriting.   800/824-3236

The *American College of Forensic Examiners* offers an extensive home study course leading to certification in questioned document examination.   417/881-3818

QUINT & ASSOCIATES
Quint & Associates is a top level research company available for high difficulty subjects. Barbara Quint,

owner, is former head of reference of the Rand Corporation and Editor-in-Chief of *Searcher* Magazine.　　310/451-0252

>RAILROADS
Jane's World Railways has reference information on over 450 railway systems in 120 countries. Information includes routes, organizational structures, political and financial information, locomotive and rolling car inventory and more. Available in book form, diskette, and CD ROM ($390 - $975). *Jane's Information Group*　　703/683-3700

Railroad Research and Development, Federal Railroad Administration　　202/366-0453

National Association of Railroad Safety Consultants and Investigators　　615/255-6288

Amtrak National Communications Center is a good place to start if you're looking for information on passenger reservation histories, contractors, vendors, employees or incident reports. For most of this you'll need to be law enforcement or have an appropriate subpoena in hand.　　800/331-0008

Or, consider filing a FOIA request, as *Amtrak* is a federal agency. This is their FOIA office number:　　202/906-3000

Railroad maps are available through *Railroad Information Service*　　512/863-6886

Association of American Railroads　　360/733-1571

RAILWAY ACCIDENT DATA-BASE
The *Federal Railroad Administration* maintains a database of rail accidents　　202/632-3125

>RAND
RAND (an acronym for research and development) is an elite think tank where over 500 research professionals, most holding doctorate degrees, study subjects from national defense to criminal justice. The end goal is producing clear information to aid public policy makers. The Internet was conceived by *RAND* researcher Paul Baran in 1962. (His concept of "distributed

communications" ultimately was put
into practice as ARPANET, the fore-
runner of what we know call the Internet.)
For more information, check out their
website, *http://www.rand.org*

Rand Headquarters	310/393-0411
Washington, D.C. Office	202/296-5000

REAL PROPERTY OWNERSHIP
Establishing who owns a given piece
of property -- or to find out if a given
person owns any real property -- can
be done through any one of several
sources:

Local county recorders and/or tax
assessors will always have information on who owns a particular
piece of land. However, their information is often impractical to access.

More economical and time saving is
to use one of the following public
record providers.

Dataquick offers real property
ownership records in part or all
of 40 different states. Many areas
include title plants. Information is
available by fax, mail, or online

800/523-3765
310/306-4295

Experian (formerly TRW Redi) offers
online access to real estate ownership
information in several states, including California, Hawaii, Colorado,
Nevada, Michigan, Ohio, Alabama,
Georgia, Mississippi, North Carolina, South Carolina, Tennessee,
New York, Illinois, Minnesota, Montana, Wisconsin, New Jersey, Oklahoma, Texas, Maryland, Virginia,
DC Metro, Delaware, Connecticut,
Pennsylvania, Oregon, Washington
and Utah. Data is available by
property address or by owner's name

800/421-1052

Also see...*DATABASE PROVIDERS*,
many of whom include real property
ownership data on their menus.

>Away from your computer or real
estate records source? See...*HOME
PRICE SEARCH* for property sale
information available by phone,
24 hours a day.

Land Registry Information does real property ownership searches throughout England

011-44-1812-881418

RESEARCH DEPARTMENT
Research Department is a private research company, excellent at retrieving media coverage on a given subject or individual.

800/953-INFO
909/337-5151

RESEARCH PAPERS
>*University Microfilms* has over one half million doctoral dissertations on file. There's a computerized index system to search by subject.

800/521-0600

Over 18,500 research papers are available on variety of subjects.

310/477-8226

>*Academic Research, Inc.* has over 20,000 research files on file, available by fax or overnight delivery.

800/47-RESEARCH
201/939-0189

>REVERSE ANSWERING MACHINE
See...*AT&T TRUE MESSAGES.*

REVERSE DIRECTORY
A reverse directory contains the same information as the published telephone directory -- only the information is searchable by address, or telephone number -- not by name. For example, the reverse directory can tell you who lives at 123 Elm Street, or who's phone number is 202/456-1414. The catch is this: Only published information is included.

The *Haines Directory* is one of the oldest and most respected providers of reverse directory information. They cover all fifty states. Look ups are available on a call in basis to subscribers on a charge per call basis:
Customer Service
Subscriber's Info Line

216/966-5543
800/466-3355

Another service, called *Uni-Directory*, also offers a limited reverse directory, accessed by a 900# pay per call line. An automated attendant converts the phone number you punch in into a

name and address. The price can't be
beat: $1 per minute.   900/933-3330

Metronet offers searches by phone,
including a nationwide reverse directory. They charge $3 for the first min-
ute and $2 for each additional minute.   900/288-3020

>Yet another firm that sells reverse
directory information is *Match A
Name*. For $1.89 a minute, their
operators will provide look up information.   900/884-1212

A very well kept secret is that a select few phone companies offer a
free reverse directory for their service areas:

In the *Chicago* area, call   312/796-9600

In *North Suburban Chicago*, call   708/796-9600

In *Hawaii*, GTE offers a limited reverse directory. For 75 cents per call,
you give the operator up to 2 numbers. Address and registrant information is given -- if it's a published number   808/976-1212

>In *Louisiana*, information operators
will convert a published phone number to a physical address as part of
their standard service.   504/555-1212
    318/555-1212

Also see...*SELECTPHONE* for a CD
ROM reverse directory.

Also see...*PHONEDISC POWER-
FINDER* for a CD ROM reverse directory.

>REWARDS OFFERED

WeTip is a non-profit anti-crime
group that offers rewards, nationwide,
to any informant whose tip leads
to the arrest and conviction of a
perpetrator of a felony or serious misdemeanor. The investigating police
officer is then asked to rate the tip on
a scale of 1-10, according to its use-
fulness. A reward is then paid in
an amount of $50 to $1,000 to the
tipster, based on the rating of the
police officer and the severity of the
crime. The reward program is avail-

able in all fifty states and there are no restrictions on the type of crime reported. To date over 5,000 convictions have been credited to the program and well over $400,000 paid out in rewards. (Private Investigators who pass on tips learned while on duty are eligible for reward money, too.) *WeTip* also offers "extraordinary" rewards for select high profile or unusually serious crimes. The organization acts as a safe keeper for reward money that has been posted by an interested party.

800/78-CRIME

Did you know that the Internal Revenue Service has a reward program for snitching on tax cheats? (Now that you do know, are you surprised?) Depending on the quality of information provided, and the money recovered, rewards payments can be up to $100,000. For specific information leading to recovery, the reward will be ten percent of the first $75,00 recovered, and 5% of the next $25,000, tapering down to 1% of any additional recovery, capped at $100,000 in total reward money. Be sure to cite Section 7623 of the IRS Code and ask for form 211 to file your claim. Your information should be directed to the Criminal Investigative Division in the office of any District Director, or the Criminal Investigative Branch of any IRS Service Center. See... *INTERNAL REVENUE SERVICE* for a listing of criminal investigation offices.

Stop an act of espionage against the United States and you're entitled to a reward of up to $500,000 as set forth by federal law (Title 18, U.S.C., Section 3071). The reward money is controlled by the United States Attorney General. To report the suspected espionage, contact your nearest FBI office and speak with its ANSIR (Awareness of National Security Issues and Response) coordinator.

Stop an act of terrorism against American citizens and/or property and you may be eligible for a reward of up to 4 million dollars through a program funded by the U.S. Department of State in conjunction with the Airline Pilots Association and the Air Transport Association. Call this number to hear a recorded message by Charlton Heston for more details.

800/HEROES-1

The *United States Postal Service* offers a variety of rewards for information leading to the arrest and conviction of any person for any one of numerous crimes. The largest reward offered is $100,000 for information leading to an arrest and conviction where an USPS employee has been murdered. Other crimes and their rewards:

Assault on employee:	*$15,000.00*
Mailing bombs or explosives:	*$50,000.00*
Postage or meter tampering:	*$50,000.00*
Robbery:	*$25,000.00*
Burglary of a post office:	*$10,000.00*
Money laundering:	*$10,000.00*
Offenses involving postal money orders:	*$10,000.00*
Theft/destruction of mail:	*$10,000.00*
Child Pornography through mail:	*$10,000.00*
Poisons/controlled substances through mail:	*$10,000.00*

Contact the Postal Inspector in Charge at the nearest division office. (See...*POSTAL INSPECTORS.*) Or:
Chief Postal Inspector

202/268-4563

Todd and Associates is a California based firm that specializes in recovering stolen boats. They have a popular website that shows stolen boats with reward money offered for the safe recovery of the vessel. Reward amount varies from boat to boat. The Internet address is *www.boatman.com/mari time/stolens.html*

CENTBOM is the FBI's code name for the bombing at Atlanta's Olympic Park on the evening of July 27, 1996. Seeing how the Richard Jewell thing never panned out, they're now offering up to $500,000 for information that leads to a suspect and subsequent conviction.

888/324-8404

>ROLEX WATCHES
Many people consider Rolex watches to be the best in the world. This certainly includes *Pulp Fiction* types, as Rolexes are the frequent target of both street thugs and professional burglars. The watches are frequently used in

insurance scams, too.

Now, did you know that every Rolex bears a unique serial number and that a database exists of activity related to the serial numbers? (The serial number can be found on the outside of the watch casing, at the six o'clock end. Remove the bracelet and between the lugs will be found the serial number.)

The Rolex database includes dates of service when a watch has been worked on at an authorized service center. Also included in the database is the serial numbers of watches reported stolen. If a stolen watch is brought into an authorized service center for service, the watch will be confiscated. Information from the database is available to persons with a legitimate need to know, including law enforcement, insurance investigators, jewelers, and others. Telephone requests are not honored. Fax your request on company letterhead to *Rolex, (fax) 212/980-2166.*
Rolex   212/758-7700

>FYI: One way to tell a real Rolex from a possible counterfeit is to observe the sweep of the second hand. Real ones have a continuous sweep, (some) fakes stop and start at each second.

RUSSIAN INVESTIGATIONS
>If you're investigating organized crime in Russia, or organized crime in the United States perpetrated by Russian immigrants, you may wish to consult with a former professor of the National Police Academy in Moscow. *Alexander Gorkin* is now located in the United States and can provide background and other information on how Russian organized crime operates. Today's most common forms of criminal activity are forgery, health care and insurance scams, and antiquities swindles, according to *Gorkin.*   303/316-4893

SAFE DEPOSIT BOXES
The *American Safe Deposit Box Association* specializes in locating the safe deposit boxes of deceased persons.   317/888-1118

SCOTLAND YARD
Main #   011-44-171-230-1212

SCREEN ACTOR'S GUILD
Screen Actor's Guild, also known as
SAG is the primary union of film and
television actors. Through the union's
representation office, members can
be located or contacted.   213/954-1600

SEARCH AND RESCUE
The *U.S. Coast Guard* maintains a
database of past search and rescue
operations.   202/267-1948

SEARCHER MAGAZINE
Searcher Magazine is for information
professionals, researchers, etc.   609/654-4888

SEARCHERS
Searchers specializes in locating lawsuits -- anywhere in America. Give
them the name of the case and they
will find it.   612/687-7740

SECRET SERVICE, U.S.
>*Headquarters*   202/435-5700

Intelligence Division   202/435-5000

Public Information Office   202/435-5708

>Direct Freedom of Information Act
requests to: *United State Secret Service, Freedom of Information Request,
1800 G Street NW, Washington, DC
20223.*

The Secret Service *Fraud Division* investigates the fraudulent use of credit
cards, computers, and telephones.   202/435-6900

Bank Fraud/Treasury Note Fraud   202/435-6100

Counterfeit Division   202/435-5756

Financial Crimes Division (includes
forgery and electronic crimes)   202/435-5850

Forensic Services Division   202/435-5926

Visual Information Bureau   202/435-5843

Investigative Support Division   202/435-5773

Special Investigations & Security   202/435-5830

Presidential Protective Division	202/395-4112
Vice Presidential Protective Division	202/634-5890
Dignitary Protective Division	202/435-7500

Secret Service Field Offices:
Albany, GA	912/430-8442
Albany, NY	518/431-0205
Albuquerque, NM	505/248-5290
Anchorage, AK	907/271-5148
Atlanta, GA	404/331-6111
Atlantic City, NJ	609/487-1300
Austin, TX	512/916-5103
Bakersfield, CA	805/861-4112
Baltimore, MD	410/962-2200
Bangkok, Thailand	011-662-255-1959
Baton Rouge, LA	504/389-0763
Birmingham, AL	205/731-1144
Bismarck, ND	701/255-3294
Boise, ID	208/334-1403
Bonn, Germany	11-49-228-339-2587
Boston, MA	617/565-5640
Buffalo, NY	716/551-4401
Canton, OH	216/489-4400
Charleston, SC	803/724-4691
Charleston, WV	304/347-5188
Charlotte, NC	704/523-9583
Chattanooga, TN	423/752-5125
Cheyenne, WY	307/772-2380
Chicago, IL	312/353-5431
Cincinnati, OH	513/684-3585
Cleveland, OH	216/522-4365
Colorado Springs, Co	719/632-3325
Columbia, SC	803/765-5446
Columbus, OH	614/469-7370
Concord, NH	603/228-3428
Dallas, TX	214/655-2500
Dayton, OH	513/222-2013
Denver, CO	303/866-1010
Des Moines, IA	515/284-4565
Detroit, MI	313/226-6400
El Paso, TX	915/540-7564
Erie, PA	814/734-1365
Fresno, CA	209/487-5204
Grand Rapids, MI	616/454-4671
Great Falls, MT	406/452-8515
Greenville, SC	803/233-1490
Harrisburg, PA	717/782-4811
Honolulu, HI	808/541-1912
Houston, TX	713/868-2299
Irving, TX	214/655-2500
Indianapolis, IN	317/226-6444
Jackson, MS	601/965-4436
Jacksonville, FL	904/724-4530

Kansas City, MO	816/374-6102
Knoxville, TN	423/545-4622
Las Vegas, NV	702/388-6571
Lexington, KY	606/233-2453
Little Rock, AR	501/324-6241
London, England	011-44-171-408-8091
Los Angeles, CA	213/894-4830
Louisville, KY	502/582-5171
Lubbock, TX	806/743-7347
Madison, WI	608/264-5191
McAllen, TX	512/630-5811
Melville, NY	516/249-0404
Memphis, TN	901/766-7632
Miami, FL	305/591-3660
Milwaukee, WI	414/297-3587
Minneapolis, MN	612/348-1800
Mobile, AL	334/441-5851
Montgomery, AL	205/223-7601
Nashville, TN	615/736-5841
Newark, NJ	201/984-5760
New Haven, CT	203/865-2449
New Orleans, LA	504/589-4041
New York, NY	212/637-4500
Norfolk, VA	804/441-3200
Oklahoma City, OK	405/297-5020
Omaha, NE	402/221-4671
Orlando, FL	407/648-6333
Paris, France	011-33-1-4312-7100
Philadelphia, PA	215/597-0600
Phoenix, AZ	602/640-5580
Pittsburgh, PA	412/644-3384
Portland, ME	207/780-3493
Portland, OR	503/326-2162
Providence, RI	401/331-6456
Raleigh, NC	919/790-2834
Reno, NV	702/784-5354
Richmond, VA	804/771-2274
Riverside, CA	909/276-6781
Roanoke, VA	540/857-2208
Rochester, NY	716/263-6830
Sacramento, CA	916/498-5141
Saginaw, MI	517/752-8076
Salt Lake City, UT	801/524-5910
San Antonio, TX	512/229-6175
San Diego, CA	619/557-5640
San Francisco, CA	415/744-9026
San Jose, CA	408/535-5288
San Juan, PR	809/277-1515
Santa Ana, CA	714/836-2805
Santa Barbara, CA	805/963-9391
Savannah, GA	912/248-4401
Scranton, PA	717/346-5781
Seattle, WA	206/220-6800
Shreveport, LA	318/676-3500
Sioux Falls, SD	605/330-4565
Spokane, WA	509/353-2532

Springfield, IL	217/492-4033
Springfield, MO	417/864-8340
St. Louis, MO	314/539-2238
Syracuse, NY	315/448-0304
Tampa, FL	813/228-2636
Toledo, OH	419/259-6434
Trenton, NJ	609/989-2008
Tucson, AZ	520/670-4730
Tulsa, OK	918/581-7272
Tyler, TX	903/534-2933
Ventura, CA	805/339-9180
Washington, D.C.	202/435-5100
West Palm Beach, FL	407/659-0184
White Plains, NY	914/682-6300
Wichita, KS	316/267-1452
Wilmington, DE	302/573-6188
Wilmington, NC	919/343-4411
Youngstown, OH	330/726-0180

SECURITIES & EXCHANGE COMMISSION (SEC)

The *SEC* regulates the interstate sale of financial instruments, such as stocks and bond and also monitors the financial markets against insider trading and other potential abuses.

SEC General Information Line	202/942-8088
>Investor Information Service	800/SEC-0330
>Public Reference Desk will do name look ups for licensing status on stock broker types	202/942-8090
>FOIA Office	202/942-4320
>Insider Trading, Enforcement	202/942-4542
>Press Room	202/942-0038
>Public Affairs	202/942-0020
Los Angeles Office	213/965-3998
New York Office	212/748-8000

>FYI: *The Securities and Exchange Commission* publishes its own phone directory, with over 7,000 employees listed inside. The phone book is available through the Government Printing Office. Or, try calling this *SEC Personnel Locator* number to locate a *SEC* employee. 202/942-4150

>Hard copy of SEC filings made by publicly owned companies are available through *Disclosure*, a private information provider. 800/638-8241

>*Washington Service Bureau* also sells SEC filings. They also publish *SEC Today*. 202/508-0600

*Also see...NATIONAL ASSOCIATION
OF SECURITIES DEALERS.*

SECURITIES - LOST & STOLEN

*The Securities Information Center,
Inc.* maintains a computerized database of lost, stolen, counterfeit and
forged securities. Used by investment
professionals, access to *SIC* is restricted
and is not available directly to the general public. *SIC* is over-seen by the
Securities and Exchange Commission.   617/345-4900

>*The Bureau of Public Debt* maintains
information on who purchased and/or
redeemed certain U.S. Savings Bonds
and other securities. If U.S. Savings
Bonds have been stolen, lost or destroyed, an application for relief can be made
to this agency.   304/480-6112

>Do you know of someone who has died,
but their life insurance policy can't be
located? Try contacting *The American
Council of Life Insurance.* It's members
will search their archives for a modest
charge.   800/942-4242

>Direct inquiries or claims relating to lost,
stolen or unclaimed postal money orders
to the *US Post Office Money Order
Branch*   800/868-2443

>Have you come across some old stock
certificates and believe they may have value?
Stock Search International will research the
value of the certificates for a modest fee.   800/537-4523

>SELECTPHONE

If you run an active investigation agency
or unit, having fast, reliable and cheap
access to both reverse directory and
directory assistance information is
vital. Having the data on CD ROM
might be your best bet. There are two
major publishers of this data: PhoneDisc
and *SelectPhone.* For around $99 you
can buy the current national version
of SelectPhone. For around $209 you
can buy a one year subscription, where
you'll automatically be sent quarterly
updates.   800/367-6646

>SEX OFFENDER REGISTRIES

All fifty states now have a sex offender registry in place. However, who can access the information in each state's registry varies widely from state to state. This is a state by state profile of rules for accessing each state's sex offender registry as of our publication date. This is the first time such a list has been published.

Note: Laws regulating release of sex offender information are continually changing. Before relying on information contained in this section, contact local authorities to verify the current accuracy of information contained in this section.

ALABAMA

Alabama is still in the process of automating its statewide registry, which currently contains the names of 300 persons convicted of felony sex offenses. When completed, the statewide database will be available to law enforcement only. However, when a registered offender is released into the community, information is sent to the local police department where the offender will be moving into. This information, in the form of flyers, will be publicly posted at local police stations for inspection.

ALASKA

Alaska has over 1,600 persons in its Sex Offender Registration Central Registry. All persons in the registry either completed their sentences, parole or probation after July 1, 1984. The public can access the database three different ways: By stopping in an Alaska State Trooper station; by logging onto the Internet at *www.dps.state.ak. us/sorcr*; or by sending a mail request to *Alaska State Troopers, Attn: Permits & Licensing, 117 W. 4th Ave., Anchorage, AK 99501*. Telephone name checks are not available.

ARIZONA

Arizona has registered sex offenders since the early 1970's and currently has over

TURMAN, VERNON C

TURNER, GARY R

TURNER, JESSE G

TURNER, MILTON W

TURNER, STEVEN C   122964

TURPEN, ALLIE J   062852

TURPIN, RAYMOND E   091755

TURPIN, WENDELL T   051970

TUTTLE, MICHAEL D   101266

TWEDDELL, EDWARD L   030354

TYNER, MELVIN E   051139

TYSON, MICHAEL G   063066

ULREY, JERRY D   051252

UMPHREY, RONALD T   030173

UNDERHILL, NIEL   090559

UNDERWOOD, DALAN   110664

UNDERWOOD, LEON   061457

UPDEGRAFF, LOWELL   091139

Excerpt from the State of Indiana's Sex Offender Registry identifying boxer Mike Tyson as a registrant. The now former heavyweight champion was convicted of rape in 1992.

(Tyson photo courtesy Marion County, Indiana Sheriff's Department.)

8,000 names in its database. The statewide database is currently available to law enforcement only. As of June 1, 1996 a community notification law went into effect that allows local law enforcement to notify a neighborhood if a high risk offender moves into the area. In this case, local police are required to go door to door with flyers. Each local police precinct maintains a notebook of previous notifications. These are available for viewing by local residents. Sex offenders released before June 1, 1996 are generally not included in the community notification program.

(FYI: Driver's licenses issued to sex offenders in Arizona contain a special tag identifying their holder as a sex offender. The information is only available to law enforcement, though. A standard, non-law enforcement driver's license check will not show this special tag.)

The Arizona Department of Public Safety has a long term goal of putting up a website containing identifying information on its registered sex offenders.

ARKANSAS
Arkansas passed its sex offender registry legislation on August 1, 1997. The new law requires sex offenders to register upon release from custody with local law enforcement. The information will be available to the public in some form – although guidelines are currently being put into place.

CALIFORNIA
California has the oldest and most advanced notification program. First started in 1945, information about the state's 68,000 plus registered sex offenders can be obtained several different ways.

Now located at (many but not all) police and sheriff stations throughout the state are computers loaded with a CD ROM containing detailed profiles of the state's sex offender population. The computerized information is available to any member of the general public, with the exception of the registered sex offenders themselves. The database is searchable several different ways. The two most common ways are a name search and a zip code search. If there is a hit on a name, a computerized dossier comes up on the subject which typically includes the offenders photograph, current zip code of residence (not actual address), information on tattoos and other physical identifiers, plus background on his or her criminal history.

There is a sub-database of the main sex offender population devoted to convicted child molesters. This database has over 35,000 names in it and is accessible through either the above CD ROM or through the state's 900 Pay Per Call system, called the Child Molester Identification Line. Calls cost ten dollars each (billed to your phone) and up to two names can be checked at a time. To complete a record check, you must know the subject's name and at least one other unique identifier, such as street address, date of birth, social security number or driver's license number.

900/463-0400

For organizations that have multiple names to screen through the Child Molester Identification Line database, there is also the option of making requests by mail. The cost is $4 per name checked. To request a form write to: *Department of Justice, Child Molester Identification Line, Rm. B-216, P.O. Box 903387, Sacramento, CA 94203-3870* or call:

916/227-3743

COLORADO
Colorado's statewide registry of over 3,500 names is available to law enforcement only. Local law enforcement maintains information on locally registered offenders that can be viewed by the public. However, there is another way to get all of this information and more. Colo.ado allows access to any persons "rap sheet" (arrests and convictions, going back to the seventies) by the general public. See...*CRIMINAL RECORDS* for details on obtaining a person's criminal history in Col-

orado.

CONNECTICUT
Connecticut has a limited sex offender registry law that it's own state officials were hard pressed to explain. In short, sex offenders are required to register with either their local police department or resident state trooper. The records are not confidential to law enforcement only. However, when we spoke with a highly placed source within the state's Attorney General's office, the source was unable to state what procedure a member of the public would follow to access this information. There is no publicly available statewide name check at the present time.

DELAWARE
Delaware's registry contains over 600 names of persons convicted of sex offenses after 1994. (Persons convicted before 1994 are NOT registered.) The statewide registry is open to law enforcement only. Local police, at their discretion, have the option of notifying local child care organizations and neighbors when a high risk offender moves into the area.

DISTRICT OF COLUMBIA
Our nation's capital has jumped on the Megan's Law bandwagon with its own version of the law, requiring sex offenders to register. Only problem is, the law hasn't been put into practical service. In fact, the Washington Post recently quoted local police officials as saying they had never heard of the law.

FLORIDA
The Florida Department of Law Enforcement offers one of the nation's best Internet site for identifying Sexual Predators (*www.fdle.state.fl.us/Sexual_Predators*). ("Sexual Predator" is the most serious classification of sexual offender.) One can search by city, county or name. If a hit is received, both a photograph of the sexual predator and other pertinent information are seen.

Both Sexual Predators and regular

sex offenders can be identified through
a 24 hour a day, 7 day a week toll
free hotline
Toll free, from within Florida   888/FL-PREDATOR
From outside Florida: 850/413-9387

GEORGIA

Georgia's sex offender registry has over
1,100 names of persons convicted of
sex offenses after July 1, 1996. *Offend-*
ers convicted before this time will
not be found in the registry. The statewide list is currently available to law
enforcement only. The general public
can request information at their local
sheriff station on locally registered
offenders. ("Regular" sex offenders
are required to register for ten years.
"Sexual Predators", the most serious
category, are required to register every
90 days for life.) By the end of 1998,
an Internet site is scheduled to be up
with the entire statewide registry available for viewing. For more details,
call the *Georgia Bureau of Investi-*
gation: 404/244-2895

HAWAII

Hawaii has a statewide sex offender
registry that's available to law enforcement only. There is no current form
of community notification. However,
legislation is pending which may make
some form of notification possible.

However, Hawaii is a state that makes
statewide criminal histories available.
See...CRIMINAL RECORDS.

IDAHO

Idaho's statewide sex offender registry
is public information. A name will be
checked within 10 days. Requests are
accepted by mail only. Information
required to conduct a search includes
the subject's name and either date
of birth or address. The state strongly
prefers that requests be made on
their form, *"Central Sex Offender*
Registry Request for Public Infor-
mation". The address to obtain the
forms from, and to send search requests to is: *Idaho Department of*
Law Enforcement, Bureau of Crim-
inal Identification, P.O. Box 700,
Meridian, ID 83680-0700. The

forms can also be obtained from
local police and sheriff stations.
The Idaho Bureau of Criminal Identification will absolutely NOT conduct
search requests over the phone.   208/884-7135

ILLINOIS
Illinois maintains a statewide felony
sex offender database with over 8,600
names. Within this group of 8,600,
there is a sub-registry of roughly 7,000
convicted child sex offenders. The
main database is available to law
enforcement only. There is no statewide
check for the child sex offender sub-
registry. However, by traveling to a
local sheriff or police department, one
can learn what child sex offenders are
registered in that particular county.

INDIANA
Indiana offers an advanced sex offender
registry program giving the public
several different options for accessing
information on the state's 8,000 plus
registered offenders. The registry is updated three times per year and is sent
to public libraries, schools, daycare
facilities, and other agencies that work
with children. Hard copy of the registry
is also available to anyone who requests
it – including private investigation
agencies. However, the registry is
roughly 300 pages long. If you don't
really need the hard copy, you can save
a tree by having a name checked one
of several different ways. Both name
checks and requests for complete copies
of the state's entire registry can be made
at this number: 317/232-1233

Names can also be checked over the Internet at *www.state.in.us/cji/index.html.*

Names can also be checked by mail. Send
requests to the *Indiana Criminal Justice
Institute, 302 W. Washington Street,
Rm. E-209, Indianapolis, IN 46204.*

IOWA
Iowa currently has 1,800 plus names in
its sex offender registry. The public
can learn if a given person is in the
registry by visiting their nearest sheriff
station. The sheriff will have access to
both information on locally registered

offenders as well as the statewide registry itself. To check a name, however, an address must also be provided along with the name. Although the local sheriff may not know it, he is authorized by state statute to check the statewide registry at the request of any member of the public. There is no statewide telephone or information-by-mail program to access the list. For further information, contact the Iowa Department of Public Safety Division of Criminal Investigations. 515/281-5138

KANSAS
Kansas maintains a sex offender registry for persons who committed violent sexual crimes after April 14, 1994. Currently there are roughly 700 names in the registry. There is one way and one way only for non-law enforcement persons to access the list: Over the Internet at *www.ink.org/public/kbi.* Every sheriff's station maintains publicly accessible information on offenders registered in that county alone. To learn about a person's overall criminal history in Kansas, including sex crimes committed before April of 1994, consider requesting a statewide criminal history through the Kansas Bureau of Investigations. See *CRIMINAL RECORDS* for further details.

KENTUCKY
Kentucky has a limited database with 500 names. It's available to law enforcement only. The state currently has no community notification program.

LOUISIANA
Louisiana is in the process of setting up a statewide sex offender registry. Government officials there indicate that it will not be open to the public. However, parties whose responsibilities include child protection, such as school superintendents, will have access to the information. For further information, contact the Louisiana State Police, Bureau of Identification. 504/925-6095

MAINE
Maine's Sex Offender Registry contains over 200 names of persons convicted after June 30, 1992. The information is public

record. There is no name check per se. Rather, for a small fee, the entire registry is mailed out to anyone who requests it. Send $7.00 to *Maine State Police, Bureau of Identification, 3600 Hospital Street, Augusta, ME 04330.*

Maine is also a state with available statewide adult criminal conviction histories. To learn about a person's entire adult criminal history in Maine, see our *CRIMINAL RECORDS* section.

MARYLAND
Maryland has a very limited sex offender database that only includes crimes committed after October 1, 1995. No statewide check of the database is presently available – to either the public or law enforcement. However, local law enforcement agencies are authorized to release information on locally registered offenders.

MASSACHUSETTS
In Massachusetts, anyone can visit a local police station to learn the identities of convicted sex offenders who live or work within a one mile radius. No system is in place for conducting a name check with the statewide registry.
From inside Massachusetts   800/936-3426
From outside Massachusetts   617/660-4600

MICHIGAN
Michigan's statewide sex offender registry contains 17,000 names and is available to law enforcement only, through LEIN (Law Enforcement Information Network). However, sex offenders are required to register at local police agencies nearest their residence and this information is open to the general public.

MINNESOTA
Minnesota has a restrictive information release policy. The state maintains a registry with over 6,500 sex offenders. However, the information is available to law enforcement only. Local law enforcement does have the authority to notify the community when a high risk offender moves into an area. However, the public has no way of checking on any certain individual to learn if he or she is in the registry.

MISSISSIPPI

Mississippi's statewide registry is available to both law enforcement and the public. Information available includes the offender's name, address, place of employment and conviction information. Sheriffs maintain information on local registrants. A name can be checked through the statewide registry for a $5 fee. The state has 14 days to respond. Name checks are done by mail only: *Mississippi Department of Public Safety, Sex Offender Registry, P.O. Box 958, Jackson, MS 39205-0958.*

MISSOURI

Missouri has a statewide sex offender registry, available to law enforcement only. There is no current form of community notification. However, legislation is pending which may make some form of notification possible.

MONTANA

Montana has a statewide sex offender registry, available to law enforcement only. With a court order, local law enforcement is allowed to notify the community of a dangerous ex-offender.

NEBRASKA

Nebraska has a statewide sex offender registry, available to law enforcement only. There is no current form of community notification. However, legislation is pending which may make some form of notification possible.

NEVADA

Effective January 1, 1998 a publicly available statewide sex offender registry went into effect in Nevada. A member of the public can check a name against the list of roughly 6,000 registrants. If there is a hit, information released by the *Nevada Highway Patrol* is sharply limited to the offender's date of arrest and the penal code section he or she was convicted under. Name checks will be available through a state hotline, which was not established by our publication date. However, by calling the *State Criminal Records Repository* the hotline number can be obtained.   702/687-5713

NEW HAMPSHIRE

New Hampshire's sex offender database of 1300 names is available to law enforce-

ment only. However, local police chiefs
do have the discretion to notify local organizations who have care over children when
an offender moves into the area. There may
be a liberalization of who can access the
information in the near future.

NEW JERSEY

New Jersey's sex offender registry contains 4,200 names of persons convicted
of sexual offenses from indecent expo-
sure to violent sexual assaults. Offenders
are required to register with their local
police department. Local law enforcement will then notify neighbors and
community groups if a high risk offender is in the area. Statewide name checks
are available to law enforcement only.

NEW MEXICO

New Mexico has a statewide sex offender registry, available to law enforcement only. There is no current form
of community notification. However,
legislation is pending which may make
some form of notification possible in
the future.

NEW YORK

New York has a sex offender registry
which contains over 5,600 names…
only release of the information has
been temporarily, and possibly
permanently, struck down by a class
action law suit. The state formerly
operated a 900 pay-per-use telephone
hotline which identified sex offenders.
This has been shut down, too.

However, a much smaller list (34 names)
of "Level 3" high risk offenders has
been circulated to local police, where
the public can view the information.

NORTH CAROLINA

Currently, North Carolina's statewide
registry is available to law enforcement only. However, records are collected at the county level and the public
can inspect information on locally registered sex offenders at any sheriff's
station. Organizations that work with
children or the elderly have a right to
copies of any county's registry. The
statewide registry contains roughly
1,200 names and is a compilation of

the county registries. An Internet site
may go up in the near future, making
the statewide list, or portions of it,
available to all.

NORTH DAKOTA

North Dakota maintains a unique dual
sex offender registry system. The official
Sex Offender Registry that complies with
federal law has 598 names and is closed to
the public. However, if local law enforcement perceives a threat to the community,
they are allowed to notify the community.

Of greater note is what is referred to as the
Non-Registration List. This contains over
900 names of convicted sex offenders and
persons convicted of having committed
offenses against children. The information
is culled from the state's Criminal Record
History System and is open to the public
at no charge. The only drawbacks are that
address information on the offenders may be
out of date as the information comes from
the offenders last interaction with the state's
criminal justice system. Secondly, persons
who committed their sex offenses out of state
would also not be on the list. The entire
Non-Registration List is available free of
charge upon request, or, name checks can be
done on a name by name basis. All requests
must be made in writing, there are no checks
done by telephone. To check if a person is
in the Non-Registration List, send a letter
with the persons full name and any
other identifiers to the *North Dakota
Bureau of Criminal Investigation,. P.O.
Box 1054, Bismarck, ND 58502.*   701/328-5500

OHIO

Ohio does not have a central statewide
registry. Rather, Sex Offenders are required
to register with the local sheriff in any one
of Ohio's 88 counties. Information about
the most serious level of offenders, Sexual
Predators, and some of the second level,
Habitual Sexual Offenders, are publicly
available to anyone who visits a local
sheriff's office. Further, the Sheriff must
actively notify neighbors, the local school
superintendent, child care facilities and
others when a Sexual Predator moves into
the area.

OKLAHOMA

The Oklahoma Department of Corrections

maintains the state's sex offender registry of over 2,000 names. The information is publicly available and a name can be checked by telephone or by mailing a request for information to: *Oklahoma Department of Corrections, Att: Records, P.O. Box 11400, Oklahoma City, OK 73136* or by e-mail to *osjimr@doc.state. ok.us*.

405/425-2500

Local law enforcement agencies also maintain information for public inspection on offenders registered in their localities.

OREGON
Oregon offers practically no meaningful information from its Sex Offender Registry of 7,000 plus names to non-law enforcement parties. A watered down state law is in effect which allows the Oregon State Police to release information on Sexual Predators — the most dangerous catagory of offenders. However, presently there are only 20 or so such names available for the entire state. Efforts are underway to increase the number of reported Sexual Predators. For further information, call the Oregon State Police and ask for the Sex Offender Registry Unit.

503/378-3720

PENNSYLVANIA
Pennsylvania has two registries: One is for law enforcement only and, statewide, contains 1,456 names. There's a second list, of Sexual Predators, who committed their crimes on or after April 21, 1996. There's no statewide check available as of yet – as all of these individuals are still incarcerated. Upon their release, notification will be made to local police in the community into which a Sexual Predators is moving. Local police are authorized to release this information to the public upon request.

RHODE ISLAND
Rhode Island has a sex offender registry that allows local law enforcement to notify the community if a dangerous predator is present. No statewide name check is available to the general public.

SOUTH CAROLINA
Although South Carolina maintains a

statewide sex offender registry, information in it is available to law enforcement only. Information on registered
offenders is available on the local level
to members of the public living in the
county where the offender is registered.
A written request must be made to
the local county sheriff to view such
information.

SOUTH DAKOTA
Local law enforcement in South Dakota
is notified when a registered offender moves
into the area. A file on the registrant is
kept at local police stations for inspection
by the public. There is a statewide registry
containing over 700 names, but this is available to law enforcement only.

TENNESSEE
Tennessee's sex offender registration program
is in a state of suspension due to a pending
federal court case. If the state wins the case,
information about sex offenders convicted after July 1, 1997 will be publicly available.

TEXAS
Texas has a Sex Offender Registry, but it
doesn't include many older offenders who
have completed prison sentences and/or
parole and probation. However, there's
a better way to get this information,
now that Texas allows statewide criminal
history checks. Because of shortcomings
in which offenders are required to register,
a statewide criminal history is recommended in place of checking the sex offender registry. See the Texas section in *CRIMINAL
RECORDS* for details.

If you're still intent on checking the Texas
sex offender registry, send a written request with the person's name you want
checked, along with any available identifiers to *Texas Department of Public
Safety, Special Crime Services, Sex Offender Registry, P.O. Box 4087, Austin, TX
78773-0426.*   512/424-2200

Information on registered offenders is also
available to any member of the public who
wishes to visit their local police or sheriff
station. The sex offender registry may be
available online, possibly over the Internet, in the future.

UTAH

Utah's sex offender registry is limited to law enforcement, the state Board Of Education and "Petitioners". There is no publicly available statewide source of information where a single name can be checked to determine if a person is a registered sex offender. A "Petitioner" is a citizen who files a request for information about sex offenders living in his or her area. After the Petitioner's request is verified by the Department of Corrections, a list of registered offenders in the Petitioner's local zip code is sent to the Petitioner. To request forms to file a petition, send a request to: *Utah Department of Corrections, Records Bureau, 6100 South Fashion Blvd, Murray, UT 84107.*

Probation and parole records are public information in Utah. Therefore, to learn if a person is on probation or parole, for a sex offense, or any other crime, call the Utah Department of Corrections: 801/265-5500

VERMONT

Vermont has a sex offender registry containing 200 names. Who can access it? No one – including law enforcement. However, when law enforcement runs a criminal check on a subject, the fact that the offender is in the registry will be indicated. Why have a sex offender registry if no one can access it – including law enforcement? "Because it's a federal regulation to have one," stated one well placed government source.

VIRGINIA

Virginia's sex offender registry began in 1994 and currently has over 5,000 names. Access to the information is limited to law enforcement, school boards, social service agencies, and prospective employers of child caregivers who have the signed authorization of the person who is being checked. (The form for this is called *SP 230* and can be obtained by calling the phone number below.) *Virginia* currently has no community notification when a potentially dangerous offender moves into a neighborhood. However, this may change in the future if amendments to the current law are passed. 804/674-2022

Also see...*CRIMINAL RECORDS* for information on Virginia's *Know thy Neighbor* program which releases information on parolees.

WASHINGTON

The State of Washington's entire list of 10,657 Registered Sex Offenders is not available to the public. By making a trip to your local Sheriff's office, information on certain local sex offenders can be obtained. One can learn if any given individual is on the list by requesting a criminal history through the Washington State Patrol. (Statewide criminal conviction histories are public record in Washington.)

Request a *Background Check Form* from: *Washington State Patrol, P.O. Box 42633, Olympia, WA 98504-2633*. You'll need to complete the form and provide the name and DOB of the person to be checked, plus a $10 fee. You'll receive back a print out of his or her criminal convictions, and whether or not he or she is on the sex offender list. Eventually there will probably also be an Internet site with the information available online. In the meantime, further questions can be directed to the *Washington State Patrol's Identification and Criminal History Section,*   360/705-5100

WEST VIRGINIA

West Virginia offers a limited community notification program. Child care and youth organizations must sign a confidentiality agreement to get on the state's notification list. Once on the list, the organization receives a notification when a sex offender registers in the area. To apply for the notification list, contact the *West Virginia State Police*:   304/746-2133

WISCONSIN

Any member of the public can call the Wisconsin Sex Offender Registry This is a state of the art 24 hour a day automated telephone information system. By entering a person's name, the caller can learn if the person is one of the state's 10,000 registered sex offenders. The date of birth, social security number and driver's license number of the person being checked may also be necessary to verify the sex offender's identity. *However, note that the registry only contains information on offenders who were convicted or released since December 25, 1993.* The state also has a proactive community notification program where local law enforcement is authorized to go door to door, if necessary, to alert persons residing near a high risk offender. 800/398-2403

WYOMING
Wyoming's registry is open to police only. If a high risk offender moves into any area, authorities can notify the area.

SHERMAN FOUNDATION LIBRARY
The *Sherman Foundation Library* is a unique private library that houses an enormous collection of old phone books and city directories. Due to a staff shortage, they have a strictly limited policy on doing checks by phone. 714/673-1880

However, local researcher *Victor Cook* is available to conduct on site research at a reasonable cost. 714/675-5407

SHIP INFORMATION
Lloyd's Maritime maintains a database on over 79,000 ocean going vessels. Information includes ship ownership, casualties, and ship movements. 800/423-8672
203/359-8383

Also see...MARITIME INFORMATION SYSTEM.

Also see...MERCHANT VESSEL DATABASE.

SHOE PRINTS
Ernest D. Hamm specializes in the forensic identification of footwear prints. 904/724-0250

SIRCHIE FINGER PRINT LABORATORIES, INC.
Sirchie Fingerprint Laboratories, Inc. manufactures invisible ink for marking paper money. When put under ultra violet light, the ink becomes visible. Used for documenting the money trail in illegal drug transactions, among other things. Sirchie offers other products, as well. 800/356-7311

SMARTLAW
Smartlaw is a free automated information service, sponsored by the L.A.
County Bar Association, but available
to anyone who calls. There are over
200 pre-recorded messages on a variety of legal subjects - from bankrupt-
cy to rights of arrestees.   213/243-1500

SOCIAL SECURITY NUMBER
VERIFICATION
The only true way to verify a social
security number is through the *Social
Security Administration*. However, the
SSA will only verify if a social security number is legitimate to an employer seeking to verify the validity of a
social security number provided by an
already hired worker.

The employer must be prepared to
provide his/her company's Federal
Employer Identification Number, and
then the full name, social security number, and date of birth of the person in
question.   800/772-1213

*Cambridge Statistical Research
Associates* will tell if a social security
number has previously been used in a
death claim.   800/327-2772
                                             714/653-2101

>All investigators know about Social Se-
curity Numbers ("SSNs"), and most
know about Federal Employer Identification Numbers ("FEINs"), which is
the taxpayer identification system for
businesses. Did you know that there is
now a new THIRD numbering system
that's recently been put into use by the
IRS? *Individual Taxpayer Identification
Numbers* (ITINs) are a new taxpayer identification numbering system for resident and
non-resident aliens who have a U.S. federal
income tax responsibility, but who are
ineligible to obtain valid SSNs. *ITINs* are
configured like SSNs, but always begin
with the digit "9": 9XX-XX-XXXX. Be
aware: If you come across a SSN in the
future that begins with "9", don't automatically assume that it's a fraudulent
number. It may be an *ITIN*.

>To report fraudulent usage of a social security number, once place you might want to start is the *Social Security Administration's Fraud Hotline*.　　800/269-0271

At the end of this book, and published widely elsewhere, is a social security number identification chart. It decodes the first three digits and tells the number's place of issuance. You can take decoding a step or two further a couple of different ways:

>The Social Security Administration does a regular monthly mailing called *Highest Group Issued* list, which will tell you if a number has or has not been issued yet. To get on the list, send a written request on your agency or company letterhead to: *Social Security Administration, Attn: John Wells, 3-D-20 Operations, 6401 Security Blvd, Baltimore, MD 21235*. However, this list may be too cumbersome and user unfriendly for many of us. One alternative is:

>The *Computerized SSN Guide* is Social Security Number verification software that tells you where the number was issued and if the number itself is valid and is within a group that has been issued. (It doesn't tell who the number has been issued to.) Costs about $30.　　800/247-8713

SOFTWARE COPYRIGHT VIOLATIONS
>*Microsoft Anti-Piracy Hotline*　　800/RU-LEGIT

>The *Business Software Alliance* operates this snitch line for pirated software. No rewards offered.　　888/NO PIRACY

Software Publishers Association seeks to prevent the violation of copyrights on software.　　301/975-2000

The FBI's National Computer Crime Squad investigates pirated software.　　202/324-9164

SOFTWARE RESEARCHERS
Softsearch claims to be able to locate any commercially available software anywhere in the world.　　800/667-6503

SOUND ENHANCEMENT
National Audio/Video Forensic Laboratory is a private lab that can en-

hance the quality of poor audio tape
recordings   818/989-0990

>SOUTHERN POVERTY LAW CENTER

Started in 1971 in Montgomery, Alabama,
the *Southern Poverty Law Center* began
as an activist civil rights organization,
waging battles in courtrooms throughout
the south. In recent years, they've been
gathering and disseminating intelligence
on right wing hate groups. *Klanwatch*
produces a quarterly *Intelligence Report*
that updates law enforcement and others
on activities of the KKK. Even more
cutting edge is their *Militia Task Force*.
Started six months before the April 19,
1995 bombing of the federal building in
Oklahoma City, *Militia Task Force*
began identifying Militia members and
organizations. After Oklahoma City, one
of the first places the FBI turned to for
information on militia groups was the
Southern Poverty Law Center. Their
website names names of militia members
and organizations in a growing, publicly
available database. (*www.splcenter.
org/klanwatch/kw-1.html*)   334/264-0286

SPECIAL INVESTIGATION UNITS

*International Association of Special
Investigation Units*   410/931-8100

SPY GEAR

Interested in spy gear? Highly reco-
mended is Lee Lapin's book, "The
Whole Spy Catalog". He's tested just
about every gadget out there and
writes about what he learns in simple,
non-technical talk. The book can be
ordered through his company, *Intelligence, Incorporated*.   650/513-5549

Shomer-Tec offers an amazing catalog of gadgets, including several unique
devices to use with a telephone.   360/733-6214

>*Private Eye Enterprises* is a
Dallas based company offering
spy gear and investigative and
security products. If you read
PI Magazine, you've no doubt
seen their big double page spread
of offerings.   972/960-2266

Also see...*HIDDEN CAMERAS.*

Also see...*NIGHTVISION EQUIPMENT.*

STALKING

Gavin de Becker is widely considered to be a leading expert in the subject of stalking, and in particular, in the stalking of celebrities, politicians, and other high profile persons. His company, *Gavin de Becker, Inc.* has assessed and managed over 19,000 cases, including the case of Tina Marie Ledbetter who is alleged to have sent over 6,000 death threats to actor Michael J. Fox. His firm maintains a library containing over 350,000 pieces of threatening and/or obsessive letters.   818/505-0177

Dr. Park Dietz is a well known forensic psychiatrist who directed a five year study for the U.S. Department of Justice on mentally disordered persons who threaten and stalk public figures. His firm, *Threat Assessment Group,* is active in the assessment and management of stalkings for businesses, lawyers and celebrities.   714/644-3537

>Los Angeles is home to the stars — and stalkers. The *LAPD Threat Management Unit* investigates threats against both the well known and just average citizens.   213/893-8339

STATE DEPARTMENT, U.S.
Main #   202/647-4000

Counter Terrorism Programs Office   202/647-8941

International Narcotics Matters   202/647-8464

International Parental Child Abduction   202/647-2688

The Department of State, Overseas Citizen Services, helps locate U.S. citizens missing in foreign lands, and monitors the arrests/trials of U.S. citizens abroad.   202/647-5226

The U.S. State Department has a Country Officer assigned to just about every foreign country. The Country Officers should be knowledgable in the current affairs of the country.   202/647-4000

STANDARD & POOR'S ON-LINE REGISTRY
Standard & Poor's Online Registry is a database of information on publicly and privately owned companies, their owners, and key executives. Also available through Dialog online service.   800/237-8552

STATE BAR ASSOCIATIONS
All fifty states have a state bar association which licenses attorneys and provides discipline, when necessary. Other background information typically available is basic biographical data, such as school attended.

Alabama	334/269-1515
Alaska	907/272-7469
Arizona	602/252-4804
Arkansas	501/682-6849
California	415/561-8200
Colorado	303/860-1115
Connecticut	860/568-5157
Delaware	302/739-5278
D.C.	202/626-3475
Florida	904/561-5600
Georgia	404/527-8700
Hawaii	808/537-1868
Idaho	208/334-4500
Illinois	217/522-6838
Indiana	317/639-5465
Iowa	515/243-3179
Kansas	913/234-5696
Kentucky	502/564-3795
Louisiana	504/566-1600
Maine	207/623-1121
Maryland	410/974-3341
Massachusetts	617/357-1860
Michigan	517/372-9030
Minnesota	612/296-2254
Mississippi	601/948-4471
Missouri	573/635-4128
Montana	406/444-3858
Nebraska	402/475-7091
Nevada	702/329-4100
New Hampshire	603/271-2646
New Jersey	609/984-7783
New Mexico	505/842-6132

New York	212/417-5872
North Carolina	919/828-4620
North Dakota	701/255-1404
Ohio	614/487-2050
Oklahoma	405/524-2365
Oregon	503/224-4280
Pennsylvania	717/238-6715
Rhode Island	401/421-5740
South Carolina	803/799-6653
South Dakota	605/224-7554
Tennessee	615/741-3234
Texas	512/463-1463
Utah	801/531-9077
Vermont	802/223-2020
Virginia	804/775-0500
Washington	206/727-8201
West Virginia	304/558-2456
Wisconsin	608/257-3838
Wyoming	307/632-9061

Also see...*ATTORNEYS.*

STATE HOTLINES
Trying to locate a particular state
agency or office through regular
directory assistance can often
be frustrating. Every state now
has a general information operator who should be able to guide
you to the right place with less
effort:

Alabama	334/242-8000
Alaska	907/465-2111
Arizona	602/542-4900
Arkansas	501/682-3000
California	916/322-9900
Colorado	303/866-5000
Connecticut	860/566-4200
Delaware	302/739-4000
D.C.	202/727-1000
Florida	904/488-1234
Georgia	404/656-2000
Hawaii	808/586-2211
Idaho	208/334-2411
Illinois	217/782-2000
Indiana	317/232-3140
Iowa	515/281-5011
Kansas	913/296-0111
Kentucky	502/564-2500
Louisiana	504/342-6600
Maine	207/582-9500
Maryland	410/974-3591
Massachusetts	617/727-2121
Michigan	517/373-1837
Minnesota	612/296-6013

Mississippi	601/359-1000
Missouri	573/751-2000
Montana	406/444-2511
Nebraska	402/471-2311
Nevada	702/687-5000
New Hampshire	603/271-1110
New Jersey	609/292-2121
New Mexico	505/827-4011
New York	518/474-2121
North Carolina	919/733-1110
North Dakota	701/328-2000
Ohio	614/466-2000
Oklahoma	405/521-2011
Oregon	503/986-1388
Pennsylvania	717/787-2121
Rhode Island	401/277-2000
South Carolina	803/734-1000
South Dakota	605/773-3011
Tennessee	615/741-3011
Texas	512/463-4630
Utah	801/538-3000
Vermont	802/828-1100
Virginia	804/786-0000
Washington	360/753-5000
West Virginia	304/558-3456
Wisconsin	608/266-2211
Wyoming	307/777-7011

>STATE POLICE AGENCIES AND HIGHWAY PATROLS

Alabama Department of Public Safety	334/242-4371
Alaska State Troopers	907/269-5611
Arizona Department of Public Safety	602/223-2000
Arkansas State Police	501/221-8200
California Highway Patrol	916/657-7261
Colorado State Police	303/239-4500
Connecticut State Police	860/685-8000
Delaware State Police	302/739-5901
Florida Highway Patrol	904/487-3139
Georgia Department of Public Safety	404/657-9300
Idaho State Police	208/884-7200
Illinois State Police	217/782-6637
Indiana State Police Department	317/232-8248
Iowa State Patrol	515/281-5824
Kansas Highway Patrol	913/296-6800
Kentucky State Police	502/695-6300
Louisiana State Police	504/925-6006
Maine State Police	207/624-7000
Maryland State Police	410/486-3101
Massachusetts State Police	508/820-2300
Michigan State Police	517/332-2521
Minnesota State Patrol	612/297-3935
Mississippi Highway Safety Patrol	601/987-1212
Missouri State Highway Patrol	573/751-3313
Montana Highway Patrol	406/444-3780
Nebraska State Patrol	402/471-4545

Nevada Highway Patrol	702/687-5300
New Hampshire State Police	603/271-3636
New Jersey Division of State Police	609/882-2000
New Mexico State Police	505/827-9000
New York State Police	518/457-6811
North Carolina State Highway Patrol	919/733-7952
North Dakota State Highway Patrol	701/328-2455
Ohio State Highway Patrol	614/466-2990
Oklahoma Department of Public Safety	405/425-2000
Oregon State Police	503/378-3720
Pennsylvania State Police	717/783-5599
Rhode Island State Police	401/444-1000
South Carolina State Highway Patrol	803/896-7894
South Dakota Highway Patrol	605/773-3105
Tennessee Department of Safety	615/741-3954
Texas Department of Public Safety	512/424-2000
Utah Highway Patrol	801/965-4518
Vermont Department of Public Safety	802/244-8727
Virginia Department of State Police	804/674-2000
Washington State Patrol	360/753-6540
West Virginia State Police	304/746-2100
Wisconsin State Patrol	608/266-3212
Wyoming Highway Patrol	307/777-4301

>STATE PRISONS

Several states (including Texas and California) will provide a state prison history, telling if any given person has a state prison incarceration history. Here's a master list of state department of corrections:

Also see...*BUREAU OF PRISONS (FEDERAL)* for a federal prison history check.

Alabama Department of Corrections	334/240-9501
Alaska Department of Corrections	907/269-7400
Arizona Department of Corrections	602/542-5536
Arkansas Department of Correction	501/247-6200
California Department of Corrections, operates 24 hours a day, 7 days a week. Call with subject name and DOB and they will tell if the person has been incarcerated in a state prison since 1977.	916/445-6713
Colorado Department of Corrections	719/579-9580
Connecticut Department of Correction	860/566-4457
Delaware Department of Correction	302/739-5601
District of Columbia Department of Corrections	202/673-7316
Florida Department of Corrections	904/488-5021
Georgia Department of Corrections	404/656-4593
Hawaii Department of Public Safety	808/587-1288
Idaho Department of Correction	208/334-2318
Illinois Department of Corrections	217/522-2666

Robert Scott

Indiana Department of Correction	317/232-5715
Iowa Department of Corrections	515/281-4811
Kansas Department of Corrections	913/296-3310
Kentucky Department of Corrections	502/564-4726
Louisiana Department of Public Safety and Corrections	504/342-6007
Maine Department of Corrections	207/287-4360
Maryland Department of Public Safety and Correctional Services	410/764-4003
Massachusetts Executive Office of Public Safety	617/727-7775
Michigan Department of Corrections	517/373-0720
Minnesota Department of Corrections	612/642-0200
Mississippi Department of Corrections	601/359-5621
Missouri Department of Corrections	314/751-2389
Montana Department of Corrections	406/444-3930
Nebraska Department of Correctional Services	402/471-5119
Nevada Department of Prisons	702/887-3285
New Hampshire Department of Corrections	603/271-5600
New Jersey Department of Corrections	609/292-9860
New Mexico Corrections Department	505/827-8709
New York Department of Correctional Services	518/457-8126
North Carolina Department of Correction	919/733-4926
North Dakota Department of Corrections and Rehabilitation	701/328-6390
Ohio Department of Rehabilitation and Correction	614/752-1164
Oklahoma Department of Corrections	405/425-2500
Oregon Department of Corrections	503/945-0920
Pennsylvania Department of Corrections	717/975-4860
Rhode Island Department of Corrections	401/464-2611
South Carolina Department of Corrections	803/896-8555
South Dakota Department of Corrections	605/773-3478
Tennessee Department of Correction	615/741-2071
Texas Department of Criminal Justice	409/295-6371
Utah Department of Corrections	801/265-5500
Vermont Department of Corrections	802/241-2442
Virginia Department of Corrections	804/674-3000
Washington Department of Corrections	360/753-1573
West Virginia Department of Military Affairs and Public Safety	304/558-2037
Wisconsin Department of Corrections	608/266-4548
Wyoming Department of Corrections	307/777-7405

STOLEN VEHICLE INVESTIGATIONS

The National Insurance Crime Bureau (NICB) is an insurance industry funded investigative agency formed to combat insurance fraud. They are very active in combating vehicle theft. 708/430-2430

See...*PASSENGER VEHICLE IDENTI-*

FICATION MANUAL.

STOLEN VESSEL INVESTIGATIONS

The International Association of Marine Investigators has a membership that includes both law enforcement and private sector investigators.

508/927-5110

Todd & Associates is a Southern California based marine surveying and investigative firm that specializes in boat theft cases, relying on not only good old fashioned gum shoe investigation, but also high tech information gathering. They operate a website where stolen boats are posted with rewards offered for information leading to the safe recovery of the vessel. They also operate a fax broacast system. When on the trail of a stolen vessel, they'll fax a wanted poster to 7,000 marine locations. They boast a 62% recovery rate.

619/226-1895

STREET GANGS
See...GANG INVESTIGATIONS.

>STREETS PLUS
Microsoft's *Streets Plus* contains a map of virtually every street in the United States on one CD ROM. Load it into your computer and you can take a bird's eye view of several states, or move in closer for a look down at a single neighborhood. How can this benefit investigators? Several ways: Different locations can be pinpointed to show spatial relationships. For example, one can create a customized map showing the relationship between where a crime scene is located and where a suspect lives. Need to roll investigators out to an address in an unfamiliar area? Just type in the destination address and a customized map of that area will come up. Forgot to log your miles on a field assignment? There's a handy built in routing tool. Just trace your route with an electronic marker and miles traveled are instantly computed. Sells for around $40. Available at many local software stores, or can be obtained by mail through:
Tiger Direct

800/888-4437

>SUPREME COURT, U.S.
Main Number   202/479-3000
Public Information Office   202/479-3211
Library   202/479-3177
If you know either the Supreme Court
case number, or the name of one of
the parties to the case, the case status
can be learned through this automated
touchtone information line: 202/479-3034

SURVEILLANCE
Inphoto Surveillance claims to be the
nation's largest surveillance company
with investigators in city's both nationwide and in Latin America, the
Caribbean and elsewhere abroad.
Their primary specialty is investigation of bodily injury claims primarily
for insurance companies.   800/822-8220

TELEGRAMS
Urgent matter? Consider using a mail-
gram or telegram through *Western
Union*.   800/325-6000

TELEPHONE BOOKS
See...*PHONE BOOKS*.

TELEPHONE SECURITY
Interactive Information Systems offers
its "Blindline" which makes available
outgoing calls through an untraceable
PBX switching system. Blindline de-
feats Caller ID and Call Return, and
keeps the caller's originating phone
number from being trapped.   800/495-0888

>Unsure if the telephone you are making
a call from blocks Caller ID or not? Call
the main switchboard at *2600*, the hacker
magazine. Enter the phone services section and an automatic attendant will tell
you if Caller ID is or is not blocked.   516/751-2600

>*Tip:* Are you on a blocked line, trying
to make a phone call to a number that
won't accept blocked calls? Hit *82
and your blocking will be disabled for
the next phone call made.

Shomer-Tec offers several gadgets that
attach to your telephone as tap detectors.
Call for their catalog: 360/733-6214

Also see...*DEBUGGING*..

Also see...*AUTOMATIC NUMBER IDENTI-FICATION.*

>TELE-TRACK
Tele-Track could be called the "Fourth Credit Bureau". It's a great source for locating hard to find low income and transient persons. *Tele-Track* collects information from what are referred to as "Sub-Prime" businesses. These are businesses that cater to high risk consumers and include rent to own furniture stores, check cashing facilities, used car dealers, secured credit card issuers, cable TV companies and others. Once you've opened an account with *Tele-Track*, they work on a no hit, no fee basis. You provide them with a name, social, and last known address. If they get a recent hit through their database, you pay $25 for the information.

800/729-6981
770/449-8809

TELEVISION - INVESTIGATIVE

American Journal	800/334-8466
America's Most Wanted	800/CRIME-TV
Current Affair	800/552-9699
CNN	404/827-1500
Dateline, NBC TV, 30 Rockefeller Plaza, #408, New York, NY 10112	212/664-7501
Hard Copy	213/956-5808
Inside Edition	800/457-5546

Twenty-Twenty prefers that story ideas be mailed to: *Story Editor, 20/20, ABC News, 147 Columbus Ave, New York, NY 10023.* To send an e-mail, direct your correspondence to *2020@ABC.com*   212/456-2020

Sixty Minutes prefers that story ideas be mailed to: *Don Hewitt, Executive Producer, 60 Minutes, CBS-TV, 524 West 57th Street, New York, NY 10019*   212/975-2009

Unsolved Mysteries (ask for New Story Department)   800/876-5353

TENANT SCREENING COMPANIES
Trans Registry Limited is a tenant screening organization that links the records of 4,100 member subscribers to track problem tenants. Database is available online or by call in service to apartment building owners. 301/881-3400

Unlawful Detainer Registry maintains a database of persons who have been evicted from rental housing in California, Nevada and Arizona. Available to landlords. 213/873-5014
818/785-4025

National Tenant Network offers coverage in several states. Service is available to landlords. 503/635-1118

>TEXAS DRIVER'S LICENSE STATUS
Here's a quick and free way to check the basic status of a Texas driver's license. Call this Texas Department of Public Safety number with a Texas DL number. The operator will verify the name and supply status — clear/suspended/revoked. 512/424-2600

THOMAS PUBLICATIONS
Thomas Publications' catalog is the mother of all investigative catalogs - and then some. Virtually every book that has been published for investigators in the last several years will be found inside. There's plenty of spy gadgets, how-to videos and other items, too. When someone asks how they can learn about becoming a PI, tell them to start by getting this catalog. 512/420-9292

TIME
The *Naval Observatory Master Clock* offers the most accurate time available, broken down to 370 trillionths of a second. 202/653-1800

TIRE TRACK EXPERT
Ernest D. Hamm 904/724-0250

TOXIC CHEMICALS
>*The Registry of Toxic Effects of Chemical Substances* (RTECS) is a mega-master list of all known toxic substances. Produced by the National

Institute for Occupational Health and Safety, the database currently contains 133,000 chemicals, and the concentrations at which toxicity is known. The database is available through several commercial information vendors, including:

Chemical Information Systems	800/247-8737
DataStar	415/254-7000
Dialog	800/334-2564
Silver Platter Information	800/343-0064

The *National Institute for Occupational Safety and Health* publishes *The Pocket Guide to Chemical Hazards*.   800/356-4674

The *Environmental Protection Agency Library* maintains reference material on toxic substances.   202/260-5922

Chemtrek is the chemical industry's emergency hotline for chemical spills.   800/424-9300

>*Chemical Accident Reconstruction Services* is an Arizona based firm specializing in analysis of chemical spills.   800/645-3369

>*The National Hazardous Material Information Exchange* includes the participation of FEMA and DOT (Department of Transportation).   800/752-6367

>*National Pesticides Telecommunications Network*   800/858-PEST

TRACKING DEVICES -- VEHICLES

>*National Systems and Research Co.* of Colorado Springs, Colorado offers its *OpenLink GPS* system. Makes use of GPS (Global Positioning System) and the control channel of the cell phone frequency. System is affordable — just $650 for the hardware and around $500 for the software, which allows you to view a map on your computer screen to see where the target vehicle is. There's one problem, though: The system takes a minimum of 30 minutes to install on a car. It can't be slapped on a vehicle's underbelly because its antenna won't be able to receive signals from GPS satellites.   719/590-8880

Teletrac also makes vehicle tracking devices, but they only sell to first party users and law enforcement. The LAPD uses this tracking system for undercover investigations.

816/474-0055

Tracking Products, Inc. makes and sells radio signal tracking devices.

303/444-2273

TRADEMARK INFORMATION
U.S. Patent and Trademark Office

800/786-9199

The *U.S. Trademark Association* will answer questions regarding usage of trademarks.

212/986-5880

The *Trademark Register* offers online access to the federal trademark registry on a subscription basis. Reasonable rates. >The entire database can also be purchased outright for around $365.

800/888-8062
202/662-1233

Government Liaison Services, Inc. offers hand searches of paper records at the Trademark Research Library for applications that have not yet been entered into the more widely available computerized database of trademarks.

800/642-6564
703/524-8200

TRANS UNION
One of the Big Three credit bureaus.

800/858-8336

TRAP LINES
If you don't already know about trap lines, we're not going to give it away here. Here's a company that may:
Interactive Information Systems

800/495-0888

TRAVEL ADVISORIES
U.S. Department of State Travel Advisory Hotline

202/647-5225

Centers for Disease Control, Traveler's Advisory Hotline

404/332-4559

Pinkerton Risk Assessment Services monitors political, terrorist, and travel threats in foreign lands. Publishes daily bulletin.

703/525-6111

DataStar online service offers the *BBC Monitoring Summary of World*

Broadcasts, which recaps political and economic TV/radio transmissions, from around the world, but with a focus on the Third World.   800/334-2564

TRAVELER'S CHECKS - LOST OR STOLEN
Although this *American Express* number is for merchant verification, they will tell if a traveler's check is reported lost or stolen.   800/221-7282

Visa International will also verify their traveler's checks.   800/227-6811

>TRUSTLINE
PI's doing background checks on child caregivers in California may want to know about *TrustLine*. This is a state run and sponsored registry of child caregivers. All persons on the list have passed a California criminal history check and have no disqualifying convictions. Some have undergone a nationwide FBI check, too. The cost of the background checks ($90) are borne by the caregivers, who are then free to add the *TrustLine* registry to their resumes as a reference. Call these numbers to learn if a person is in the registry:
Inside California   800/822-8490
From outside California   415/882-0234

TRW CREDIT BUREAU
See....*EXPERIAN*.

>TUGBOAT LOCATOR
Thousands of tugboat workers are out on the rivers and waterways of America at any one time. Sometimes, they're gone for weeks at a time. *Water-Com* is a phone company that will place a call for you directly to anyone of the tugboats. You only need to know the name of the tugboat. *Water-Com*   800/258-9329

>UNCLAIMED FUNDS
Unclaimed Funds can have many faces including unclaimed bank accounts, stocks, bonds and insurance pay outs. Various laws seek to protect the rights of the rightful owners of these funds,

which are kept in the unclaimed property offices in each state. The identity of the rightful owners is public information and who they are can be learned from these state offices. Typically, the state unclaimed property offices will give away for free, or sell, a list of the names. Some enterprising private investigators have found it worthwhile to locate and reunite these persons with their money, in exchange for a commission based fee.

The *National Association of Unclaimed Property Administrators* is the national organization of the state unclaimed property offices and is a central repository for legal and other questions relating to unclaimed funds.   701/258-8667

Here are the phone numbers for each state's unclaimed property office:

Alabama	334/242-9614
Alaska	907/465-4653
Arizona	602/542-4643
Arkansas	501/682-9174
	800/252-4648
California	916/445-8318
Toll free, within California	800/992-4647
Colorado	303/894-2443
Connecticut	860/702-3050
Delaware	302/577-3349
District of Columbia	202/727-0063
Florida	904/488-0357
Georgia	404/656-4244
Hawaii	808/586-1589
Idaho	208/334-7623
Illinois	217/785-6995
Indiana	317/232-6348
Iowa	515/281-5367
Kansas	913/296-4165
Kentucky	502/564-4722
Louisiana	504/925-7407
Maine	207/287-6668
Maryland	410/225-1700
Massachusetts	617/367-0400
Michigan	517/ 335-4327
Minnesota	612/296-2568
Mississippi	601/359-3600
Missouri	573/751-0840
Montana	406/444-2425
Nebraska	402/471-2455
Nevada	702/486-4140
New Hampshire	603/271-2649
New Jersey	609/984-8234
New Mexico	505/827-0767

New York	518/474-4038
North Carolina	919/733-6876
North Dakota	701/328-2805
Ohio	614/466-4433
Oklahoma	405/521-4275
Oregon	503/378-3805
Pennsylvania:	
Claims Inquiries	800/222-2046
Reporting Questions & Instructions	800/379-3999
Rhode Island	401/277-6505
South Carolina	803/734-2629
South Dakota	605/773-3378
Tennessee	615/741-6499
Texas	512/463-3120
Utah	801/533-4101
Vermont	802/828-2301
Virginia	804/225-2393
Washington	360/586-2736
West Virginia	304/343-4000
Wisconsin	608/267-7977
Wyoming	307/777-5590

The Swiss Bankers Association is actively attempting to identify owners or heirs to dormant Swiss bank accounts, opened before the end of World War II. To view a list of the account holders, or for more information, either log onto the world wide web at *www.dormantaccounts.ch* or call: 800/662-7708

Pension Benefit Guaranty Corporation is an agency of the federal government that seeks to reunite missing persons with their pensions. Typically, either the pensioner has moved and left no forwarding address, or, the pension fund or company itself became financially troubled and was taken over by government caretakers. The database of persons whom pension money is being held for is called the Pension Search Directory and can be found on the Internet at *http://search.pbcg.gov.*   800/326-LOST

The Bureau of Public Debt maintains information on who purchased and/or redeemed certain U.S. Savings Bonds and other securities. If U.S. Savings Bonds have been stolen, lost or destroyed, an application for relief can be made to this agency.   304/480-6112

Do you know of someone who has died, but their life insurance policy can't be located? Try contacting *The American*

Council of Life Insurance. It's members will search their archives for a modest charge.   800/942-4242

Have you come across some old stock certificates and believe they may have value? *Stock Search International* will research the value of the certificates for a modest fee.   800/537-4523

The American Safe Deposit Association can aid in the locating the safe deposit boxes of dead persons.   317/888-1118

To make a claim or inquiry about a lost or uncashed postal money order, contact the *US Post Office Money Order Branch*.   800/868-2443

UNDERWRITER'S LABORATOR-IES
Underwriter's Laboratories can provide information on any product marked "UL Approved".   847/272-8800

UNITED NATIONS, THE
Main #   212/963-1234
U.S. Mission   212/415-4000

>U.S. CAPITOL POLICE
Cops that watch the Capitol grounds.   202/224-1677

>U.S. CENSUS BUREAU
Source of general statistical information on not only the general population, but also for business, education, income and other areas.
Public Information Office   301/457-3030

U.S. CITIZENS - ARRESTED OVERSEAS
The U.S. Department of State monitors the arrests/trials of U.S. citizens in foreign lands through its *Overseas Citizens Unit*.   202/647-5226

U.S. CITIZENS - MISSING OVERSEAS
The Department of State, Overseas Citizen Services, helps locate U.S. citizens missing in foreign lands.   202/647-5226

>U.S. COURT DIRECTORY
The United States Court Directory is published by the Government Printing Office and contains address and other

pertinent information on the individual
courts of the federal court system. It's
612 pages and sells for $51.   212/512-1800

>Ever wonder who keeps all the various
federal courts organized? Try *The Administrative Office of the United States
Courts.*   202/273-0107

>U.S. FAX WATCH
U.S. Fax Watch, a program of the Government Printing Office, offers popular
documents and information about available government documents and CD
ROMS by phone. Information available
includes popular editions of the Federal
Register, the Code of Federal Regulations,
and listings of government information
indexed by 200 subject listings.   202/512-1716

>U.S. GOVERNMENT MANUAL
Government publication is over 900
pages long and details bureaus, divisions,
services, offices and departments within
the Federal government. Cost is $33;
available through the Government
Printing Office.   202/512-1800

U.S. HOUSE OF REPRESENTA-
TIVES
Main #   202/224-3121

House Staff Locator   202/225-3121

U.S. MARSHALS SERVICE
Headquarters   703/285-1131

Contact the *Communications Center*
of the *U.S. Marshals Service* to report
federal fugitives from justice.   202/307-9100

>*Con Air* is the division of the US
Marshals Office that transports prisoners
by air. (Yes, it was the also basis of the
Hollywood movie by the same name.) It's
also known as *Justice Prison and Alien
Transportation System.*   816/374-6060

>U.S. PARTY/CASE INDEX
The U.S. Party/Case Index is a new
nationwide database containing information from nearly all federal
district, bankruptcy, appellate and Court
of Federal Claims indices. Operated by
Pacer, the information is available by
computer for just sixty cents per minute.

To subscribe, call *Pacer*: 800/676-6856

U.S. POSTAL SERVICE
See...*POSTAL SERVICE.*

U.S. SENATE
Main # 202/224-3121

Senate Staff Locator 202/224-3207

>U.S. TAX COURT
When the Internal Revenue Service files
a Notice of Deficiency against a taxpayer,
the taxpayer has three options: Pay the
taxes; don't pay the taxes and become
delinquent, or, sue the IRS in *U.S. Tax
Court* and seek to overturn the tax bill.

At any one time, the *U.S. Tax Court* has
roughly 27,000 pending cases and many
times this amount in closed cases. This
little known *constitutionally mandated*
court has 19 sitting judges. Although
all Tax Court cases must be filed in
Washington, D.C., the judges actually
go on the road, traveling to 80 cities,
where hearings and trials take place.

Why should investigators care about
this? Because when a person or business
takes on the IRS in Tax Court, they put
their once private financial affairs into the
realm of public record. Most of the U.S.
Tax Court cases will include the tax returns of the filing party. Why do very few
PI's know about Tax Court? Most likely,
because the Court has refused to sell its
indices to any database vendors. There is
no computer database to log into, outside
of the court, to find out who's filed cases
here. The good news is the Tax Court
will do name checks over the phone,
limited to one name per call. 202/606-8764

After you've found a case in Tax Court
that's of interest, you'll want to obtain
a copy of it. One local Washington, D.C.
public record retrieval company that is
familiar with the U.S. Tax Court is
Federal Document Retrieval. 800/874-4337

VEHICLES
See...*STOLEN VEHICLES.*

Also see...*TRACKING DEVICES.*

VERDICT RESEARCH
Verdict Research maintains a database profiling the prior decisions of individual judges. Additional databases help to determine the worth of a civil lawsuit based upon past judgments   619/487-1579

VETERAN'S AFFAIRS, DEPT OF
Main #   800/827-1000

Veteran's Benefits Administration   202/418-4343

VICTIM'S RESOURCES
National Victim Resource Center   800/627-6872

National Organization for Victim Assistance (NOVA)   202/232-6682

VIDEO ARCHIVES
>*Vanderbilt TV News Archives* maintains one of the most extensive libraries of news footage, dating back decades.   615/322-2927

UCLA Film & TV Archives   310/206-5388

Also see...*VIDEO MONITORING SERVICE OF AMERICA.*

VIDEO IMAGE ENHANCEMENT
See ... *NATIONAL AUDIO/VIDEO FORENSIC LABORATORY.*

VIDEO MONITORING SERVICE OF AMERICA
Video Monitoring Service of America is a news clipping service for television. If it's appeared on TV in the last thirty days, there's a good chance this company can provide a copy of it. They also have a computerized subject index that can be searched by phone.   213/993-0111

VIDEOTAPE PIRACY
The *Motion Picture Association of America* initiates 1,500 to 2,000 investigations per year into pirated movies. A reward of up to $15,000 may be paid for information that leads to the arrest and conviction of persons engaged in piracy. A separate reward program, called *Bounty for Pirates,* offers $2,500 to the first person who reports a pirate lab where arrests

and/or seizure of pirate product or equipment occurs. The lab must have 30 or more VCRs at one location used to produce unauthorized copies of MPAA member company motion pictures.

800/NO-COPYS

Also see...*National Anti-Piracy Association* for information on investigation of pirated pay-per-view.

Also see...*CABLE TV - THEFT OF SERVICE.*

>VIOLENT CRIMINAL APPREHENSION PROGRAM (VICAP)

Violent Criminal Apprehension Program (VICAP) is a little known FBI data collection center that catalogs nationwide information relating to unsolved serial murders and other crimes of violence. Information collected focuses on apparently random killings. The purpose is to cross index the data to identify signature aspects of the homicides, hopefully pointing to a single suspect.

800/634-4097

VOICE PRINT IDENTIFICATION

Voice Print Identification is the scientific identification of a tape recorded voice. See...*NATIONAL AUDIO/ VIDEO FORENSIC LABORATORY.*

VOTER REGISTRATION RECORDS

Aristotle Publishing is the central commercial source for nationwide voter registration records. They have the registered voter files of 49 states. (North Dakota is not available.) However, the records of only 19 states can be used for commercial purposes. Access to the information is available online, directly from *Aristotle* now. However, most, if not all, of this same information can also be obtained from any number of online database providers.

800/296-2747
202/543-8345

>If you're looking for a subject who resides in Franklin County, Ohio (which includes Columbus,

the state capitol), you'll want to know that locally registered voters can be found via a computerized telephone system. After entering the person's social security number, you'll receive back their name and current address.

614/462-3100

>WASHINGTON DOCUMENT SERVICE
Washington Document Service is a private company that specializes in retrieving public documents from federal agencies in Washington, D.C.

800/728-5200

WEATHER DATA
National Climatic Data Center

704/271-4800

Falconer Weather Information Service is a private research service specializing in weather, flood, and storm information.

800/428-5621
518/399-5388

Compu Weather, Inc. is a private weather forecasting service.

800/825-4445

National Weather Service

301/713-0622

National Oceanic & Atmospheric Administration

202/482-6090

WESTLAW
West Law offers an extensive database of legal information for attorneys.

800/937-8529

>WE TIP HOTLINE
See...*REWARDS OFFERED.*

WHITE HOUSE, THE
Main #

202/456-1414

>WOMEN INVESTIGATORS ASSOCIATION
WIA is run by Los Angeles PI Debra Burdette. Membership includes a newsletter, networking, and free or discounted books and other products for investigators.

800/603-3524
818/340-6890

WORKPLACE VIOLENCE
>*Crisis Prevention Institute* offers books, videos, and seminars on non-violent crisis intervention. Areas

of focus include verbal diffusion
skills and how to react to weapons
in the workplace. Shouldn't some-
body tell the post office about this?

800/558-8976
414/783-5787

Threat Assessment Group, Inc.
(aka *TAG*) is a consulting firm
specializing in the assessment and
management of workplace threats.
TAG is made up of forensic psy-
chiatrists, psychologists and crimi-
nalists. Numerous Fortune 500
companies rely upon the firm
when it comes to close encounters
with dangerous current and former
employees, stalkers, and anonymous
letter writers.

714/644-3537

WORLD FACTBOOK, THE
The *World Factbook* is published
by the CIA and contains a factual
profile of each of the world's nations.
Available through the National
Technical Information Service.The
most recent edition available is 1996.
Sells for $45 in book form, $40 on
CD ROM.

800/553-NTIS
703/487-4650

>ZIP CODE INFORMATION
Need to know a zip code for a given
address or what area a given zip code
corresponds to? The *U.S. Postal Service* now has a single 800 number for
all of the above.

800/275-8777

Appendix

Directory
of
North American
Area Codes

201 New Jersey	319 Iowa
202 District of Columbia	320 Minnesota
203 Connecticut	323 California
204 Manitoba	330 Ohio
205 Alabama	334 Alabama
206 Washington	340 US Virgin Islands
207 Maine	345 Cayman Islands
208 Idaho	352 Florida
209 California	360 Washington
210 Texas	401 Rhode Island
212 New York	402 Nebraska
213 California	403 Alberta
214 Texas	404 Georgia
215 Pennsylvania	405 Oklahoma
216 Ohio	406 Montana
217 Illinois	407 Florida
218 Minnesota	408 California
219 Indiana	409 Texas
228 Mississippi	410 Maryland
240 Maryland	412 Pennsylvania
242 Bahamas	413 Massachusetts
246 Barbados	414 Wisconsin
248 Michigan	415 California
250 British Columbia	416 Ontario
253 Washington	417 Missouri
254 Texas	418 Quebec
264 Anguilla	419 Ohio
268 Antigua	423 Tennessee
281 Texas	425 Washington
284 British Virgin Is.	435 Utah
301 Maryland	440 Ohio
302 Delaware	441 Bermuda
303 Colorado	443 Maryland
304 West Virginia	450 Quebec
305 Florida	456 Int'l Inbound
306 Saskatchewan	473 Grenada
307 Wyoming	501 Arkansas
308 Nebraska	502 Kentucky
309 Illinois	503 Oregon
310 California	504 Louisiana
312 Illinois	505 New Mexico
313 Michigan	506 New Brunswick
314 Missouri	507 Minnesota
315 New York	508 Massachusetts
316 Kansas	509 Washington
317 Indiana	510 California
318 Louisiana	512 Texas

513 Ohio	704 North Carolina
514 Quebec	705 Ontario
515 Iowa	706 Georgia
516 New York	707 California
517 Michigan	708 Illinois
518 New York	709 Newfoundland
519 Ontario	710 US Government
520 Arizona	712 Iowa
530 California	713 Texas
540 Virginia	714 California
541 Oregon	715 Wisconsin
561 Florida	716 New York
562 California	717 Pennsylvania
573 Missouri	718 New York
580 Oklahoma	719 Colorado
600 Canada/Services	720 Colorado
601 Mississippi	724 Pennsylvania
602 Arizona	732 New Jersey
603 New Hampshire	734 Michigan
604 British Columbia	740 Ohio
605 South Dakota	757 Virginia
606 Kentucky	758 St. Lucia
607 New York	760 California
608 Wisconsin	765 Indiana
609 New Jersey	767 Dominica
610 Pennsylvania	770 Georgia
612 Minnesota	773 Illinois
613 Ontario	780 Alberta
614 Ohio	781 Massachusetts
615 Tennessee	784 St. Vincent/Gren.
616 Michigan	785 Kansas
617 Massachusetts	787 Puerto Rico
618 Illinois	800 800 Services
619 California	801 Utah
626 California	802 Vermont
630 Illinois	803 South Carolina
649 Turks & Caicos	804 Virginia
650 California	805 California
660 Missouri	806 Texas
664 Montserrat	807 Ontario
670 CNMI	808 Hawaii
671 Guam	809 Caribbean
678 Georgia	810 Michigan
700 IC Services	812 Indiana
701 North Dakota	813 Florida
702 Nevada	814 Pennsylvania
703 Virginia	815 Illinois

816 Missouri	954 Florida
817 Texas	956 Texas
818 California	970 Colorado
819 Quebec	972 Texas
830 Texas	973 New Jersey
831 California	978 Massachusetts
843 South Carolina	
847 Illinois	
850 Florida	
860 Connecticut	*>FYI: California now*
864 South Carolina	*holds the lead as the*
867 Yukon and North-	*state with the most area*
west Territories	*codes with 23. Texas is*
868 Trinidad and Tobago	*second with 15, Florida,*
869 St. Kitts/Nevis	*Illinois and New York*
870 Arkansas	*each follow with 9 each.*
876 Jamaica	
880 PAID 800 Service	
881 PAID 888 Service	
877 800 Serv. Expansion	
888 800 Serv. Expansion	
900 900 Service	
901 Tennessee	
902 Nova Scotia	
903 Texas	
904 Florida	
905 Ontario	
906 Michigan	
907 Alaska	
908 New Jersey	
909 California	
910 North Carolina	
912 Georgia	
913 Kansas	
914 New York	
915 Texas	
916 California	
917 New York	
918 Oklahoma	
919 North Carolina	
920 Wisconsin	
925 California	
931 Tennessee	
937 Ohio	
940 Texas	
941 Florida	
949 California	

Directory
of International
Telephone
Country Codes

International calls from North America: Dial "011" plus country code plus phone number. For Caribbean countries not found here, refer to Directory of North American Area Codes. For International Directory Assistance from the United States, dial "00".

93 Afghanistan
355 Albania
213 Algeria
684 American Samoa
376 Andorra
244 Angola
54 Argentina
374 Armenia
297 Aruba
247 Ascension Island
61 Australia
672 Australian External Territories
43 Austria
994 Azerbaijan
973 Bahrain
880 Bangladesh
375 Belarus
32 Belgium
501 Belize
229 Benin
975 Bhutan
591 Bolivia
387 Bosnia and Herzegovina
267 Botswana
55 Brazil
673 Brunei Darussalm
359 Bulgaria
226 Burkina Faso
257 Burundi
237 Cameroon
238 Cape Verdi
236 Central African Republic

235 Chad
56 Chile
86 China (People's Republic)
886 China (Taiwan)
57 Colombia
269 Comoros and Mayotte
242 Congo
682 Cook Islands
506 Costa Rica
385 Croatia
53 Cuba
357 Cyprus
42 Czech Republic
45 Denmark
246 Diego Garcia
253 Djibouti
593 Ecuador
20 Egypt
503 El Salvador
240 Equatorial Guinea
291 Eritrea
372 Estonia
251 Ethiopia
500 Falkland Islands
298 Faroe (Faeroe) Islands
679 Fiji
358 Finland
33 France
590 French Antilles
594 French Guiana
241 Gabon)
220 Gambia
995 Republic of Georgia
49 Germany
233 Ghana
350 Gibraltar
30 Greece
299 Greenland
671 Guam
502 Guatemala
224 Guinea
245 Guinea-Bissau
592 Guyana
509 Haiti

504 Honduras	377 Monaco
852 Hong Kong	976 Mongolia
36 Hungary	212 Morocco
354 Iceland	258 Mozambique
91 India	95 Myanmar
62 Indonesia	264 Namibia
98 Iran	674 Nauru
964 Iraq	977 Nepal
353 Ireland	31 Netherlands
972 Israel	599 Netherlands Antilles
39 Italy	687 New Caledonia
225 Ivory Coast	64 New Zealand
81 Japan	505 Nicaragua
962 Jordan	227 Niger
254 Kenya	234 Nigeria
855 Khmer Republic	683 Niue
(Cambodia/Kampuchea)	670 North Mariana Is-
686 Kiribati Republic	lands (Saipan)
(Gilbert Islands)	47 Norway
82 Korea - South	968 Oman
850Korea - North	92 Pakistan
965 Kuwait	680 Palau
996 Kyrgyz Republic	507 Panama
371 Latvia	675 Papua New Guinea
856 Laos	595 Paraguay
961 Lebanon	51 Peru
266 Lesotho	63 Philippines
231 Liberia	48 Poland
370 Lithuania	351 Portugal (includes
218 Libya	Azores)
352 Luxembourg	974 Qatar
853 Macao	262 Reunion (France)
389 Macedonia	40 Romania
261 Madagascar	7 Russia
60 Malaysia	250 Rwanda
265 Malawi	378 San Marino
60 Malaysia	239 Sao Tome and
960 Maldives	Principe
223 Mali	966 Saudi Arabia
356 Malta	221 Senegal
692 Marshall Islands	381 Serbia and Montene-
596 Martinique	gro
222 Mauritania	248 Seychelles
230 Mauritius	232 Sierra Leone
52 Mexico	65 Singapore
691 Micronesia	42 Slovakia
373 Moldova	386 Slovenia

677 Solomon Islands
252 Somalia
27 South Africa
34 Spain
94 Sri Lanka
290 St. Helena
508 St. Pierre &
Miquelon
249 Sudan
597 Suriname
268 Swaziland
46 Sweden
41 Switzerland
963 Syria
689 Tahiti
255 Tanzania (includes
Zanzibar)
66 Thailand
228 Togo (Togolese Republic)
690 Tokelau
676 Tonga
216 Tunisia
90 Turkey
688 Tuvalu (Ellice Islands)
256 Uganda
380 Ukraine
971 United Arab Emirates
44 United Kingdom
598 Uruguay
678 Vanuatu (New Hebrides)
379 Vatican City
58 Venezuela
84 Viet Nam
681 Wallis and Futuna
685 Western Samoa
969 Yemen
967 North Yemen
243 Zaire
260 Zambia
263 Zimbabwe

>*FYI: The world's nation with the highest number of telephone lines per 1000 inhabitants? Sweden, with 683. The United States comes in second with 602. Four countries are tied for last with the fewest. Cambodia, Chad, Niger and The Republic of Congo (formerly Zaire) each have one phone line per 1,0000 residents.*

The nation with the most cell phones per 1,000 persons is also Sweden, with 158. The U.S. is fifth with 91.

Source: World Telecommunication Report, 1997, The United Nations.

Phonetics

A	"Adam"
B	"Boy"
C	"Charlie"
D	"David"
E	"Edward"
F	"Frank"
G	"George"
H	"Harry"
I	"Ida"
J	"John"
K	"King"
L	"Lincoln"
M	"Mary"
N	"Nora"
O	"Ocean"
P	"Peter"
Q	"Queen"
R	"Robert"
S	"Sam"
T	"Tom"
U	"Union"
V	"Victor"
W	"Walter"
X	"X Ray"
Y	"Young"
Z	"Zebra"

Perpetual
Calendar

YEAR

1800 - 1900				1900 - 2000			
01	29	57	85		25	53	81
02	30	58	86		26	54	82
03	31	59	87		27	55	83
04	32	60	88		28	56	84
05	33	61	89	01	29	57	85
06	34	62	90	02	30	58	86
07	35	63	91	03	31	59	87
08	36	64	92	04	32	60	88
09	37	65	93	05	33	61	89
10	38	66	94	06	34	62	90
11	39	67	95	07	35	63	91
12	40	68	96	08	36	64	92
13	41	69	97	09	37	65	93
14	42	70	98	10	38	66	94
15	43	71	99	11	39	67	95
16	44	72		12	40	68	96
17	45	73		13	41	69	97
18	46	74		14	42	70	98
19	47	75		15	43	71	99
20	48	76		16	44	72	
21	49	77	00	17	45	73	
22	50	78		18	46	74	
23	51	79		19	47	75	
24	52	80		20	48	76	
25	53	81		21	49	77	00
26	54	82		22	50	78	
27	55	83		23	51	79	
28	56	84		24	52	80	

HOW TO USE THE PERPETUAL CALENDAR:

The perpetual calendar computes what day of the week any date between 1800-2000 fell on, or will fall on. (Example: January 26, 1973)

1. Find year from chart on this page. (Example: 1973 would be the 21st row down, second column from the right.)

2. Move horizontally across the page to the month chart on the facing page to the desired month. (Example: January would be the first column, "1".)

3. Add "1" plus the day number, refer to day chart on facing page to compute day of week. (Example: "1", plus, day number 26, equals 27, falling on a Friday.)

MONTH											
J	F	M	A	M	J	J	A	S	O	N	D
4	0	0	3	5	1	3	6	2	4	0	2
5	1	1	4	6	2	4	0	3	5	1	3
6	2	2	5	0	3	5	1	4	6	2	4
0	3	4	0	2	5	0	3	6	1	4	6
2	5	5	1	3	6	1	4	0	2	5	0
3	6	6	2	4	0	2	5	1	3	6	1
4	0	0	3	5	1	3	6	2	4	0	2
5	1	2	5	0	3	5	1	4	6	2	4
0	3	3	6	1	4	6	2	5	0	3	5
1	4	4	0	2	5	0	3	6	1	4	6
2	5	5	1	3	6	1	4	0	2	5	0
3	6	6	2	4	0	2	5	1	3	6	1
5	1	1	4	6	2	4	0	3	5	1	3
6	2	2	5	0	3	5	1	4	6	2	4
0	3	3	6	1	4	6	2	5	0	3	5
1	4	5	1	3	6	1	4	0	2	5	0
3	6	6	2	4	0	2	5	1	3	6	1
4	0	0	3	5	1	3	6	2	4	0	2
5	1	1	4	6	2	4	0	3	5	1	3
6	2	3	6	1	4	6	2	5	0	3	5
1	4	4	0	2	5	0	3	6	1	4	6
2	5	5	1	3	6	1	4	0	2	5	0
3	6	6	2	4	0	2	5	1	3	6	1
4	0	1	4	6	2	4	0	3	5	1	3
6	2	2	5	0	3	5	1	4	6	2	4
0	3	3	6	1	4	6	2	5	0	3	5
1	4	4	0	2	5	0	3	6	1	4	6
2	5	6	2	4	0	2	5	1	3	6	1

DAY

SU	1	8	15	22	29	36
MO	2	9	16	23	30	37
TU	3	10	17	24	31	
WE	4	11	18	25	32	
TH	5	12	19	26	33	
FR	6	13	20	27	34	
SA	7	14	21	28	35	

Social
Security
Number
Identification
Chart

The first three numbers of a Social Security Number indicate state of issuance:

001-003	New Hampshire
004-007	Maine
008-009	Vermont
010-034	Massachusetts
035-039	Rhode Island
040-049	Connecticut
050-134	New York
135-158	New Jersey
159-211	Pennsylvania
212-220	Maryland
221-222	Delaware
223-231	Virginia
232-236	West Virginia & North Carolina
237-246	North Carolina
247-251	South Carolina
252-260	Georgia
261-267	Florida
268-302	Ohio
303-317	Indiana
318-361	Illinois
362-386	Michigan
387-399	Wisconsin
400-407	Kentucky
408-415	Tennessee
416-424	Alabama
425-428	Mississippi

429-432	Arkansas
433-439	Louisiana
440-448	Oklahoma
449-467	Texas
468-477	Minnesota
478-485	Iowa
486-500	Missouri
501-502	North Dakota
503-504	South Dakota
505-508	Nebraska
509-515	Kansas
516-517	Montana
518-519	Idaho
520	Wyoming
521-524	Colorado
525	New Mexico
526-527	Arizona
528-529	Utah
530	Nevada
531-539	Washington
540-544	Oregon
545-573	California
574	Alaska
575-576	Hawaii
577-579	District of Columbia
580	Virgin Islands
581-584	Puerto Rico
585	New Mexico

586	Guam, American Samoa
587-588	Mississippi
589-595	Florida
596-599	Puerto Rico
600-601	Arizona
602-626	California
627-645	Texas
646-647	Utah
648-649	New Mexico
650-653	Colorado
654-658	South Carolina
659-699	Not issued
700-728	Railroad Retirement
729-999	Not issued

Note: There is now a third taxpayer identification numbering system, called TIPI — Tax Payer Identification Number. These numbers are issued by the IRS to parties who may have a federal tax liability, but who are not eligible for a Social Security Number or a Federal Employment Identification Number. TIPI's begin with the number 9, and are otherwise in the same configuration as Social Security Numbers: 9XX-XX-XXXX.

Federal
Employer
Identification
Numbers

Businesses with employees are required to obtain a Federal Employer Identification Number(FEIN). FEIN's are nine digits long, with the first two digits indicating which IRS district office the number was issued through:

Alabama	Birmingham	63
Alaska	Anchorage	92
Arizona	Phoenix	86
Arkansas	Little Rock	71
California	Laguna Nigel	33
	Los Angeles	95
	Sacramento	68
	San Francisco	94
	San Jose	77
Colorado	Denver	84
Connecticut	Hartford	06
Delaware	Wilmington	51
Florida	Fort Lauderdale	65
	Jacksonville	59
Georgia	Atlanta	58
Hawaii	Honolulu	99
Idaho	Boise	82
Illinois	Chicago	36
	Springfield	37
Indiana	Indianapolis	35
Iowa	Des Moines	42
Kansas	Wichita	48
Kentucky	Louisville	61
Louisiana	New Orleans	72
Maine	Augusta	01
Maryland	Baltimore	52
Massachusetts	Boston	04
Michigan	Detroit	38
Minnesota	St. Paul	41
Mississippi	Jackson	64
Missouri	St. Louis	43
Montana	Helena	81
Nebraska	Omaha	47
Nevada	Las Vegas/Reno	88
New Hampshire	Portsmouth	02
New Jersey	Newark	22

New Mexico	Albuquerque	85
New York	Albany	14
	Brooklyn	11
	Buffalo	16
	Manhattan	13
North Carolina	Greensboro	56
North Dakota	Fargo	45
Ohio	Cincinnati	31
	Cleveland	34
Oklahoma	Oklahoma City	73
Oregon	Portland	93
Pennsylvania	Philadelphia	23
	Pittsburgh	25
Rhode Island	Providence	05
South Carolina	Columbia	57
South Dakota	Aberdeen	46
Tennessee	Nashville	62
Texas	Austin	74
	Dallas	75
	Houston	76
Utah	Salt Lake City	87
Vermont	Burlington	03
Virginia	Richmond	54
Washington	Seattle	91
West Virginia	Parkersburg	55
Wisconsin	Milwaukee	39
Wyoming	Cheyenne	83
Washington, DC	Baltimore	52

Internet
Abbreviations

The five most common abbreviations found after an internet address are:

.COM (For commercial organizations)

.NET (For network infrastructure machines and organizations)

.EDU (For 4 year, degree granting colleges and universities. Schools, libraries, and museums register under country domains)

.GOV (For United States federal government agencies. State and local governments register under country domains.)

.ORG (For miscellaneous, usually nonprofit, organizations.)

Internet addresses may contain a two letter code indicating country of origin:

AFGHANISTAN AF
ALBANIA AL
ALGERIA DZ
AMERICAN SAMOA AS
ANDORRA AD
ANGOLA AO
ANGUILLA AI
ANTARCTICA AQ
ANTIGUA AND BARBUDA AG
ARGENTINA AR
ARMENIA AM
ARUBA AW
AUSTRALIA AU
AUSTRIA AT
AZERBAIJAN AZ
BAHAMAS BS
BAHRAIN BH
BANGLADESH BD
BARBADOS BB
BELARUS BY
BELGIUM BE
BELIZE BZ
BENIN BJ
BERMUDA BM
BHUTAN BT
BOLIVIA BO
BOSNIA AND HERZEGOWINA BA
BOTSWANA BW
BOUVET ISLAND BV
BRAZIL BR
BRITISH INDIAN OCEAN TERRITORY IO
BRUNEI DARUSSALAM BN
BULGARIA BG
BURKINA FASO BF
BURUNDI BI
CAMBODIA KH
CAMEROON CM
CANADA CA
CAPE VERDE CV
CAYMAN ISLANDS KY
CENTRAL AFRICAN REPUBLIC CF
CHAD TD
CHILE CL
CHINA CN
CHRISTMAS ISLAND CX
COCOS (KEELING) ISLANDS CC
COLOMBIA CO
COMOROS KM

CONGO CG	GUAM GU
COOK ISLANDS CK	GUATEMALA GT
COSTA RICA CR	GUINEA GN
COTE D'IVOIRE CI	GUINEA-BISSAU
CROATIA HR	GW
CUBA CU	GUYANA GY
CYPRUS CY	HAITI HT
CZECH REPUBLIC	HEARD AND MC
CZ	DONALD ISLANDS
DENMARK DK	HM
DJIBOUTI DJ	HONDURAS HN
DOMINICA DM	HONG KONG HK
DOMINICAN REPUB-	HUNGARY HU
LIC DO	ICELAND IS
EAST TIMOR TP	INDIA IN
ECUADOR EC	INDONESIA ID
EGYPT EG	IRAN (ISLAMIC RE-
EL SALVADOR SV	PUBLIC OF) IR
EQUATORIAL	IRAQ IQ
GUINEA GQ	IRELAND IE
ERITREA ER	ISRAEL IL
ESTONIA EE	ITALY IT
ETHIOPIA ET	JAMAICA JM
FALKLAND ISLANDS	JAPAN JP
(MALVINAS) FK	JORDAN JO
FAROE ISLANDS FO	KAZAKHSTAN KZ
FIJI FJ	KENYA KE
FINLAND FI	KIRIBATI KI
FRANCE FR	KOREA, DEMO-
FRANCE,	CRATIC PEOPLE'S
METROPOLITAN FX	REPUBLIC OF KP
FRENCH GUIANA	KOREA, REPUBLIC
GF	OF KR
FRENCH POLYNESIA	KUWAIT KW
PF	KYRGYZSTAN KG
FRENCH SOUTHERN	LAO PEOPLE'S DEMO-
TERRITORIES TF	CRATIC REPUBLIC
GABON GA	LA
GAMBIA GM	LATVIA LV
GEORGIA GE	LEBANON LB
GERMANY DE	LESOTHO LS
GHANA GH	LIBERIA LR
GIBRALTAR GI	LIBYAN ARAB
GREECE GR	JAMAHIRIYA LY
GREENLAND GL	LIECHTENSTEIN LI
GRENADA GD	LITHUANIA LT
GUADELOUPE GP	LUXEMBOURG LU

MACAU MO	PANAMA PA
MACEDONIA, THE	PAPUA NEW
FORMER YUGOSLAV	GUINEAPG
REPUBLIC OF MK	PARAGUAY PY
MADAGASCAR MG	PERU PE
MALAWI MW	PHILIPPINES PH
MALAYSIA MY	PITCAIRN PN
MALDIVES MV	POLAND PL
MALI ML	PORTUGAL PT
MALTA MT	PUERTO RICO PR
MARSHALL ISLANDS	QATAR QA
MH	REUNION RE
MARTINIQUE MQ	ROMANIA RO
MAURITANIA MR	RUSSIAN FEDERA-
MAURITIUS MU	TION RU
MAYOTTE YT	RWANDA RW
MEXICO MX	SAINT KITTS AND
MICRONESIA, FEDER-	NEVIS KN
ATED STATES OF	SAINT LUCIA LC
FM	SAINT VINCENT AND
MOLDOVA, REPUB-	THE GRENADINES
LIC OF MD	VC
MONACO MC	SAMOA WS
MONGOLIA MN	SAN MARINO SM
MONTSERRAT MS	SAO TOME AND
MOROCCO MA	PRINCIPE ST
MOZAMBIQUE MZ	SAUDI ARABIA SA
MYANMAR MM	SENEGAL SN
NAMIBIA NA	SEYCHELLES SC
NAURU NR	SIERRA LEONE SL
NEPAL NP	SINGAPORE SG
NETHERLANDS NL	SLOVAKIA (Slovak
NETHERLANDS AN-	Republic) SK
TILLES AN	SLOVENIA SI
NEW CALEDONIA NC	SOLOMON ISLANDS
NEW ZEALAND NZ	SB
NICARAGUA NI	SOMALIA SO
NIGER NE	SOUTH AFRICA ZA
NIGERIA NG	SOUTH GEORGIA
NIUE NU	AND THE SOUTH
NORFOLK ISLAND NF	SANDWICH ISLANDS
NORTHERN MARI-	GS
ANA ISLANDS MP	SPAIN ES
NORWAY NO	SRI LANKA LK
OMAN OM	ST. HELENA SH
PAKISTAN PK	ST. PIERRE AND
PALAU PW	MIQUELON PM

SUDANSD
SURINAME SR
SVALBARD AND JAN
MAYEN ISLANDS SJ
SWAZILANDSZ
SWEDEN SE
SWITZERLAND CH
SYRIAN ARAB REPUB-
LIC SY
TAIWAN, PROVINCE
OF CHINA TW
TAJIKISTAN TJ
TANZANIA, UNITED
REPUBLIC OF TZ
THAILAND TH
TOGO TG
TOKELAU TK
TONGA TO
TRINIDAD AND TO-
BAGO TT
TUNISIA TN
TURKEYTR
TURKMENISTAN TM
TURKS AND CAICOS
ISLANDS TC
TUVALU TV
UGANDAUG
UKRAINEUA
UNITED ARAB EMI-
RATES AE
UNITED KINGDOM GB
UNITED STATES US
UNITED STATES MI-
NOR OUTLYING IS-
LANDSUM
URUGUAYUY
UZBEKISTANUZ
VANUATU VU
VATICAN CITY STAT-
EVA
VENEZUELA VE
VIET NAM VN
VIRGIN ISLANDS
(BRITISH) VG
VIRGIN ISLANDS
(U.S.) VI
WALLIS AND FUTUNA

ISLANDS WF
WESTERN SAHARA EH
YEMEN YE
YUGOSLAVIA YU
ZAIRE ZR
ZAMBIA ZM
ZIMBABWE ZW

Fair Credit Reporting Act: Permissible Purposes

(Excerpts)

The Fair Credit Reporting Act (15 USC 1681) is the Federal law governing information contained in consumer credit reports. This is an excerpt of portions most applicable to private sector investigators. However, other portions not contained in this excerpt may also be applicable to the work of private investigators.

"...Any consumer reporting agency may furnish a consumer report under the following circumstances and no other:

(1) In response to the order of a court having jurisdiction to issue such an order, or a subpoena issued in connection with proceedings before a Federal grand jury.

(2) In accordance with the written instructions of the consumer to whom it relates.

(3) To a person which it has reason to believe

(A) intends to use the information in connection with a credit transaction involving the consumer on whom the information is to be furnished and involving the extension of credit to, or review or collection of an account of, the consumer; or

(B) intends to use the information for employment purposes; or

(C) intends to use the information in connection with the underwriting of insurance involving the consumer; or

(D) intends to use the information in connection with a determination of the consumer's eligibility for a license or other benefit granted by a governmental instrumentality required by law to consider an applicant's financial responsibility or status; or

(E) intends to use the information, as a potential investor or servicer, or current insurer, in connection with a valuation of, or an assessment of the credit or prepayment risks associated with, an existing credit obligation; or

(F) otherwise has a legitimate business need for the information

> (i) in connection with a business transaction that is initiated by the consumer; or

> (ii) to review an account to determine whether the consumer continues to meet the terms of the account."

Excerpt from FCRA includes changes effective October 1, 1997.

Anatomy
of a
Check

The series of numbers at the bottom of the check is referred to as the *MICR Line*, short for *Magnetic Ink Character Recognition*. The *MICR Line* includes the paying bank's ABA (American Banking Association) routing number, the account number of the writer of the check, and usually the sequential check number. The dollar amount of the check will be entered on the MICR line by the bank of first deposit as the first step in the processing of the item.

Check number

Small type is referred to as the fractional form of the ABA routing number. If the bottom of the check is damaged and the MICR line becomes unreadable, the bank on whom the check was issued can be identified through these numbers.

Amount Field. The dollar amount of the check will be encoded in this area by the bank of first deposit.

Date Code . If present, this optional information indicates the month and year when the account was opened.

Charles Ponzi
123 Scheme St.
Your Town, TX 12345

101
44-44/1199

DATE *April 1, 1998*

PAY
TO THE   *Ponzi Fund for Widows and Orphans*

One Thousand Dollars and 00/100

1000.00/100

Dollars

0695

BANK NAME ADDRESS

Charlie Ponzi

MEMO

⑆119900449⑆ 101 ⑈ 9900 33333 ⑈

This area of the *MICR Line* is used for the printing of the check writer's account number and (usually) the sequential check number and other information. The configuration of this information is not standardized, as it is used only by the paying bank. In this example, the sequential check number is followed by the account number.

This 9 digit *Routing Number*, may also be referred to as the *ABA Number*. The first 4 digits are the *Fed Routing Symbol*. The first 2 digits identify the Federal Reserve District (see chart, following pages) in which the presentment point of the paying bank is located. A mismatch between the location of the bank and Federal Reserve District could indicate a possible counterfeit check. Digits 5 through 8 constitute the institution identifier and identify the paying institution. The 9th digit is a check digit which allows automated check processing equipment to verify that it has read the first 8 digits correctly.

Federal Reserve District Codes

01   *Boston*, includes Massachusetts, Maine, New Hampshire, Connecticut, Vermont, Rhode Island.

02   *New York*, includes New York, New Jersey, Connecticut.

03   *Philadelphia*, includes Pennsylvania, Delaware, New Jersey.

04   *Cleveland*, includes Ohio, Pennsylvania, Kentucky, West Virginia.

05   *Richmond*, includes Virginia, Maryland, North Carolina, District of   Columbia, South Carolina, West Virginia.

06   *Atlanta*, includes Georgia, Alabama, Florida, Tennessee, Louisiana, Mississippi.

07   *Chicago*, includes Illinois, Michigan, Indiana, Iowa, Wisconsin.

08   *St. Louis*, includes Missouri, Arkansas, Kentucky, Tennessee, Indiana, Illinois, Mississippi

09   *Minneapolis*, includes Minnesota, Montana, North Dakota, South Dakota, Wisconsin, Michigan.

10   *Kansas City*, includes Missouri, Colorado, Oklahoma, Nebraska, Iowa, Wyoming, Kansas, New Mexico.

11   *Dallas*, includes Texas, Arizona, New Mexico, Louisiana.

12   *San Francisco*, includes California, Oregon, Washington, Utah, Hawaii, Alaska, Idaho, Nevada, Arizona.

Note: Other prefixes may be used which indicate any one of a number of special exceptions to the above chart, including checks from thrifts and credit unions, postal money orders and traveler's checks.

The
Death Penalty:

State by State
Profile

State	Death Penalty?	Lethal Inj.	Electrocution	Gas Chamber	Hanging	Firing Squad
AL	Y		Y			
AK	N					
AZ	Y	Y		Y		
AR	Y	Y	Y			
CA	Y	Y		Y		
CO	Y	Y				
CT	Y	Y				
DE	Y	Y			Y	
DC	N					
FL	Y		Y			
GA	Y		Y			
HI	N					
ID	Y	Y				Y
IL	Y					
IN	Y					
IA	N					
KS	Y	Y				
KY	Y		Y			
LA	Y	Y				
ME	N					
MD	Y	Y		Y		
MA	N					
MI	N					
MN	N					
MS	Y	Y		Y		

Source: Death Penalty Information Center

State	Death Penalty?	Lethal Inj.	Electrocution	Gas Chamber	Hanging	Firing Squad
MO	Y	Y		Y		
MT	Y	Y				
NB	Y		Y			
NV	Y	Y				
NH	Y	Y			Y	
NJ	Y	Y				
NM	Y	Y				
NY	Y	Y				
NC	Y	Y		Y		
ND	N					
OH	Y	Y	Y			
OK	Y	Y	Y			Y
OR	Y	Y				
PA	Y	Y				
RI	N					
SC	Y	Y	Y			
SD	Y	Y				
TN	Y		Y			
TX	Y	Y				
UT	Y	Y				Y
VT	N					
VA	Y	Y	Y			
WA	Y	Y			Y	
WV	N					
WI	N					
WY	Y	Y		Y		

Sample
Miranda
Warning

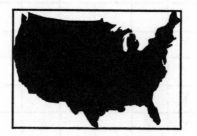

You have the right to remain silent.

Anything you say can and will be used against you in a court of law.

You have the right to consult with an attorney, and to have an attorney present both before and during questioning.

If you cannot afford to hire an attorney, one will be appointed by the court, free of charge, to represent you before any questioning, if you wish.

You can decide at any time to exercise these rights and not answer any question or make any statements.

To secure a waiver of these rights, the following questions should be asked and an affirmative answer received:

Do you understand these rights I have just explained to you?

With these rights in mind, are you willing to talk to me now?

CALIBER COMPARISON CHART

(Common Handgun Rounds)

Source: *Death Investigator's Handbook, 1993, by Louis Eliopulos.* Published by Paladin Press, 1993.

Common Round Name	Avail-ability	Inch Size	Metric Equiv.	Bullet Diameter
.22	Revolver or Semi-Auto	.22	5.6mm	●
.25	Semi-Auto	.25	6.38mm	●
.32	Revolver or Semi-Auto	.31	7.65mm	●
9mm	Semi-Auto	.356	9mm	●
.380	Semi-Auto	.356	9mm	●
.357	Revolver	.357	9.1mm	●
.38	Revolver	.357	9.1mm	●
.40 s&w	Semi-Auto	.40	10.16mm	●
.44	Revolver	.429	10.91mm	●
.45	Semi-Auto	.451	11.47mm	●

Beyond a
Reasonable
Doubt

This is the legal definition of "Reasonable doubt" as read to all criminal juries in California. A very similar version is used in the the 49 other states and in federal criminal cases:

"Reasonable doubt is defined as follows: It is not a mere possible doubt; because everything relating to human affairs, and depending on moral evidence, is open to some or imaginary doubt. It is the state of the case which, after the entire comparison and consideration of all the evidence, leaves the minds of the jurors in that condition that they cannot say they feel an abiding conviction, to a moral certainty, of the truth of the charge."

Freedom of Information Act Request Template

(Your name)
(Your street address)
(Your city/state/zip)
(Your phone number)

FOIA Officer
(Federal Agency)
(Agency address)

(Date)

re: FREEDOM OF INFORMATION ACT REQUEST.

Dear FOIA Officer:

Under the provisions of the Freedom of Information Act, 5 U.S.C. 552, I am requesting access to:

(Specify requested information as accurately and clearly as possible.)

If there are fees associated with fulfilling this request, or for copying, please advise me of the anticipated cost prior to exceeding *(XXX)* dollars in expense.

As you may know, the Freedom of Information Act does allow you to reduce or waive fees altogether if the information is primarily benefiting the public.

I believe that my request qualifies for this fee waiver and/or reduction because *(your reason)*.

If all or any part of my request is denied, please inform me as to the specific exemptions of the FOIA that you believe justifies your refusal to release the information.

If all or any part of my request is denied, also please inform me as to the appeals procedure available to me under the law.

Your prompt handling of this request is appreciated and I look forward to hearing from you within 10 days as the law indicates.

Very truly yours,
(Your signature)

DIRECTORY
OF INVESTIGATIVE
SERVICES
& PRODUCTS

When a skip has our card, you've got his number.

Give a skip a free calling card, and he'll give you all the information you need to determine his whereabouts. That is, as long as it's an 800 ID Calling Card, the innovative new skiptracing tool from IIS.

No other service is as effective — or as simple. It works like this: We'll send our free calling card — charged with 60 minutes of prepaid phone time — anywhere your skip could be receiving mail. When he uses it (and he will; it's free), we'll notify you instantly of the number he's calling from and the number he's calling to. So you can immediately pursue the possibilities, and your skip.

Our 800 ID Calling Card is the most powerful tool yet in your skiptracing arsenal. And at $35 for 60 minutes of calling time, with a no find, no fee guarantee, it's also the most cost-efficient.

Call IIS today at 800-495-0888 to find out more about this exciting new service. Or fax your orders now to 303-595-8825. We'll put a calling card in your skip's hand. And soon he'll be eating out of ours.

1-800-495-0888

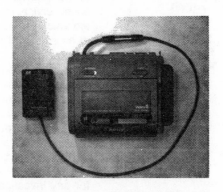

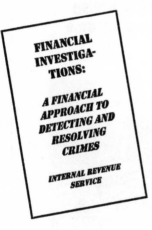

RE-ORDER FORM

☑ ☑ ☑

☐ Yes, please send me The Investigator's Little Black Book 2 @ $19.95 per copy plus $2.75 S&H. *(Shipments to California addresses add 8.25% Sales tax — $1.65.)*

☐ Don't send me your book! Instead, please put me on your mailing list to receive notice of future Crime Time Publishing Co. products.

Okay to Photocopy this Form!

Name:	
Company:	
Street:	
City/State:	
Zip:	
E-mail or Phone:	

Mail to:

Crime Time Publishing Co
289 S. Robertson Blvd., Suite 224
Beverly Hills, CA 90211

Payment accepted by check, money order, or cashier's check only. Sorry, credit cards and purchase orders NOT accepted.

Phone Numbers

Phone Numbers

Found a great number for the next edition of *The Investigator's Little Black Book?* Why not let us know about it?! Mail it to: **Black Book c/o Crime Time Publishing Co., 289 S. Robertson Blvd., Suite 224, Beverly Hills, CA 90211** or e-mail it to **blackbook@pacificnet.net**

Phone Numbers

Found a great number for the next edition of *The Investigator's Little Black Book?* Why not let us know about it?! Mail it to: **Black Book c/o Crime Time Publishing Co., 289 S. Robertson Blvd., Suite 224, Beverly Hills, CA 90211** or e-mail it to **blackbook@pacificnet.net**

Phone Numbers